COMPARATIVE METHODS
IN THE SOCIAL SCIENCES

COMPARATIVE METHODS
IN THE SOCIAL SCIENCES

Neil J. Smelser

Classics of the Social Sciences

qIp

QUID PRO BOOKS

New Orleans, Louisiana

Previously published in 1976 by Prentice-Hall, Inc., Englewood Cliffs, N.J., and copyright © 1976 by Prentice-Hall; the book was originally part of the Prentice-Hall Methods of Social Science Series edited by Herbert L. Costner and Neil J. Smelser.

Published in 2013 by Quid Pro Books.

ISBN 978-1-61027-170-7 (pbk.)

QUID PRO BOOKS
Quid Pro, LLC
5860 Citrus Blvd., Suite D-101
New Orleans, Louisiana 70123
www.quidprobooks.com

qp

Publisher's Cataloging-in-Publication

Smelser, Neil J.
  Comparative methods in the social sciences / Neil J. Smelser.
      p. cm. — (Classics of the social sciences)
  Includes bibliographical references and index.
  ISBN 978-1-61027-170-7 (pbk.)

1. Sociology—Methodology. 2. Sociology—History. I. Title. II. Series.
HM24 .S527 2013   301'.01'8—dc22
                                                                  2013471673

This is an unabridged republication of the original 1976 work, also available in high-quality new ebook editions from Quid Pro Books. It is presented as part of the *Classics of the Social Sciences* Series.

Contents

3

4

5

6

7

ASSOCIATION, CAUSE, EXPLANATION, AND THEORY   196

Preface

The evolution of this volume is inseparable from my association with the Institute of International Studies at the University of California, Berkeley—more particularly, my association with a number of scholars that were and are members of that Institute's Group on Theory and Method in Comparative Studies. The Group was launched in 1965, as a kind of brainchild of David Apter, then Director of the Institute. Apter asked me to chair the Group, and I have done so ever since. Two subsequent Directors, Ernst Haas and Carl Rosberg, have given the Group their strongest support and nurturance. Cleo Stoker has managed its budget artfully, and the practical arrangements for the Group's meetings have been handled at different times by Peggy Dechant, Frances Brown, and Mirtha Hernandez, all staff members of the Institute. The Group's financial support derived from Ford Foundation funds granted to the Institute in 1965. I take this opportunity to thank those who have sustained the Group during its ten years of continuous existence.

During those years the Group had a membership of between ten and fifteen scholars from various social science departments at the University of California, Berkeley, perhaps two advanced graduate students as Re-

iv

search Apprentices, and occasionally a visitor from another university. We have met for dinner and discussion approximately every three weeks continuously for ten years. We have read and criticized one another's work; we have invited visitors whose work in comparative studies has excited our attention; we have read and discussed critically many of the important studies in comparative social science that have been published during the past decade; and we have published *Comparative Methods in Sociology*,[1] which was organized and edited by my colleague and friend, the late Ivan Vallier.

One of the remarkable features of the Group is that, despite the duration and continuity of its membership, its individuals have steadfastly refused to adopt stereotyped and reiterated intellectual positions. Its discussions have been open and free-ranging, and forever taking unexpected turns. The morale of the Group has always been high, and, as a consequence, really hard-hitting criticism has been given and taken in an atmosphere of collegiality and friendship. And, most important, the Group has always insisted on observing the highest standards of scholarship in its critical work. It maintained this scholarly posture consistently through the turbulent 1960s and the sparse 1970s. For many of us it has been a haven for intellectual intercourse during a period when our academy was threatened by political and economic forces from many quarters.

It was in the context of the Group that many of the ideas in this book were invented, probed, refined, and solidified. Though the book is my responsibility, I feel that in many respects my colleagues in the Group have been collaborators. I shall not mention all those who have been members or visitors in the Group over the years, but I would like to thank those who discussed an earlier version of this book on the evening of January 23, 1975. These included Robert Bellah, Elbaki Hermassi, Leo Lowenthal, Arthur Stinchcombe (Sociology); Elizabeth Colson, Eugene Hammel (Anthropology); Reinhard Bendix, Carl Rosberg (Political Science); Martin Malia, Frederic Wakeman, Irving Scheiner (History); Albert Fishlow (Economics); Lawrence Dickey, John Zammito (graduate students, History); and Stephan Nowak (Sociology, University of Warsaw and Fellow of the Center for Advanced Study in the Behavioral Sciences). I should also mention Charles Y. Glock (Sociology), who was not present at that meeting, but from whose methodological wisdom I have profited over the years.

While the book thus emerged as a kind of cumulative product, the last phases of research and the drafting were done during 1973–1974, when I

---

[1] Ivan Vallier, ed., *Comparative Methods in Sociology: Essays on Trends and Applications* (Berkeley and Los Angeles: University of California Press, 1971).

was away from Berkeley on sabbatical leave. I was sustained in inflation-ridden Europe that year both by sabbatical leave salary from the University of California and by a John Simon Guggenheim Memorial Fellowship. Incidental research expenses were carried by a small supplementary grant from the Institute of International Studies. About half of that year was spent in London, where I relied on the libraries of the British Museum and the London School of Economics and Political Science, where I was an academic visitor. I should like to thank the staffs of both those libraries—and, during an earlier period, the staffs of the various libraries of the University of California, Berkeley—who responded with efficiency and cheer to my voracious demands for books and journals. Most of the actual drafting was executed over a period of months when my family and I were living in a villa named "Ma Vie" in Cagnes-sur-mer on the Côte d'Azur and in a villa in Maderno on the Lago di Garda in northern Italy. The year abroad was a glorious experience, and any notes of optimism to be found in the pages that follow should be discounted accordingly.

In November 1973, when my family and I were vacationing in Barcelona, thieves broke into our camper and absconded with a number of valuables, among them the only copy of my notes comparing the methodological positions of Emile Durkheim and Max Weber. I experienced some pleasure at the thieves' obviously cultivated intellectual tastes, but this did not match my consternation at the loss. In desperation I wrote to several graduate students in the Department of Sociology at Berkeley who had taken my course in sociological theory in which I had discussed the methodologies of the two scholars. Several students—Joyce Bird, Robert Dunn, Megali Sarfati Larsen, Maxine Raz, Lucy Sells, and Erik Wright—responded to the call and sent me xeroxed copies of their lecture notes. Pieced together, those notes seemed to make more sense and contain more insights than the original set that had disappeared into the Spanish underworld. I am certain that chapter three reads better as a result of the whole episode.

The crucial draft was completed more or less in isolation from professional colleagues, so I asked a number of people to give the manuscript a critical reading on my return to the U.S. The reactions of the members of the Group on Theory and Method in Comparative Studies suggested a number of needed revisions. In addition, the following people gave me benefit of their detailed reactions based on careful readings: James Beniger (University of California, Berkeley), Herbert Costner (University of Washington), Marshall Meyer (University of California, Riverside), Whitney Pope (University of Indiana, Bloomington), Frederic Pryor (Swarthmore College), and James Wood (University of California, Riverside).

These readers' comments were often penetrating. They led me to eliminate a number of inelegancies and *bêtises,* and in a number of instances spurred me to undertake a significant amount of revision. I thank them all, and add the customary disclaimer that they bear no responsibility for the final product.

NEIL J. SMELSER
Berkeley, California

COMPARATIVE METHODS
IN THE SOCIAL SCIENCES

1

The Objectives of This Book

Human beings who organize into a society cannot remain indifferent to others who conduct their social life differently from their own. Why should this be so? The reasons are several. First, a group that has chosen a different pattern of morals and customs poses a *threat* to the home society; it suggests that their own morals and customs may not be right, sacred, or universal—as they are generally held to be. People usually respond to such a threat with hostility or disgust, which may in turn become an instrument used to punish or otherwise control those of their own kind who may be tempted to be different.[1] Or they may treat the threat as harmless but nonetheless alien or bizarre; this response, too, may be used for purposes of social control. Or they may invent some way to "tolerate" the threat of difference; that is, to trivialize it by incorporating it into a more inclusive universe of similarity. Alternatively, a foreign way of life may be an *attraction* as well, particularly for those who perceive the morals and customs of their own group as constraining or oppressive in some way.

---

[1] Emile Durkheim, *The Division of Labor in Society,* trans. George Simpson (Glencoe, Ill.: The Free Press, 1949), bk. 1, ch. 2. This observation is not different from Durkheim's explanation of society's response to crime and related forms of deviance.

The worship of the "noble savage" or the life of pastoral simplicity is invariably accompanied—explicitly or implicitly—by a posture of alienation from contemporary society. The fascination with differences, in short, must be regarded as reflecting people's ambivalence toward those forces of socialization and social control that work to produce sameness within the home society.

In this universal tendency to view differences in the mirror of domestic ambivalence lies another tendency—to distort those differences. Insofar as a group reacts to a different group in terms of its own preoccupations, it is not likely to perceive the way of life of the different group as that group experiences it. Or, to make the point in cognitive terms, insofar as a group insists on regarding the experiences of others mainly within its own categories of experience, it is likely to generate errors of understanding and prediction about the others, who invariably organize their experience and act on the basis of categories other than those of the home group.

Only recently in the history of human thought has this tendency for human groups to distort their perceptions of "the different" become widely appreciated. Correspondingly, serious efforts to overcome that distortion by inventing ways to understand differences in social life through categories that transcend a single group are also of relatively recent origin. Most of these efforts have been made in the social sciences, especially in anthropology, sociology, political science, and history. Such efforts have been labeled differently, such as "comparative studies," "cross-cultural analysis," and "cross-national analysis." Whatever their label, however, they are a part of the common enterprise of describing, explaining, and developing theories about socio-cultural phenomena as they occur in social units (groups, tribes, societies, cultures) that are evidently dissimilar to one another.

My main objective in this book is to evaluate some of these efforts. I want to ask what kinds of problems arise in generating knowledge about dissimilar social units; how investigators have contrived to address these problems in their research; and how successful they have been in overcoming them.

I must qualify this statement of purpose immediately and in two ways. First, I do not regard "comparative social science," or the study of dissimilar social units, as a species of inquiry independent from the remainder of social-scientific investigation. "Comparative sociology," Durkheim observed, "is not a particular branch of sociology; it is sociology itself, in so far as it ceases to be purely descriptive and aspires to account for facts."[2] Others have endorsed that view. Swanson, for example, remarked:

[2] Durkheim, *The Division of Labor,* p. 139.

Thinking without comparisons is unthinkable. And, in the absence of comparisons, so is all scientific thought and all scientific research. No one should be surprised that comparisons, implicit and explicit, pervade the work of social scientists and have done so from the beginning: comparisons among roles, organizations, communities, institutions, societies, and cultures.[3]

To press this point further, I might note that even the act of applying general *descriptive* words to a situation—words such as "densely populated" or "democratic"—presupposes a universe of situations that are more or less populated or more or less democratic, and assumes that the situation being described lies somewhere *in comparison with* the others.

If that be true, then the analysis of phenomena in evidently dissimilar units (especially different societies or cultures) should have no methodological problems unique to itself. All methodological problems appear in the analysis of relatively similar units as well (for example, cities in the same region of the same country, white middle-class American males between the ages of 30 and 40), because such analysis involves comparing units that differ from one another in *some* respects. So the methodological problems facing "comparativists" are the same as those facing all social-scientific investigators. The main reasons for concentrating on evidently dissimilar units are that, on the positive side, these methodological problems—such as establishing equivalent measures, or controlling for third variables—stand out with great clarity when comparing dissimilar units, and that, on the negative side, the efforts to overcome them are likely to be plagued with more serious and transparent difficulties. On all other counts, however, the methodological observations ventured in this book are of general significance for the social sciences.

The second qualification is that my conception of "methodology" is broader than that which the term sometimes connotes. I conceive the term to refer to the critical evaluation of investigative activity in relation to the normative standards of scientific inquiry. Some of this evaluation concerns problems of research design, measurement, and other technical procedures—selecting appropriate indices to test given hypotheses, designing questionnaires for cross-national surveys, sampling, coding responses, and the like. I shall devote attention to these procedures as they are employed in studying evidently dissimilar social units. Methodological evaluation, however, should also focus on the conceptual aspects of scientific inquiry, be-

[3] Guy E. Swanson, "Frameworks for Comparative Research: Structural Anthropology and the Theory of Action," in Ivan Vallier, ed., *Comparative Methods in Sociology: Essays on Trends and Applications* (Berkeley and Los Angeles: University of California Press, 1971), p. 145.

cause the adequacy of scientific research is affected by the philosophical assumptions and the theoretical frameworks employed by an investigator, and by the ways he moves between his body of conceptual presuppositions and his empirical research operations. Accordingly, I shall stress the methodology of theory construction—and touch on some issues in the philosophy of science—as these are related to the adequacy of efforts to generate scientific knowledge of a comparative character.

My main strategy in this book will be to examine critically a variety of comparative studies. Moreover, I shall move, by a series of stages, *from* considering illustrative studies that employ neither a self-conscious methodology nor sophisticated empirical measures or research techniques *to* considering illustrative studies that do both. I shall begin by summarizing and evaluating the comparative observations of Alexis de Tocqueville on the United States and France (chapter two). Tocqueville never wrote a methodology for his studies; he relied heavily on impressionistic data; and he did not develop a deliberately systematic theory to inform his comparative observations (though, as we shall see, his thought is quite well organized). Despite the relative informality of his work, however, we can identify certain definite methodological issues he faced because in fact he was attempting (though often implicitly) to generate comparative explanations. In addition, we can assess the ways he arrayed the data available to him to make his arguments.

At the next stage I shall examine the comparative research of two giants in the tradition of comparative studies, Emile Durkheim and Max Weber. Both these scholars issued ambitious methodological manifestos on the nature of sociological inquiry and the place of comparative work within it. In addition, both scholars conducted extensive comparative studies, which remain among the best, even though the quality of data and the research techniques available to them were inferior to those developed since their time. In chapter three I shall examine critically the programs for sociology enunciated by these two men, programs which are fundamentally opposed on several counts. As each turned to the exigencies of empirical investigation, however, each adapted his theoretical starting-points in several ways, and these adaptations brought the two scholars closer substantively and methodologically. In chapters four and five I shall examine many of their comparative empirical studies, identifying their research procedures, noting the problems each faced, assessing their attempted solutions to these problems, and noting the emerging patterns of similarities and differences between them.

In the remainder of the book I shall focus on comparative studies since the time of Durkheim and Weber. I do not intend to survey these studies historically, and I intend to illustrate rather than exhaust the different strategies and techniques that have been developed to improve comparative knowledge. I shall include, however, ample reference to the "cross-cultural" tradition as it has developed in anthropology over several decades; to the "cross-national" tradition as it has burgeoned in political science and sociology more recently; and to the continuing comparative efforts to study the process of modernization in its economic, political, and social aspects. I shall make some reference to the efforts of psychologists who study personality and conduct experiments on a cross-cultural basis. These several traditions of research have grown amid—indeed, have been made possible by—the improvement of data production, storage, and retrieval; the development of sophisticated inference procedures; and the increase in methodological and theoretical self-consciousness on the part of investigators. Chapters six and seven, then, will be a critical evaluation of portions of recent comparative research. Chapter six will concern methodological issues that arise in classifying, describing, and measuring empirical phenomena in evidently dissimilar social units. Chapter seven will concern methodological issues that arise in attempting to establish associations and causal relations in comparative studies, and to organize these into theoretical models that apply to dissimilar units.

I shall move, then, from the less systematic to the more systematic as the book develops. As the analysis proceeds, it will be possible to discern an extraordinary diversity of substantive concerns in comparative studies —how to explain variations in the social structure of grandparenthood, how to measure and account for cross-cultural differences in mental health, how to account for the rise and consolidation of democratic political systems, how to account for national differences in response to stressful situations, to name a few. Moreover, it will be possible to discern a bewildering array of specific strategies and techniques that have been developed to improve the quality of comparative analysis. Despite this diversity in substance, strategy, and technique, the methodological principles governing comparative investigation will turn out to be very few in number. More particularly, it will be possible to discern a striking continuity among all the comparative studies reviewed in this book—both classical and modern. This continuity stems from the fundamental fact that all the theorists and empirical investigators we shall examine were attempting to *gain control over and manipulate* various causal conditions in social life, and thus to establish a case for one or another selected condition. The specific methods of gaining control will be shown to vary greatly in type, in effectiveness, and in scientific utility, but all the methods to be studied can be understood—and, indeed, compared with one another—as efforts to explain social phenomena by establishing controls over conditions and causes of variations in those phenomena.

2

Alexis de Tocqueville as Comparative Analyst

Alexis de Tocqueville has been widely hailed and extensively analyzed as a perceptive and brilliant commentator on American society;[1] as a profound prophet;[2] as a theorist of mass society;[3] as an original thinker

Note: This chapter is a revised version of my earlier essay, "Alexis de Tocqueville as Comparative Analyst," which appeared in *Comparative Methods in Sociology: Essays on Trends and Applications,* edited by Ivan Vallier. Copyright © 1971 by The Regents of the University of California; reprinted by permission of the University of California Press.

[1] Alexis de Tocqueville, *Democracy in America;* vol. 1 first published in 1835, vol. 2 in 1840. All references in this chapter are to the Vintage Book edition (New York: Knopf and Random House, 1945).

[2] Especially for his prediction of the emergence of the United States and Russia as the two great world powers in Tocqueville, *Democracy in America,* 1:452. See also his predictions of continued social stability in Great Britain, written in September 1833, in J. P. Mayer, ed., *Alexis de Tocqueville: Journeys to England and Ireland* (Garden City, N.Y.: Doubleday, 1968), pp. 51–59.

[3] See, for example, William Kornhauser's interpretation of this aspect of Tocqueville's work in *The Politics of Mass Society* (Glencoe, Ill.: The Free Press, 1959).

on the history and sociology of revolutions;[4] and, to a lesser extent, as a political figure involved in and around the Revolution of 1848 in France.[5] However, his work has not been extensively analyzed from the standpoint of comparative analysis,[6] even though his comparative emphasis is widely appreciated.

In undertaking such an analysis, I intend to treat Tocqueville's two classic works—*Democracy in America* and *The Old Regime and the French Revolution*—as a single study in comparative sociological explanation. At first glance this may seem unjustified, because the publication of the two works was separated by more than 20 years, and because the former is primarily an attempt to describe, account for, and examine the consequences of the conditions of social equality in an entire nation; and the latter is an attempt to account for the rise, development, and consequences of a monumental historical event. Study of the works reveals, however, that in both of them Tocqueville was preoccupied with a set of intellectual issues concerning equality and inequality, freedom and despotism, and political stability and instability. Furthermore, the works constitute something of a double-mirror; Tocqueville's analysis of the condition of America is continually informed by his diagnosis of French society, and vice versa.[7] And finally, as I hope to demonstrate, a single perspective on social structure and social change informs his insights about each nation and renders the two nations comparable.

The chapter will be divided into three sections. In the first I shall outline Tocqueville's view of Western social structure—with special reference to equality—and its historical development. In the second I shall outline his account of different conditions of equality and his account of the differences between the United States and France. And in the third section I

---

[4] Alexis de Tocqueville, *The Old Regime and the French Revolution*, originally published in 1856. References in this chapter are to the Doubleday Anchor Edition (Garden City, N.Y., 1955), and *The Recollections of Alexis de Tocqueville*, ed. with an introduction by J. P. Mayer (Cleveland and New York: World Publishing Company, 1965).

[5] See Mayer, ed., *The Recollections of Alexis de Tocqueville*.

[6] An exception is Melvin Richter, "Comparative Political Analysis in Montesquieu and Tocqueville," *Comparative Politics*, 1(1969): 129–60.

[7] Tocqueville revealed his comparative perspective on the first page of his "Author's Introduction" to *Democracy in America*, where he observed that the quality that most distinguishes the United States—"the general equality of condition among the people"—is furthest developed in that country, and is in the process of unfolding in Europe. Later in the introduction, he noted that "as the generating cause of laws and manners in the two countries is the same [that is, equality of condition], it is of immense interest for us to know what it has produced in each of them." Tocqueville, "Author's Introduction" to *Democracy in America*, 1:14. See also George Pierson, *Tocqueville in America* (Garden City, N.Y.: Doubleday, 1959), pp. 53–54.

shall identify his comparative strategies—the kinds of empirical data and logical argumentation he used to buttress his case.

Tocqueville's General Perspective on Society and Change

It is possible to discern in Tocqueville's work an overriding preoccupation with a single issue, without reference to which most of his observations or insights cannot be appreciated. This issue is social equality versus social inequality.

In considering this issue, moreover, Tocqueville tended to think of two extreme ways of structuring equality in society—the aristocratic, in which equality was minimized, and the democratic, in which it was maximized. And though Tocqueville did not develop anything like a methodology of the "ideal type," his use of the notions of aristocracy and democracy throughout his work suggests that they are, indeed, abstract concepts to which no empirical instance corresponds perfectly, but to which different degrees of historical approximation may be found.[8]

Tocqueville looked back to 11th-century France to find an approximation of the pure case of a society organized according to aristocratic values: "the territory was divided among a small number of families, who were the owners of the soil and the rulers of the inhabitants; the right of governing descended with the family inheritance from generation to generation; force was the only means by which man could act on man; and landed property was the sole source of power."[9] While unequal from the standpoint of distribution of wealth and power, France and other societies in medieval Europe were nonetheless regulated by a web of customs and understandings that inhibited the development of despotism.

> There was a time in Europe when the laws and the consent of the people had invested princes with almost unlimited authority, but they scarcely ever availed themselves of it. I do not speak of the prerogatives of the nobility, of the authority of high courts of justice, of corporations and their chartered rights, or of provincial privileges, which served to break the blows of sovereign authority and keep up a spirit of resistance in the nation. Independently of these political institutions, which, however opposed they might be to personal liberty, served to keep alive the love of freedom in the mind and which may be esteemed useful in this respect, the manners and opinions of the nation confined the royal authority within barriers that were not less

[8] Richter, "Comparative Political Analysis," pp. 154–56.
[9] Tocqueville, *Democracy in America*, 1:4.

powerful because less conspicuous. Religion, the affections of the people, the benevolence of the prince, the sense of honor, family pride, provincial prejudices, custom, and public opinion limited the power of kings and restrained their authority within an invisible circle. The constitution of nations was despotic at that time, but their customs were free. Princes had the right, but they had neither the means nor the desire of doing whatever they pleased.[10]

For an approximation of the pure case of democratic society, Tocqueville looked toward the United States of America. Writing in 1835, he saw America as the nation where the social evolution toward equality "seems to have nearly reached its natural limits."[11] In direct contrast to aristocratic society, its laws of inheritance call for equal partition of property, which makes for a "constant tendency [for property] to diminish and . . . in the end be completely dispersed."[12] Tocqueville commented on Americans' love of money, but added that "wealth circulates with inconceivable rapidity, and experience shows that it is rare to find two succeeding generations in the full enjoyment of it."[13]

Tocqueville argued that democratic societies are likely to become despotic as men turn away from public affairs, as government becomes more centralized, and as public opinion develops into a tyranny of the majority. Yet Tocqueville found in America a number of social forces that "allow a democratic people to remain free."[14] He singled out various "accidental" factors contributing to this effect, such as the absence of hostile neighboring powers,[15] but he emphasized laws and customs as the most important forces. Among the laws, he identified the principle of federal union, the institutionalization of townships, and the judicial system; and among the customs he stressed the presence of a common religion that encourages liberty, the separation of church and state, a common language, and a high level of education.[16] Comparing the impact of laws and customs, he found the latter more decisive.[17] He also regarded the freedom of the press and the presence of voluntary political associations as important mechanisms to forestall the development of despotism.[18]

Nothing stands out more clearly in Tocqueville's work than his convic-

[10] Ibid., 1:338–39.
[11] Ibid., 1:14.
[12] Ibid., 1:51.
[13] Ibid., 1:53.
[14] Ibid., 1:342.
[15] Ibid., 1:299.
[16] Ibid., vol. 1, ch. 17.
[17] Ibid., 1:330–34.
[18] Ibid., vol. 1, chs. 11–12.

tion of the inexorability of the Western historical transition from aristocracy to democracy, from inequality to equality. In 1832 he wrote that the development of the principle of equality is "a providential fact. It has all the chief characteristics of such a fact: it is universal, it is lasting, it constantly eludes all human interference, and all events as well as all men contribute to its progress."[19] Writing in 1848, he professed not to be surprised at the events of the recent revolution in France, because of his long awareness of the universality and irresistability of the advance of the principle of equality.[20] And in 1856 he wrote that "all our contemporaries are driven on by a force that we may hope to regulate or curb, but cannot overcome, and it is a force impelling them, sometimes gently, sometimes at headlong speed, to the destruction of aristocracy."[21]

Furthermore, Tocqueville found many of the roots of despotism, tyranny, and instability in the transition between aristocracy and democracy. If any single proposition dominates his interpretation of the cause of the French Revolution and its excesses, it is this: France had historical origins similar to many other European—and indeed American—societies. But in the 18th century France had experienced certain changes that had *partially* destroyed aristocratic society and *partially* advanced the principle of equality. It was this unstable mixture of the two principles that made for the dissatisfaction, selfishness and self-seeking, conflict, despotism, and diminished national morale that culminated in the revolutionary convulsion late in the century.[22] One of the advantages that America possessed, moreover, was that it was able to start afresh, to establish a democracy without having to go through the pains of destroying an aristocracy. "[America] is reaping the fruits of the democratic revolution which we are undergoing, without having had the revolution itself."[23]

Two fundamental distinctions thus inform Tocqueville's comparative work. The first is the distinction between aristocracy and democracy; the second is between either of these conditions, institutionalized consistently, and the social condition built on a mixture of both. The comparison between 18th-century France and 19th-century America, then, becomes one of a society that had proceeded part way along the transition from aristocratic to democratic, with one that had been born democratic, as it were, and manifested the characteristics of a democratic system in relatively pure form. Within this kind of comparison, furthermore, a number of specific questions emerged: By what historical process is aristocratic society eroded

[19] Ibid., 1:6.
[20] Ibid., 1:ix.
[21] Tocqueville, *The Old Regime and the French Revolution*, p. xii.
[22] Ibid., pp. xii–xiv.
[23] Tocqueville, *Democracy in America*, 1:14.

by the principles of equality? How does this contrast with the historical development of the principle of equality *de novo?*[24] What consequences for ideas and social outlook are generated by these two conditions of society?[25] What are the political consequences that follow from these ideas, particularly with respect to political revolution and the development of despotism?[26]

Tocqueville's Explanation of the Differences Between France and America

France versus America: equality obtained at the cost of aristocracy versus "pure" equality

Two historical trends were especially powerful in undermining the principle of aristocracy in 18th-century France, according to Tocqueville: the centralization and paternalization of government and the partial advance of certain social classes in French society toward equality.

Tocqueville devoted much of the early part of his work on the *ancien régime* to describing the extensive centralization of powers in the government in Paris.

> We find a single central power located at the heart of the kingdom and controlling public administration throughout the country; a single Minister of State in charge of almost all the internal affairs of the country; in each province a single representative of government supervising every detail of the administration; no secondary administrative bodies authorized to take action on their own initiative; and, finally, "exceptional" courts for the trial of cases involving the administration or any of its officers.[27]

Why had this centralization taken place? Tocqueville noted simply that the

[24] Tocqueville devoted most of part two of *The Old Regime and the French Revolution* to the first question. He characterized this part as an effort to specify the "circumstances remote in time and of a general order which prepared the way for the great revolution." P. 138. Most of the first volume of *Democracy in America* was devoted to the second question.

[25] Tocqueville's analysis of the characteristics of the revolutionary ideology in *The Old Regime and the French Revolution* addressed itself to these questions, as did the first three books of volume two of *Democracy in America.*

[26] Tocqueville addressed this question in his discussion of the impact of the French Revolution in *The Old Regime and the French Revolution.* He discussed the same set of issues in the fourth book, volume two, of *Democracy in America,* which is entitled "Influence of Democratic Ideas and Feelings on Political Society."

[27] Tocqueville, *The Old Regime and the French Revolution,* p. 57.

government "merely yielded to the instinctive desire of every government to gather all the reins of power into its own hands."[28]

Far as these tendencies proceeded, they had not gone all the way. Local assemblies still existed, though they had no real power;[29] those who had been previously in the ruling classes still possessed their ranks and titles, "but all effective authority was gradually withdrawn from them."[30] The old aristocratic order was in a state of partial eclipse.

Other groups had also experienced changes in their social condition, but unlike the aristocracy—which was being edged out of its former position of influence—they had enjoyed partial advances. The bourgeois class had improved its situation with respect to wealth, education, and style of life, but it had failed to gain access to various feudal rights.[31] The peasants owned more land than in times past and had been freed from the harshness of government and landlords, but were still subjected to certain traditional duties and taxes. In addition, "in an age of industrial progress [the peasants] had no share in it; in a social order famed for its enlightenment they remained backward and uneducated."[32]

Why should these changes have been unsettling to all these groups? To answer this question Tocqueville invoked—though only implicitly—a version of the social-psychological principle we now refer to as "relative deprivation." The social changes experienced in 18th-century France produced a number of groups which were losing in some respects while retaining or gaining in others. For Tocqueville these inconsistencies were psychologically more unsettling than the social arrangements of aristocratic feudalism, for under that system men might have been worse off in some absolute sense, but their access to the good things in life was organized according to a consistent principle. On the basis of this assumption, Tocqueville argued that the various groups—noblemen, middle classes, and peasants—were more dissatisfied with the state of affairs in France than they had been in the past.

This complicated system of social inequities had the consequence of isolating these groups and setting them at odds with one another. Each group tried to clutch those privileges that it had, to gain those it did not have, and to rid itself of burdens not shared by other groups. Relative deprivation also appeared to foster a peculiar form of social aloofness and antagonism:

[28] Ibid., p. 58.
[29] Ibid., p. 50.
[30] Ibid., p. 51.
[31] Ibid., pp. 80–81.
[32] Ibid., p. 133.

While the bourgeois and nobleman were becoming more and more alike in many ways, the gap between them was steadily widening, and these two tendencies, far from counteracting each other, often had the opposite effect . . . the bourgeois was almost as aloof from the "common people" as the noble from the bourgeois.[33]

The central government itself welcomed this social divisiveness, since the consequence was that no single group could muster the strength to challenge its power.[34] The cumulative effect of all these conditions was to leave 18th-century France in a very precarious state of integration:

Once the bourgeois had been completely severed from the noble, and the peasant from both alike, and when a similar differentiation had taken place within each of these three classes, with the result that each was split up into a number of small groups almost completely shut off from each other, the inevitable consequence was that, though the nation came to seem a homogeneous whole, its parts no longer held together. Nothing had been left that could obstruct the central government, but, by the same token, nothing could shore it up. This is why the grandiose edifice built up by our Kings was doomed to collapse like a card castle once disturbances arose within the social order on which it was based.[35]

By contrast Tocqueville saw in America a multitude of factors making for a general equality of condition, and inhibiting the development of either aristocracy or centralization. Many factors inherited from the colonial tradition contributed to this: the unifying effect of a common language; the common social origins of most of the immigrants; land in plenty; an emphasis on education; and a religious tradition that nourished a spirit of liberty.[36] He identified the township as a particularly important corrective to centralization. The township was "the nucleus around which the local interests, passions, rights, and duties collected and clung. It gave scope to the activity of a real political life, thoroughly democratic and republican."[37] The township was able to resist the incursion of the states and the federal government; it was, in fact, the generalization of the loyalty to the small township at the national level that gave American patriotism its distinctive character.[38] Interestingly, Tocqueville found a point of common origin to the French parish and the North American township—the

---

[33] Ibid., pp. 84, 89.
[34] Ibid., p. 106.
[35] Ibid., pp. 136–37.
[36] Tocqueville, *Democracy in America*, vol. 1, ch. 2.
[37] Ibid., 1:42.
[38] Ibid., 1:62, 68, 170.

medieval rural parish. In America, however, the parish had been "free to develop a total independence" as it grew into the township, whereas in Europe it had been "controlled at every turn by an all-powerful government." The French and American systems of local government thus "resembled each other—in so far as a dead creature can be said to resemble one that is very much alive."[39]

Out of their colonial origins the Americans had created a federal constitution, electoral and party systems, and a free press, all of which contributed to the political liberty of the people. Tocqueville repeatedly stressed that the Americans were a people dominated by uniform customs and by the sway of public opinion; but politically America contrasted with many of the European countries in that relatively little control over the lives of the people was exercised by a centralized government.

What effect did these conditions of equality and liberty have on feelings of relative deprivation, and on the relations among groups and classes in society? Tocqueville certainly saw the Americans as an ambitious, restless, and chronically dissatisfied people. And he believed that these characteristics arose from the condition of equality. When ranks are intermingled and men are forever rising or sinking in the social scale, there always exists a class of citizens "whose fortunes are decreasing" and a class of citizens "whose fortune is on the increase, but whose desires grow much faster than their fortunes."[40] Under conditions of equality the slightest inequalities are likely to become the source of frustration and the object of envy.

> Among democratic nations, men easily attain a certain equality of condition, but they can never attain as much as they desire. It perpetually retires from before them, yet without hiding itself from their sight, and in retiring draws them on. At every moment they think they are about to grasp it; it escapes at every moment from their hold. They are near enough to see its charms, but too far off to enjoy them; and before they have fully tasted its delights, they die.[41]

The spiritual life of a democratic nation, then, reveals a kind of haunting melancholy in the midst of abundance.

Having acknowledged this great restlessness, however, Tocqueville proceeded to argue that its consequences for social instability were not significant. And in so doing he once again appealed to his distinction between aristocracy and democracy, citing 18th-century France as the mixture of the two. In aristocracies, great inequalities prevail, but dissatisfaction is

---

[39] Tocqueville, *The Old Regime and the French Revolution*, p. 48.
[40] Tocqueville, *Democracy in America*, 2:51–52.
[41] Ibid., 2:147.

low because "the people . . . get as much accustomed to poverty as the rich to their opulence. The latter bestow no anxiety on their physical comforts because they enjoy them without an effort; the former do not think of things which they despair of obtaining, and which they hardly know enough of to desire."[42]

When ranks and privileges erode, however, and when the principle of equality begins to advance, ambition runs rampant:

> The desire of acquiring the comforts of the world haunts the imagination of the poor, and the dread of losing that of the rich. Many scanty fortunes spring up; those who possess them have a sufficient share of physical gratifications to conceive a taste for these pleasures, not enough to satisfy it. They never procure them without exertion, and they never indulge in them without apprehension. They are therefore always straining to pursue or retain gratifications so delightful, so imperfect, so fugitive.[43]

The people inherit the standards of opulence of the old society, and combine them with the ambitiousness of the new. The result is a great gulf between expectations and reality.

As indicated, democratic societies are also characterized by great ambition and envy. But because social differences are less extreme, because the rich were once themselves poor, and because they do not hold themselves aloof from the poor, social distinctions are less invidious. People are ambitious, but their ambitions are limited by modest expectations. "Rich men who live amid democratic nations are . . . more intent on providing for their smallest wants than for their extraordinary enjoyments . . . thus they are more apt to become enervated than debauched."[44]

Furthermore, democracies tend to individualize ambitions, and to throw men back upon themselves. Because no group is powerful enough to sway the fortunes of the nation, people "acquire the habit of always considering themselves as standing alone. . . ."[45] The principle of aristocracy, by contrast, links men into an organized system of estates. And once again, Tocqueville saw the transitional period of popular revolution as combining both aristocratic and democratic principles. Such a revolution creates "democratic confusion," in which ambition reigns, but in which it has not yet become completely individualized. Relative deprivation is still collectivized, and as a result "implacable animosities are kindled between the

[42] Ibid., 2:137.

[43] Ibid.

[44] Ibid., 2:140. Elsewhere Tocqueville noted that "among democratic nations, ambition is ardent and continual, but its aim is not habitually lofty; and life is generally spent in eagerly coveting small objects that are within reach." Ibid., 2:258.

[45] Ibid., 2:105–6.

different classes of society."[46] In democracies, collective action and collective conflict tend to be based less on class and more on the formation of voluntary associations, which Tocqueville interpreted as a corrective both to extreme individualism and isolation and to the tyranny of the majority that endangers democracies.[47]

France versus America: revolutionary ideas versus pragmatism

Given these contrasts in social condition, it is not surprising that Tocqueville also found great differences in national ideas and outlook between France and America. Basically he found Frenchmen more speculative and revolutionary in outlook, Americans more pragmatic and conservative. Tocqueville invoked three kinds of explanations for these differences.

(1) The condition of equality itself accounts for the differences. As we have seen, Tocqueville viewed all classes in France as having moved part way toward the principle of equality, and all classes as rankling under the burden of institutional inconsistencies. An understanding of these circumstances helps to explain why a "total" revolutionary ideology developed in 18th-century France. The irregular decay of France's aristocracy had left a confused social system. All classes were experiencing inequities, but these took different forms in each class. The kind of ideology that was most likely to have widespread appeal among all classes was that which created "an imaginary ideal society in which all was simple, uniform, coherent, equitable, and rational in the full sense of the term."[48] The particularities of each class's outlook could be subsumed only under a generalized belief which reconstructed everything in society, rather than under one which tinkered only with some of its parts. Frenchmen believed that everything feudal had to be destroyed, and "all [classes] were quite ready to sink their differences and to be integrated into a homogeneous whole, provided no one was given a privileged position and rose above the common level."[49] Such were some of the pressures to revolutionize and universalize ideas about man and society in 18th-century France.

In democratic America Tocqueville found a great deal of frantic activity, which took the form of "a small, distressing motion, a sort of incessant jostling of men, which annoys and disturbs the mind without exciting or elevating it."[50] Yet great revolutionary ideas were rare. Tocqueville at-

[46] Ibid., 2:107.
[47] Ibid., vol. 1, ch. 12, and vol. 2, chs. 5–6.
[48] Tocqueville, *The Old Regime and the French Revolution*, p. 146.
[49] Ibid., p. 96.
[50] Tocqueville, *Democracy in America*, 2:44.

tributed this to the existence of equality. Democratic societies have some very wealthy and some very poor persons, but between these two groups stands "an innumerable multitude of men, who without being exactly either rich or poor, possess sufficient property to desire the maintenance of order, yet not enough to excite envy."[51] Revolutions are not attractive to this middle class, because revolutions invariably threaten the property system. The majority of people in the United States, being directed toward commercial gains, displayed little inclination for ideas that threatened to modify the laws of property. Because of the differences in equality between America and Europe, Tocqueville concluded that "in America men have the opinions and passions of democracy; in Europe we still have the passions and opinions of revolution."[52] For the same reason he saw the only serious possibility of revolution in America to lie in "the presence of the black race on the soil of the United States," a race which continued to experience inequities in a system dedicated to equality.[53]

(2) The level of political participation creates differences in political outlook. Tocqueville did perceive a penchant for generalizations among the Americans that was greater than that of the British. He attributed this also to the existence of equality in America: "He . . . who inhabits a democratic country sees around him on every hand men differing but little from one another; he cannot turn his mind to any one portion of mankind without expanding and dilating his thought till it embraces the whole."[54] Yet he found eagerness for general political ideas to be greater in France than in America, which seems paradoxical, since he viewed democracy as generally less advanced in France than in America. He explained the difference, however, not in terms of equality of condition but in terms of the level of political participation. In America, where the institutions compel all citizens to take part in government, the "excessive taste for general theories in politics which the principle of equality suggests" is diminished.[55] In France, by contrast, social conditions "led them to conceive very general ideas on the subject of government, while their political constitution prevented them from correcting those ideas by experiment and from gradually detecting their insufficiency."[56] Frenchmen experienced only frustration when trying to make their voices heard in any meaningful political way;

[51] Ibid., 2:266.
[52] Ibid., 2:270.
[53] Ibid., 2:270. Future historians, viewing the turbulences of the 1860s and 1960s, may view this passage as yet another of Tocqueville's great prophecies.
[54] Ibid., 2:16.
[55] Ibid., 2:20.
[56] Ibid., 2:19.

hence, they tended to be drawn to the more abstract principles generated by the philosophers.[57] In noting these differences Tocqueville was enunciating what has become almost a sociological axiom: political exclusion and frustration generates generalized disaffection and utopian thinking, whereas political participation generates moderation and a preoccupation with particulars.

(3) The place of religion in society creates differences in political outlook. Tocqueville noted that in America religion was not only separated from politics, but itself encouraged the principles of democracy.[58] One consequence of this is that religious controversy was separated from political controversy, and the ideologies associated with each were also separated. As a result, these ideologies were more limited in their generality. In Europe, however, where the breakdown of the feudal order was incomplete, and where the church was intimately associated with the political life of the nation, "unbelievers . . . attack the Christians as their political opponents rather than as their religious adversaries."[59] This fusion of religion and politics meant that protest became both more extreme and more generalized:

> Both religious institutions and the whole system of government were thrown into the melting pot, with the result that men's minds were in a state of utter confusion; they knew neither what to hold on to, nor where to stop. Revolutionaries of a hitherto unknown breed came on the scene: men who carried audacity to the point of sheer insanity; who balked at no innovation, and, unchecked by any scruples, acted with an unprecedented ruthlessness.[60]

France versus America: revolution and increased centralization versus stability and inhibited centralization

Everything so far indicates that Tocqueville viewed the institutions of France as predisposing her to great social revolutions, and the institutions of America as predisposing her to a social stability combined with frenetic individual activity. However, most of the conditions described—the level of centralization of government, the level of collectivized relative deprivation, and so on—are rather indeterminate in their character, and, of themselves, do not really explain the occurrence or lack of occurrence of a single historical event, such as a revolution. Rather, Tocqueville's reason-

---

[57] Tocqueville, *The Old Regime and the French Revolution*, p. 205.
[58] Tocqueville, *Democracy in America*, 1:45–46; vol. 2, ch. 5.
[59] Ibid., 1:325.
[60] Tocqueville, *The Old Regime and the French Revolution*, p. 157.

ing thus far simply helps to understand the probability of the occurrence of such events.

Tocqueville was aware of the different levels of generality in the factors he used to explain the occurrence of the French Revolution. He devoted part two of *The Old Regime and the French Revolution* to specifying the "circumstances remote in time and of a general order which prepared the way for the great revolution."[61] Most of the factors we have reviewed thus far fall into this category. Most of his explicit comparisons between France and America, moreover, were made at this level. But in order to gain a more precise explanation of the revolution, Tocqueville also examined (in part three) the "particular, more recent events which finally determined [the revolution's] place of origin, its outbreak, and the form it took."[62] These include events such as the increasing relative deprivation of various classes in the decades before the revolution;[63] various repressive measures, such as the abolition of the *parlements* in 1771;[64] hasty and ill-conceived reforms, some of which were quickly reversed;[65] and a variety of unjust practices against the poor.[66]

Thus a kind of general model of historical causation emerges—a model of general, indeterminate causes, within the scope of which more particular and determinate causes are identified. On the basis of the combination of these predisposing and precipitating conditions, Tocqueville regarded the French revolution as "a foregone conclusion."[67] The effect of the combined factors "was cumulative and overwhelming."[68]

On the last two pages of his book on the French Revolution Tocqueville had recourse to yet another explanatory factor—French national character —which made revolution "more drastic" than it was elsewhere:

Ordinarily the French are the most routine-bound of men, but once they are forced out of the rut and leave their homes, they travel to the ends of the earth and engage in the most reckless ventures. Undisciplined by temperament, the Frenchman is always more ready to put up with the arbitrary rule, however harsh, of an autocrat than with a free, well-ordered govern-

[61] Ibid., p. 138.
[62] Ibid.
[63] This took various forms, such as increasing prosperity (ibid., pp. 174–76), the increasing institutional uncertainty of the workers (ibid., p. 193), and the increasing concern for the welfare of the poor (ibid., p. 186).
[64] Ibid., p. 166.
[65] Ibid., pp. 188, 194–98.
[66] Ibid., pp. 190–91.
[67] Ibid., p. 203.
[68] Ibid., p. 211.

ment by his fellow citizens, however worthy of respect they be. . . . He is more prone to heroism than to humdrum virtue, apter for genius than for good sense, more inclined to think up grandiose schemes than to carry through great enterprises. Thus the French are at once the most brilliant and the most dangerous of all European nations, and the best qualified to become in the eyes of other peoples, an object of admiration, of hatred, of compassion, or alarm—never of indifference.[69]

This "all-or-nothing" feature of the French temperament suggests that French revolutions would be more extreme than others. Add to this Tocqueville's earlier argument that the inequities among the several classes in 18th-century France made for a total onslaught on all the archaic institutions, and the inevitable conclusion unfolds: The extreme destructiveness of the French Revolution created the setting for an even more centralized government to enforce order in its wake.

> Since the object of the Revolution was not merely to change an old form of government but to abolish the entire social structure of pre-revolutionary France, it was obliged to declare war simultaneously on all established powers, to destroy all recognized prerogatives, to make short work of all traditions, and to institute new ways of living, new conventions. . . . But beneath the seemingly chaotic surface there was developing a vast, highly centralized power. . . . This new power was created by the Revolution, or rather, grew up almost automatically out of the havoc wrought by it. True, the governments it set up were less stable than any of those it overthrew; yet, paradoxically, they were infinitely more powerful.[70]

The effect of French political ideas and actions, then, was to set in motion a circle of revolutionary instability and increasing centralization and despotism.

As we have seen, Tocqueville believed that the main forces of American democracy inhibited great revolutions and made for a generally stable social order. Yet he also saw many forces in democracies that increased the probability of despotism. In the fourth book of volume two of *Democracy in America* he set out to trace the political influence of democratic ideas, and in this effort he enunciated the following principle: "That the opinions of democratic nations about government are naturally favorable to the concentration of power."[71] Since democracy minimizes the vesting of power and privileges in separate social groups, the possibility of strict

---

[69] Ibid., pp. 210–11.
[70] Ibid., pp. 8–9.
[71] Tocqueville, *Democracy in America*, 2:306.

uniformity of laws, emanating from a central source, arises.[72] Furthermore, because democracies foster individualistic sentiments, they encourage attention to private affairs, and abandonment of public business to the state.[73] Equality breeds conditions of individual independence and powerlessness, and the tendency is to rely on the state to protect the individual against others.[74] In these ways democracy and centralization may become involved in a self-reinforcing spiral.

> [The] never dying, ever kindling hatred which sets a democratic people against the smallest privileges is peculiarly favorable to the gradual concentration of all political rights in the hands of the representative of the state alone. . . . Every central power, which follows its natural tendencies, courts and encourages the principle of equality; for equality singularly facilitates, extends, and secures the influence of a central power.[75]

Tocqueville found this spiral more pronounced in some democracies than others, and once again, he found the absence of aristocratic traditions in America to be important in diminishing the tendencies toward centralization. In America, equality was a characteristic of the people from their birth, whereas in Europe, "equality, introduced by absolute power and under the rule of kings, was already infused into the habits of nations long before freedom had entered into their thoughts."[76] When the old regime was swept away by the storm, there remained a "confused mass," which was ready to turn powers over to the central state. Thus Tocqueville invoked his explanatory principle of the transition between aristocracy and democracy once again:

> The supreme power is always stronger, and private individuals weaker, among a democratic people that has passed through a long and arduous struggle to reach a state of equality than among a democratic community in which the citizens have been equal from the first. The example of the Americans completely demonstrates the fact. The inhabitants of the United States were never divided by any privileges; they have never known the mutual relation of master and inferior; and as they neither dread nor hate each other, they have never known the necessity of calling in the supreme power to manage their affairs. The lot of the Americans is singular: they have derived from the aristocracy of England the notion of private rights

[72] Ibid., 2:307.
[73] Ibid., 2:310.
[74] Ibid., 2:311.
[75] Ibid., 2:312.
[76] Ibid., 2:315.

and the taste for local freedom; and they have been able to retain both because they have had no aristocracy to combat.[77]

Tocqueville's Comparative Methods

Thus far I have been concerned mainly with the *substance* of Tocqueville's comparisons between France and America—the general perspective that informed these comparisons, the specific explanatory problems he posed, and his explanatory account of the contrasting histories of the two nations. Now we turn to the *methods* by which he attempted to demonstrate his case. What kind of comparative arguments did he use? To what kinds of data did he refer? What, in short, were his comparative strategies?

In approaching Tocqueville's methods, it must be remembered that his national comparisons and contrasts were made in the context of a *partially formulated* model of the complex interaction of historical forces.[78] I have attempted to outline the guiding assumptions and the central propositions of this model in the foregoing pages. To facilitate the discussion of Tocqueville's comparisons, I have represented schematically, in figure 2-1, some of the "circumstances remote in time and of a general order" that predisposed France to revolutionary turmoil.

Several comments on figure 2-1 are in order. (1) I have entered as "variables" the historical forces identified by Tocqueville in *The Old Regime and the French Revolution*. The arrows indicate causal direction, as inferred from his analysis. Factors not in parentheses refer to features of French society identified by Tocqueville as critical to his analysis, whereas factors in parentheses indicate psychological assumptions and assertions employed by him to round out his analysis. (2) The chart is only a partial and illustrative representation of Tocqueville's theory. In particular, I have omitted any reference to his account of the "particular, more recent events" that affected the time and place of the Revolution's occurrence, as well as any reference to the political impact of the revolutionary ideology. These factors could, however, be represented in a way similar to figure 2-1. (3) If the figure were to be redrawn to represent the American case, different values would have to be entered for the several variables (for example, the

---

[77] Ibid., 2:316. Tocqueville cited a number of other circumstances—level of education, infrequency of wars, and strategies of the sovereign—that influence the level of centralization. His discussion implied comparisons between America and Europe, but he did not make them explicit. Ibid., pp. 316–20.

[78] I underscore the words "partially formulated" because Tocqueville himself did not state the relations of the "model" formally; and, in general, he was vigorously opposed to viewing history in terms of general laws. Richter, "Comparative Political Analysis," p. 153.

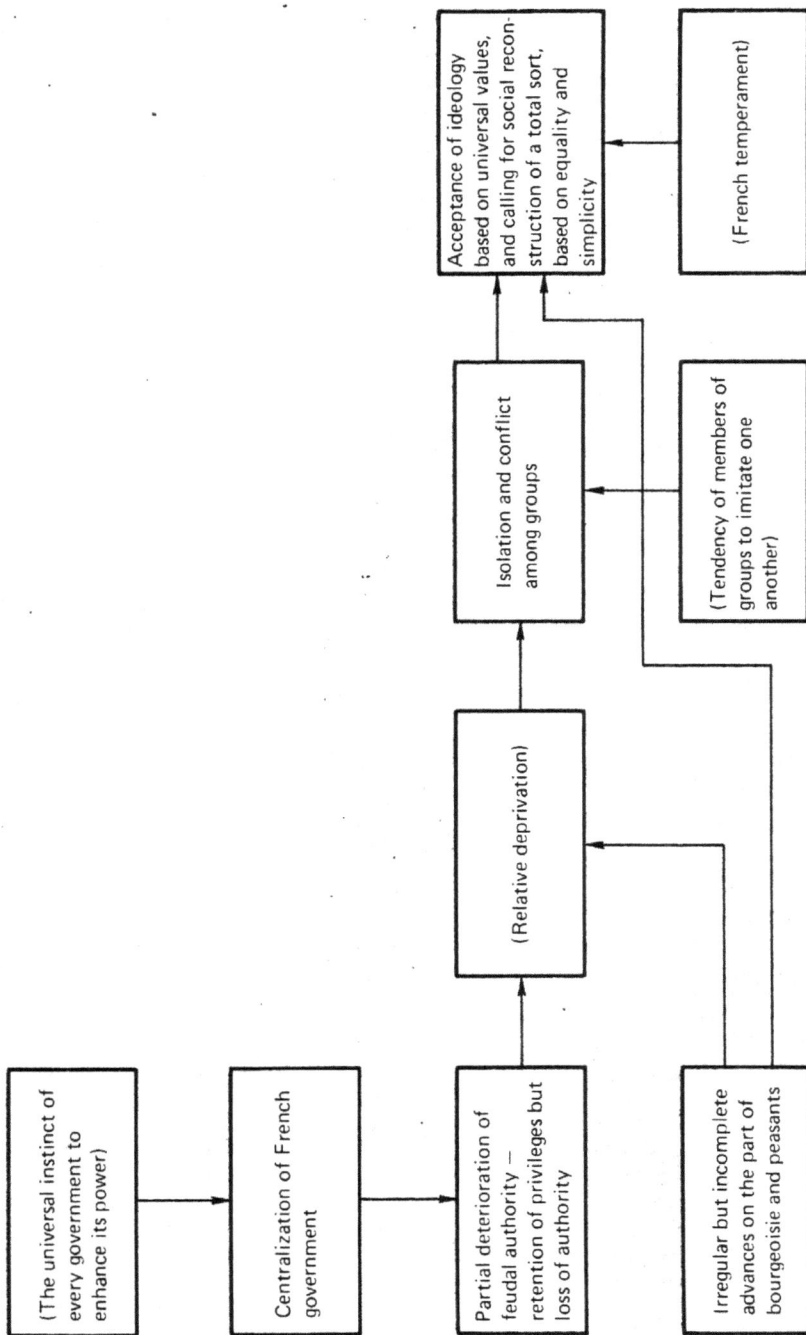

FIG. 2–1 Tocqueville's Model of "Circumstances Remote in Time and of a General Order"

The boxes in the diagram contain the following text:

(The universal instinct of every government to enhance its power)

Centralization of French government

Partial deterioration of feudal authority — retention of privileges but loss of authority

Irregular but incomplete advances on the part of bourgeoisie and peasants

(Relative deprivation)

Isolation and conflict among groups

(Tendency of members of groups to imitate one another)

Acceptance of ideology based on universal values, and calling for social reconstruction of a total sort, based on equality and simplicity

(French temperament)

variable of "centralization of French government" would be replaced by a variable such as "decentralization and the autonomy of the American township"). In addition, a different "map" of causal forces would have to be constructed to represent the distinctive patterning of socio-cultural factors in 19th-century America. Finally, the American "map" would incorporate certain "accidental" geographical and historical factors that influenced the main variables.

Given Tocqueville's guiding conceptual framework and his desire to account for the divergent historical courses taken by France and America, it is not surprising that most of his comparative illustrations focused on the *differences* rather than the *similarities* between these two countries.[79] In pursuing these illustrations, moreover, Tocqueville used a number of related but distinguishable strategies.

1. *Two-nation comparisons: different causes associated with different effects.* Tocqueville's most common strategy was to identify two sets of different characteristics of two nations with the explicit or implicit claim that the differences on one set of characteristics (effects) are to be explained with reference to the other (causes). In discussing the causes of intensive group conflict in France, for example, Tocqueville noted that in Britain the social classes are less isolated from one another than they were in France, implying that group conflict was not likely to be so bitter in England.[80] In discussing the importance of the "partial advance" of French peasants toward proprietorship and freedom, Tocqueville noted that this process had not gone nearly so far in either England or Germany,[81] thus implying that the level of "relative deprivation" among both British and German peasants was less than in France. Or again, Tocqueville contrasted the centralization of France with the local autonomy of the United States, claiming that the former encroached on the powers and responsibilities of traditional aristocratic classes—thus increasing their dissatisfactions—whereas the latter avoided this effect by safeguarding the liberty of citizens.[82]

[79] In logic this procedure follows John Stuart Mill's method of concomitant variation of cause and effect. Tocqueville's use of this method was usually very crude however, in that the "variation" consisted of the simple presence or absence of presumed causes and effects, and in that usually only two cases were compared.

[80] Tocqueville, *The Old Regime and the French Revolution*, pp. 97–98.

[81] Ibid., pp. 24–25.

[82] In a footnote in *Democracy in America* Tocqueville made explicit the different impact of the two systems of administration: "when I see the communes of France, with their excellent system of accounts, plunged into the grossest ignorance of their true interests, and abandoned to so incorrigible an apathy that they seem to vegetate rather than to live; when, on the other hand, I observe the activity, the information, and the spirit of enterprise in those American townships whose budgets are neither methodical nor uniform, I see that society is always at work." 1:95.

By dozens of such contrasts Tocqueville sought to strengthen each of the causal links in his complicated explanatory account. The common element in all these illustrations is the assertion that different outcomes in two nations (for example, revolutionary turmoil versus relative political stability) can be traced to different historical causes. Furthermore, the fact that nations differing with respect to outcomes also differ with respect to causes lends greater plausibility to Tocqueville's case than would an illustration from one nation alone.

2. *Within-nation comparisons: different causes associated with different effects.* To bolster his causal arguments further, Tocqueville attempted to replicate between-nation differences by showing that the same relations existed within nations. After pointing out that peasants in England and Germany had advanced less than those in France, Tocqueville turned to the German situation:

> It was chiefly along the Rhine that at the close of the eighteenth century German farmers owned the land they worked and enjoyed almost as much freedom as the French small proprietor; and it was there, too, that the revolutionary zeal of the French found its earliest adepts and took most permanent effect. On the other hand, the parts of Germany which held out longest against the current of new ideas were those where the peasants did not as yet enjoy such privileges.[83]

The within-Germany comparison thus yielded the same results as the France-Germany comparison. Noting that the general increase in prosperity in the second half of the 18th century aggravated the French social situation, Tocqueville observed that "it was precisely in those parts of France where there had been most improvement that popular discontent ran highest."[84] And on a number of occasions he pointed to the internal differences in the United States—particularly between New England and the South—to show that variations in the equality of social conditions produced different results.[85]

The logic of within-unit contrasts is identical to that of between-unit contrasts: to associate different effects with different causes. The objective of within-unit comparisons, moreover, is to lend greater plausibility to the causal assertion by observing the association in which it is presumably manifested in several different kinds of social units.

3. *Within-unit comparisons over time: different causes associated with different effects.* Tocqueville employed still another minor refinement on the method of citing differences. Arguing that the burst of prosperity just

[83] Tocqueville, *The Old Regime and the French Revolution*, p. 25.
[84] Ibid., p. 25.
[85] Tocqueville, *Democracy in America*, 1:211, 343ff.

before the French Revolution was of great importance in precipitating the turbulence, he noted that "a study of comparative statistics makes it clear that in none of the decades immediately following the Revolution did our national prosperity make such rapid forward strides as in the two preceding it."[86] In another passage he contrasted the severity of the 1789 revolution with the mildness of subsequent revolutions by pointing to the greater stability of the administrative system in the first half of the 19th century.[87] Once again, the logic of contrast is the same as in the previous two illustrations: the difference is that time, rather than national unit or region, is the basis of variation.

4. *Addition of a third, varying case to bolster a two-nation contrast.* Most of Tocqueville's national analysis involved two-nation references that highlighted differences relevant to his causal framework. On occasion, however, he supplemented this basic strategy by developing a contrast among three cases. I have already illustrated this strategy on a general level: both pure democracy and pure aristocracy are opposed to the transitional mixture of the two principles. Let me now turn to a more specific illustration. In the third book of the second volume of *Democracy in America,* Tocqueville set out to trace the influence of equality on manners and customs. Among the objects of his attention were the relations between masters and servants. He began by noting that these relations were most distant in England, least distant in France, with America occupying a middle position.[88] On first reading, this assertion struck me as anomalous, since in many respects Tocqueville regarded Britain as most aristocratic of the three, America as most democratic, and France as intermediate. He accounted for the differences, however, by relating them not only to the degree of equality in general, but also to the now familiar fact that aristocracy was in the process of breaking down in France. In England both masters and servants still constituted "small communities in the heart of the nation, and certain permanent notions of right and wrong are ultimately established among them." As a result, masters and servants agreed on the nature of "fame, virtue, honesty, and honor," and servants maintained themselves in a position of "servile honor."[89] In America, by contrast, the relations between masters and servants were organized in a way which made the two classes only temporarily unequal. The servant was willing to assume a subordinate role, because he knew it was organized on a contractually reciprocal and functionally specific basis.[90] England and

---

[86] Tocqueville, *The Old Regime and the French Revolution,* p. 174.
[87] Ibid., pp. 202–3.
[88] Tocqueville, *Democracy in America,* 2:187.
[89] Ibid., 2:188.
[90] Ibid., 2:191–93.

America differed, then, on the kind of rules on which the master-servant relationship was legitimized.

In France, however, it was a matter of the breakdown of aristocratic rules by the partial intrusion of democracy. In such "sad and troubled times," Tocqueville saw

> a confused and imperfect phantom of equality [haunting] the minds of servants; they do not at once perceive whether the equality to which they are entitled is to be found within or without the pale of domestic service, and they rebel in their hearts against a subordination to which they have subjected themselves and from which they derive actual profit. They consent to serve and they blush to obey; they like the advantages of service, but not the master; or, rather, they are not sure that they ought not themselves to be masters, and they are inclined to consider him who orders them as an unjust usurper of their own rights.[91]

Given the nature of the contrast Tocqueville was attempting to make—between the "pure" types and one mixed type—the selection of one comparative example that included all three types strengthened his argument more than any two-way comparison might have done.

5. *Identification of common characteristics of different nations to strengthen a preferred explanation.* One of the consequences of democracy, Tocqueville argued, was to make the daily intercourse between people relatively simple and easy. To bolster this argument he cited the differences in the behavior of Americans and Englishmen traveling abroad. Americans are at once friends because they conceive of themselves as equal. Englishmen, however, are quiet and remote unless they happen to be of the same social rank. To convince his readers that differences in equality of condition were responsible for these differences in behavior, Tocqueville pointed to the fact that "Americans are connected with England by their origin, their religion, their language, and partially by their customs; they differ only in their social condition. It may therefore be inferred that the reserve of the English proceeds from the constitution of their country much more than from that of its inhabitants."[92] The logic of this argument complements the procedure of simply citing differences: if it could be demonstrated that different outcomes (differences in daily comportment between Americans and English) are associated with similarities between the countries, this would constitute a *prima facie* case that the similarities cannot be operative as causes. Or, to put it more succinctly, a common cause

91 Ibid., 2:194–95.
92 Ibid., 2:180.

cannot have different effects, and hence, different causes must be sought within each separate nation.[93]

6. *Comparative statements with unknown comparative references.* On most occasions Tocqueville was quite explicit in identifying the units which manifested the differences he wished to explain—units such as specific nations, specific regions, or specific periods in time. On occasion, however, the comparative referent was left implicit at best. The clearest illustration of the lack of explicitness is his characterization of the importance of the French temperament as a conditioning feature of the French Revolution. After describing this temperament, he concluded that "France alone could have given birth to revolution so sudden, so frantic, and so thoroughgoing, yet so full of unexpected changes of direction, of anomalies and inconsistencies."[94] In this case no other temperaments were identified, and Tocqueville left it to the reader to fill in one or more "other" temperaments that would not have caused or permitted such turbulent effects. The argument is one variant of the method of analyzing differences so commonly found in Tocqueville's work, but in this instance the differing cases are not specified.

7. *Two rhetorical "strategies": the elimination of apparently plausible ideas and the resolution of paradoxes.* All the strategies considered up to this point have involved the explicit or implicit comparison of different data as between two—occasionally more—different social units, usually societies. In addition to using these strategies, Tocqueville sometimes made his case more convincing by using a number of conceptual and stylistic devices. These devices are not exactly "comparative strategies" in the sense discussed above, but rather are attempts to establish a point by a particular style of persuasion.

On occasion Tocqueville began an argument with a statement of what was a plausible or received view. Then he proceeded to assert and then demonstrate that the truth was the opposite, or at least more complex than that which was commonly believed. Consider the following: "How the chief and ultimate aim of the Revolution was not, as used to be thought, to overthrow religious and to weaken political authority in France."[95] Or, after describing the differences among master-servant rela-

---

[93] In using this explanatory strategy Tocqueville was moving in the direction of approximating John Stuart Mill's "method of difference," which establishes cause by grouping cases together that resemble one another in all respects except one point of disagreement, which is assigned causal status. For further discussion of the method of difference as approximated in the works of Durkheim, Weber, and more modern comparative analysts, see pp. 103–4, 146, 210–22.

[94] Tocqueville, *The Old Regime and the French Revolution*, p. 211.

[95] Ibid., p. 51.

tions in England, France, and America: "Such is the fact as it appears upon the surface of things; to discover the causes of that fact, it is necessary to search the matter thoroughly."[96] Or again: "A first glance at the administration of France under the old order gives the impression of a vast diversity of laws and authorities, a bewildering confusion of powers."[97] Going beyond this first glance, Tocqueville argued that, on the contrary, France had "a single central power located at the heart of the kingdom and controlling public administration throughout the country. . . ."[98] He then proceeded to account for this fact by one of his favorite notions: "Whenever a nation destroys its aristocracy, it almost automatically tends toward a centralization of power."[99]

Closely related to this strategy of "going behind the scenes" is Tocqueville's occasional practice of stating an apparent paradox, then resolving it by making recourse to a new way of looking at the phenomenon. In discussing the differential spread of revolutionary fervor in European countries, Tocqueville first whetted the reader's appetite with a paradox:

> At first sight it may appear surprising that the Revolution, whose primary aim . . . was to destroy every vestige of the institutions of the Middle Ages, should not have broken out in countries where those institutions had the greatest hold and bore most heavily on the people instead of those in which their yoke was relatively light.[100]

He then "resolved" this paradox by substituting a new assumption for the one that was implicit in the paradox. The new assumption was the notion of relative deprivation—that a half-decayed social system is more burdensome than a consistently organized system, even though the latter may be more oppressive.

The essence of such an argument is as follows: First, Tocqueville identified a historical phenomenon that, given "common sense" causal assumptions, appeared to be surprising or unexpected. Then, by a gradually unfolding argument, he pointed to another set of causes that made the effect "expected" after all. In this operation he was not uncovering any new data; rather he was modifying the intervening causal link and thus "making sense" of existing data.

The arguments of "eliminating plausible ideas" and "resolving paradoxes" are often persuasive. The persuasiveness, moreover, seems to me

[96] Tocqueville, *Democracy in America*, 2:187.
[97] Tocqueville, *The Old Regime and the French Revolution*, p. 33.
[98] Ibid., p. 57.
[99] Ibid., p. 60.
[100] Ibid., p. 22.

to rest on both cognitive and emotional grounds. On the one hand, they are persuasive in that they involve the creation of new hypotheses that are more nearly consistent with known data than other hypotheses. But there is a subtle emotional impact as well. By using these arguments Tocqueville led the reader to a world of new causes that other observers had either been unable to discern or had interpreted only superficially. Tocqueville's style often conveys the impression that he is sharing secret discoveries with his readers. He thereby capitalized on the considerable psychological impact that is experienced when the apparently surprising and mysterious is converted into the expected and understandable.

Assessment of Tocqueville's
Comparative Strategies

Having reviewed Tocqueville's array of comparative arguments, I turn now to what might be called a "methodological critique" of his comparative procedures. I venture this critique in a restricted sense. I do not intend to imply that Tocqueville should have proceeded differently in executing his studies, or that he ignored important concepts or sources of data. My intention is, rather, to discuss certain problems of inference that arise in his procedures and bear on the validity of his conclusions. For the moment I shall discuss these problems only with specific reference to Tocqueville's work; as the analysis of comparative methodology unfolds in various ways throughout the volume, however, we shall see that these problems are relevant to all comparative analysis and can be restated in more general terms.

I mention only in passing one large and obvious problem connected with Tocqueville's studies—the qualitative and impressionistic nature of much of the data on which he based his conclusions. Tocqueville was a thorough and indefatigable scholar, who attempted to maintain maximum objectivity in his research. Despite such qualities, much of the archival material available to him was necessarily limited. Furthermore, many of his comparisons were based on his impressions gained as a traveler, which, however penetrating, were of limited reliability.[101] As a result, appropriate qualification must be exercised in accepting his comparative observations.

Though I have stated the problem of the inadequacy of some of his data, I feel it would be tedious and unnecessary to examine in detail each

---

[101] For example, his "facts" on the differences between master-servant relations in France and England were based on an observation made by an American traveler, which Tocqueville believed confirmed his own impressions. Tocqueville, *Democracy in America*, 2:187.

of his conclusions according to the quality of data on which it was based. Instead, I shall focus on a number of more general problems in his comparative interpretations. I group these problems under three headings: (1) the use of indirect indicators for comparative variables; (2) the selection of comparative cases; (3) the imputation of causal relations to comparative associations.

1. *The use of indirect indicators for comparative variables.* From time to time Tocqueville noted in passing some of the methodological difficulties that arose in making national comparisons. At one point in *Democracy in America* he was led to inquire whether public expenditure was proportionately greater in France than in the United States. And in a remarkably detailed argument, he concluded that this could not be ascertained, both because the total wealth of neither country could be accurately known, and because the administrative and budgetary figures of the two countries were both incomplete and incomparable.[102] Furthermore, he warned that even to attempt an approximate statistical comparison would be misleading, adding wryly that "the mind is easily imposed upon by the affectation of exactitude which marks even the misstatements of statistics; and it adopts with confidence the errors which are appareled in the forms of mathematical truth."[103] Rather than adopt a direct measure, even an approximate one, however, Tocqueville gauged the prosperity of American citizens, "after having paid the dues of the state," and concluded that anyone who viewed the external appearance of Americans would "undoubtedly be led to the conclusion that the American of the United States contributes a much smaller portion of his income to the state than the citizen of France."[104] Such a measure suffers not only from being impressionistic but also from the fact—acknowledged by Tocqueville—that the total wealth of the respective nations was not known. Tocqueville should perhaps not be criticized too severely since he affirmed in principle the desirability of a direct measure. Yet the indirect measure he used includes not only the methodological problems of a direct estimate, but additional ones as well.

The example just cited is a minor one, and inconsequential, on the whole, for Tocqueville's general analysis. A more serious problem arises in connection with his reliance on what I referred to as "relative deprivation." As we have seen, Tocqueville regarded this psychological condition as an important causal factor in his explanation of social stability and instability. In particular, he argued that the incongruity of the social condition of the

102 Ibid., 1:228–31.
103 Ibid., 1:232.
104 Ibid.

population of 18th-century France—in which all the major classes were aware of discrepancies between their expectations and their experiences—made for a higher level of social dissatisfaction than existed in societies that were organized on consistently aristocratic or consistently democratic principles. This dissatisfaction, moreover, generated group conflict and ultimately revolutionary overthrow in France, phenomena which were much less in evidence in the other types of societies.

Most of the evidence that Tocqueville adduced to demonstrate the different levels of experienced deprivation in different societies is of two varieties: (1) data referring to the presumed social causes of the dissatisfaction (for example, that the French middle classes were advancing on some fronts and not others); and (2) data referring to the presumed social effects of the dissatisfaction (for example, group conflict, attraction to revolutionary beliefs). In most cases, that is, the evidence for deprivation is indirect, and refers either to its presumed causes or its presumed effects. To be sure, direct information on the psychological states of groups was scarcely available in Tocqueville's day, and the indirect measures were no doubt better than none. But with respect to the explanatory force of his argument, it is clear that without direct measures of deprivation Tocqueville's argument had to rest on the two unverified psychological generalizations: that discrepancies in status privileges are the source of greater dissatisfaction than absolute deprivations with respect to these privileges; and that these dissatisfactions manifest themselves in group conflict and revolutionary activity. Only with some direct measure of deprivation could the validity of these two generalizations—which are critical links in the chain of Tocqueville's reasoning—be established.

2. *The selection of comparative cases.* The main comparative preoccupation in Tocqueville's work lay in the systematic exploration of the similarities and differences between the United States and France. Sometimes, however, he cited other cases to underscore a point he was arguing (using England, Germany, Mexico, for example). I have already noted a number of these ancillary comparisons. In general, it is methodologically desirable to add more cases as a way of increasing the plausibility of comparative statements. Unless the investigator specifies the criteria by which additional cases are selected, however, he is likely to run two sorts of risks. First, he is likely to skip around illustratively, citing only a case or two that might support a point and ignoring other cases that may not be so clearly supportive. Second, to extract apparently similar (or different) phenomena from a variety of societies, without comparing also the socio-cultural context within which these phenomena occur, may lead to misinterpretations. As Tocqueville's work repeatedly illustrates, surface similarities between countries often turn out to be manifestations of very

opposed principles of social organization—for example, the character of rural parishes in France and the local townships in America. By and large, Tocqueville seemed to have a keen intuitive sense for the socio-cultural context of any given social item. Nevertheless, unless the criteria by which different cases are selected are made explicit—that is, unless the respective contexts are specified—there is a danger of comparing phenomena which in fact are not comparable.[105]

Tocqueville's comparative references are selective in a second sense. As we have seen, all his specific comparisons must be read in connection with the causal framework that informs his work. Most of his comparative illustrations were meant to demonstrate the validity of a single causal link in this framework, usually by pointing to salient differences between two cases. But comparative data were not brought to bear equally on all the links in the framework, and, as a result, some of the causal links are not "proved"—in so far as Tocqueville's comparative method offers limited proof—by comparative reference.

In particular, Tocqueville's most extensive comparative illustrations were made with reference to the "circumstances remote in time and of a general order," that is, to the general institutional characteristics of 18th-century France and their contrasting counterparts in America. The same cannot be said of the "particular, more recent events" preceding the French Revolution. In part three of *The Old Regime and the French Revolution*—where he examined these events—very few comparative references to America (or to any other country, for that matter) are to be found. The reason is not difficult to ascertain. When general, predisposing characteristics of a nation's culture and social structure are being compared, broad classes of events can be subsumed under general comparative categories—such as the structuring of equality or inequality, or the centralization of government. But when it comes to a comparative analysis of discrete historical events—a legislative act, a governmental decree, a strike, for example— these are most difficult to compare directly, *because they derive their meaning and significance from the context established by the general, predisposing characteristics.* It would have been difficult, for example, to compare the impact of specific changes in welfare policy in late 18th-century France and England, without at the same time investigating previous structural and cultural contexts that imbued these policies with meaning. Only when a common socio-cultural context can be reasonably assumed, is the direct comparative analysis of specific historical events possible.[106]

[105] The issue of comparability is given extensive discussion later, especially in chapter six.

[106] See pp. 185–93 for a more general discussion of the issues of comparability in context.

3. *The imputation of causal relations to comparative associations.* Because Tocqueville was dealing with historical material, the experimental method—one of the most powerful tools for establishing causal relations—was not available to him. In addition, because the number of comparative cases (countries) at his disposal was very small, his ability to prove the actual operativeness of the causes he posited was correspondingly restricted. The number of variables in his causal network vastly exceeded the number of societies he studied. As a result, it was not possible to use the procedures of multivariate analysis to rule out spurious causes, and to increase confidence in suspected causes, even if these procedures had been available to him. (These limitations, incidentally, are not peculiar to Tocqueville's work. They apply to all attempts to study multi-variable systems when only a few cases are available.) Even so, by his ingenious and extensive observation of national differences, Tocqueville moved a certain distance toward ruling out certain historical factors and creating a presumption in favor of others.

Because Tocqueville relied on a complex explanatory framework with multiple causal forces and because he dealt with so few cases, the reader is necessarily left with a sense of vagueness as to the precise weight to be given certain causal forces and as to when they might be overwhelmed or deflected by other forces. One example will illustrate this problem. As we have seen, one of Tocqueville's central propositions was that democratic nations tend toward centralization of government and concentration of power. He based this assertion on a number of arguments: that the minimization of the power of individuals and groups may encourage uniform, centrally-administered laws, that citizens with individualistic values may turn over the management of affairs to the state, and so on. However, in his prime example of a democratic nation (America), he found that this relationship did not prevail. Accordingly, he ventured a number of observations about Americans—their emphasis on freedom, the strength of local townships, the importance of voluntary associations, etc. Such reasoning gives the reader pause, and leads him to consider the actual extent of a tendency for centralization within a democracy. From Tocqueville's account alone we cannot discern the relative strengths of this system of forces and counter-forces relating to centralization. To do so we would require an array of countries defined as "democratic" in varying degrees and "centralized" in varying degrees, so that the relationship between the two conditions—and the intrusion of other conditions—could be established on a broader comparative basis.

A more subtle and complicated issue concerning causal imputation arises from the relations between Tocqueville's conceptual framework and his comparative empirical illustrations. As I attempted to demonstrate earlier, Tocqueville's analysis rested on a semi-developed model of interacting historical causes. (A partial representation of this model is found in figure 2-1.) Furthermore, since he was utilizing a nascent theoretical system, it may be assumed that the modification of one causal relation in the system would reverberate throughout the system and affect the other causal relations. For example, if the middle classes in France had been advancing steadily on all fronts in the 18th century, and had remained tranquil, this circumstance would have decreased the reaction against governmental centralization, reduced the level of group conflict, diminished the appeal of revolutionary ideas, and so on; in short, it would have affected a whole range of what were to become causes for a revolution. The logic of Tocqueville's model, therefore, rests on the assumption that a whole cluster or pattern (rather than discrete pairs) of causal links prevail. Furthermore, any one causal link contributes to an explanation only if the others do so at the same time. For example, the unhappiness of the French bourgeoisie would not have had the same impact on French society unless all the other causal relations in the model remained intact.

Such an explanatory model calls for a certain strategy of comparative empirical analysis. Instead of seeking discrete *pairs* of causal connections between two different societies—basically what Tocqueville has done—it becomes essential to try to establish *clusters* of causal empirical relations, because only the simultaneous establishment of all the interactive causes could be said to demonstrate the workability of the model. To establish only one or two causal links would not do so, because these can be operative only in the context of the operation of the other causal links.

It might be argued that Tocqueville's study of the United States and France, considered in toto, does add up to something like the comparison of a whole cluster of causal links, because with respect to almost every causal link shown in figure 2-1, he attempted to point out a consistent line of contrast between the two societies. With respect to his more ad hoc comparisons with other societies, however, his comparative strategies are more vulnerable to criticism, because he tended to contrast France (or the United States) with another society with respect to only one causal link. Even if he could have definitively established the contrast with respect to this link, however, the comparison would have been very limited in value, because all the other necessary links could not have been considered to be simultaneously established.

This line of reasoning raises a dilemma for the comparative investigator.[107] On the one hand, it is theoretically realistic to conceive of his-

[107] I am grateful to R. Stephen Warner for making explicit this dilemma as stated in this form.

torical processes as complicated networks of interacting causes. To do so, however, calls for more than establishing a number of pairs of empirical associations comparatively; it calls for a strategy of establishing a whole pattern of causal regularities. Using the former approach alone would create a discrepancy between the logic of the "model" employed as the explanatory device and the logic of comparative empirical investigation. To pursue the latter strategy, however, raises even more problems. Not only does the investigator have to investigate the operation of a large number of variables—which is difficult enough with a small number of comparative cases—but he must operate under the further constraint that these variables have to be associated in a definite causal *pattern* in order to validate the model. This further aggravates the "many variables, small N" problem that often hinders comparative analysis in any case. The student of comparative analysis, in short, must continually attempt to strike a compromise between (a) constructing complex and realistic models of the historical process which, however, cannot be validated comparatively because of the limited number of cases, and (b) positing simplified and comparatively verifiable causal relations, the causal significance of which, however, may differ among the societies in which they obtain.[108]

A Concluding Remark

Only on the rarest occasions did Tocqueville indicate a self-conscious vision of himself as a creator of theory—indeed, he was generally hostile to conceptualizations of general laws—nor did he self-consciously examine his own empirical observations in the light of any kinds of canons of validity. Neither theorist nor methodologist, he was mainly an incisive commentator on the condition of societies as they were being destroyed and built by the great historical trends in the 18th and 19th centuries. Yet, as we have been able to discern, a conceptual organization—however incomplete—emerges from his observations and insights. In addition, his style of presenting empirical material indicates a concern both with the kinds of facts that are essential for the empirical verification of an assertion, and with how these facts should be arrayed when comparing two societies. Moreover, the structure of his ideas intimately affected his empirical procedures. His preoccupation with equality, for example, turned his attention toward questions of wealth, power, privilege, and legal immunity in France and the United States, not to other features of these societies which might

[108] We have not yet finished with this dilemma. For a discussion of the efforts of both Durkheim and Weber to resolve a different version of it, see pp. 57–62 and 141–45. For a discussion of it in more general terms, see pp. 202–5.

be compared and contrasted. The importance he gave to the phenomenon of "relative deprivation" focussed his attention on certain *relations* among the distribution of different kinds of rewards rather than on the patterns of absolute distribution of these rewards. And finally, because he was constrained to demonstrate the differential impact of the development of equality in two societies, his comparative method invariably took the form of attempting to associate different causes and different effects. Even when an investigator does not explicitly acknowledge the conceptual and methodological aspects of his work, these two aspects emerge and engage in continual interplay.

3

Programs for
Comparative Sociology:
Emile Durkheim and Max Weber

Durkheim and Weber are commonly and correctly regarded as two of the foremost comparative analysts in the history of sociology. Their own comparative studies in such substantive areas as economic structure, law, politics, and religion still exert a powerful influence on those who continue to work in those areas. In their work, moreover, they faced a number of common problems that arise in comparative analysis, and attempted to overcome them in ways that are still instructive.

I shall examine the strategies of these two scholars in action—that is, the way they went about the business of comparative sociological investigation—in chapters four and five. In this chapter, however, I shall consider their work from a more general perspective. Both these men made their contribution to sociology in the late 19th and early 20th centuries, when the field was making significant strides toward establishing itself as an academic and scientific discipline. Both of them, moreover, had occasion during the course of their careers—Durkheim in 1895[1] and Weber in 1904[2]—to produce major theoretical and methodological statements on the program for sociology. Each statement was incomplete in many ways; for example, while both theorists assigned comparative sociological analysis a central place in their programs for sociology, neither developed a detailed, explicit statement of strategies for comparative analysis. Nevertheless, their reflections, considered together, expose the major methodological dilemmas encountered in comparative analysis. Their methodological writings are further instructive in that while they began with methodological perspectives that were radically opposed to one another, each made a number of significant modifications of these starting points in the course of his argument. As a result, their practical programs for sociological investigation—to say nothing of their actual empirical research—resemble one another much more than their methodological perspectives.

In this chapter, then, I shall examine the methodological contributions of Durkheim and Weber,[3] with an eye to identifying certain general issues in comparative sociology which recur, and which form a basis for discussing strategies for comparative analysis that have been developed more recently. More particularly, I shall compare and contrast Durkheim and Weber under the following headings: (1) The character of scientific knowledge and its relation to other kinds of knowledge and cultural values; (2) The appropriate range of data to be investigated by sociologists; (3) Classification in sociological investigation; (4) The nature of sociological explanation; and (5) Verification in sociology.

Scientific Knowledge in Sociology

Let me begin with Durkheim, whose program of sociological positivism was laid out clearly and forcefully. While insisting that the subject matter of

[1] Emile Durkheim, *The Rules of Sociological Method*, ed., George E. G. Catlin, and trans. Sarah A. Solovay and John H. Mueller (Glencoe, Ill.: The Free Press, 1958).

[2] Max Weber, " 'Objectivity' in Social Science Policy," in *The Methodology of the Social Sciences*, ed. and trans. Edward A. Shils and Henry A. Finch, with a foreword by Edward A. Shils (New York: The Free Press, 1969), pp. 49–112.

[3] My main focus will be on the works identified in footnotes one and two, but both Durkheim and Weber ventured methodological observations elsewhere in their work. In particular, Weber wrote an exceptionally concise methodological statement at the beginning of his *Economy and Society;* Max Weber, "The Definition of Sociology and of Social Action," in *Economy and Society: An Outline of Interpretive Sociology*, ed. Guenther Roth and Claus Wittich (New York: Bedminister Press, 1968), 1:4–24. I shall refer to these additional methodological reflections as well.

sociology is distinct from that of other sciences, Durkheim also insisted that the sociologist should approach his subject matter "in the same state of mind as the physicist, chemist, or physiologist when he probes into a still unexplored region of the scientific domain."[4] Regarding the social sciences of his day as analogous to alchemy before the rise of the natural sciences, he condemned them as having dealt "more or less exclusively with concepts and not with things."[5] By this he meant that sociologists had approached their subject matter with some abstract notion—such as evolution —in mind and attempted to ascertain how various social arrangements suit those notions. Using such preconceptions, Durkheim argued, instead of "observing, describing, and comparing things, we are content to focus our consciousness upon, to analyze, and to combine our ideas. Instead of a science concerned with realities, we produce no more than an ideological analysis."[6]

The proper strategy for sociology, Durkheim continued, is to cast aside such preconceptions and regard social phenomena as "distinct from the consciously formed impressions of them in the mind."[7] The most important characteristic of a "thing," moreover, is "the impossibility of its modification by a simple effort of the will."[8] The investigator should free his mind of all preconceptions, take a more passive relationship to social reality, and deal with phenomena "in terms of their inherent properties," and their "common external characteristics."[9] For example,

> We note the existence of certain acts, all presenting the external characteristic that they evoke from society the particular reaction called punishment. We constitute them as a separate group, to which we give a common label; we call every punished act a crime, and crime thus defined becomes the object of a special science, criminology. Similarly, we observe within all known societies small groups whose special characteristic is that they are composed preponderantly of individuals who are blood-kin, united by legal bonds. We classify together the facts relating thereto, and give a particular name to the group of facts so created, "domestic relations." We call every aggregate of this kind a family, and this becomes the subject of a special investigation which has not yet received a specific name in sociological terminology.[10]

4 Durkheim, "Author's Preface to the Second Edition," *Rules*, p. xlv.
5 Durkheim, *Rules*, p. 18.
6 Ibid., p. 14.
7 Ibid., p. 28.
8 Ibid.
9 Ibid., p. 35.
10 Ibid., pp. 35–36.

Furthermore, such classifications should not "depend on [the sociologist] or on the cast of his individual mind but on the nature of things."[11]

Durkheim's positivism is understandable as an expression of his impatience with unfounded and unverified theories of his day, and as a strategic appeal for empirical observation. Yet as a general methodological program, it evidently presents serious problems. The decisive problem concerns the possibility of ridding oneself of all preconceptions and letting the real world of empirical phenomena speak for itself. Aside from the fact that this is psychologically impossible for anyone who has been socialized in a language and in a way of regarding the world, Durkheim's position would seem to involve a logical impossibility as well. Given the complexity of empirical reality, and given the innumerable ways it may present itself, how is it possible to perceive a single set of external characteristics without actively selecting from among all the possibilities? Certainly the characteristic of "evoking punishment" is not the only possible empirical characteristic that presents itself in those acts to be defined as "crimes." And if the necessity of selection is acknowledged, does not this imply the necessity of some preconception on the part of the investigator? Without criteria for selecting aspects of the empirical world for observation and classification, is not the investigator left in a position of methodological paralysis, unable to begin?

Considerations such as these led Weber to a contrasting formulation of the character of scientific knowledge, though he did not offer his formulation as a direct polemic against Durkheim. Weber regarded scientific knowledge of society and culture as emanating from a number of "one-sided" (that is, selective) views of different aspects of cultural life. It was by selecting, over-emphasizing, and simplifying certain aspects that bodies of scientific knowledge—like formal economics—were generated. Furthermore, he argued that "the one-sidedness is intentional."[12] More important, selectivity is not determined by the "nature of things," as Durkheim held, but by the initiative of the investigator:

Is it not the "actual" interconnections of "things" but the *conceptual* interconnections of *problems* which define the scope of the various sciences. A new "science" emerges where new problems are pursued by new methods and truths are thereby discovered which open up significant new points of view.[13]

11 Ibid., p. 36.
12 Weber, " 'Objectivity' in Social Science and Social Policy," p. 67.
13 Ibid., p. 68.

Reality, even a single object, is so complex—"it presents an infinite multiplicity of successively and coexistently emerging and disappearing events, both 'within' and 'outside' ourselves"[14]—that Weber was led to a firm conclusion: "All the analysis of infinite reality which the finite human mind can conduct rests on the tacit assumption that only a finite portion of this reality constitutes the object of scientific investigation."[15]

But by what criteria is this selection—this reduction to the finite—made? According to Weber it is not made by nature, as Durkheim might argue; scientific reality is not constructed by the regular unfolding of forces dictated by abstract "laws." In particular,

> the social-scientific interest has its point of departure . . . in the *real*, i.e., concrete, individually-structured configuration of our cultural life in its universal relationships which are themselves no less individually-structured, and in its development out of other social cultural conditions, which themselves are obviously likewise individually structured.[16]

Hypothetical laws may be helpful as a set of heuristic devices in generating explanations of concrete configurations, but these configurations cannot be deduced from them.[17] Historical configurations interest the investigator, rather, because they are *culturally significant* for him. This implies further that the investigator has a "value-orientation" toward historical events and situations. Thus:

> Empirical reality becomes "culture" to us because and insofar as we relate it to value ideas. It includes those segments and only those segments of reality which have become significant to us because of this value-relevance. Only a small portion of existing concrete reality is colored by our value-conditioned interest and it alone is significant to us. It is significant because it reveals relationships which are important to us due to their connection with our values.[18]

Accordingly, the "presuppositionless" approach to empirical reality was, for Weber, an impossibility. Empirical description, to say nothing of explanation, is impossible without presuppositions and is pervaded by them. "A chaos of 'existential judgments' about countless individual events would

[14] Ibid., p. 72.

[15] Ibid.

[16] Ibid., p. 74.

[17] In making this point Weber was assuming his polemic against prevalent evolutionary and other monocausal theories of his time, which held, in one way or another, that history involved the unfolding of immutable laws. For a discussion of Weber's posture, see Guenther Roth, "Introduction" to Weber, *Economy and Society*, pp. xix–xxiv.

[18] Weber, " 'Objectivity' in Social Science and Social Policy," p. 76.

be the only result of a serious attempt to analyze reality 'without presuppositions.' "[19] To attempt to be empirically exhaustive "is not only practically impossible—it is simply nonsense."[20] It is essential to bring order out of chaos by selection of aspects of events, and we select only those parts of reality that are "interesting and *significant* to us, because only [those parts are] . . . related to the *cultural values* with which we approach reality."[21] Social or cultural reality is not that which presses itself on the uncluttered mind of the investigator; it is "a finite segment of the meaningless infinity of the world process, a segment on which *human beings* confer meaning and significance."[22]

Concluding this line of reasoning, Weber penned a passage that reads as if it were aimed directly at Durkheim:

> If the notion that [the points of view governing empirical selectivity] can be derived from the "facts themselves" continually recurs, it is due to the naive self-deception of the specialist who is unaware that it [the notion] is due to the evaluative ideas with which he unconsciously approaches his subject matter, that he has selected from an absolute infinity a tiny portion with the study of which he *concerns* himself. . . . To be sure, without the investigator's evaluative ideas, there would be no principle of selection of subject-matter and no meaningful knowledge of the concrete reality. Just as without the investigator's conviction regarding the significance of particular cultural facts, every attempt to analyze concrete reality is absolutely meaningless, so the direction of his personal belief, the refraction of values in the prism of his mind, gives direction to his work.[23]

What Durkheim wished to banish Weber wished to turn into a set of active guidelines to be used in description and explanation.

Thus Weber envisioned a more intimate connection between the investigator's value-preoccupations and his scientific inquiry than did Durkheim. In another connection Weber took an opposite position; I mention this here only in passing, since it is of little concern to my central purposes. Throughout his methodological writings Weber insisted on the strict separation of statements with empirical (scientific) validity and statements with normative (right and wrong) validity. In particular, he held that the latter cannot be derived from the former; consequently he was opposed to any effort to generate an empirically-based "science of ethics." Scientific investigators can make statements regarding the relative effective-

19 Ibid., p. 78.
20 Ibid.
21 Ibid.
22 Ibid., p. 81.
23 Ibid., p. 82.

ness and cost of alternative means to given ends; they can also often identify and make explicit goals or values which may not be acknowledged by the actors being studied. But they cannot go further: "empirical science cannot tell anyone what he *should* do."[24] Durkheim, in contrast, envisioned arriving at assessments regarding the "normal" or "pathological" character of ethical rules on the basis of empirical examinations of the appropriateness of the rule to its social context.[25] Regarding both the implications of cultural values for the conduct of scientific inquiry and the implications of scientific findings for value-judgments, then, Durkheim's and Weber's formulations appear to be firmly opposed to one another.

On the Subject Matter of Sociology

Durkheim's methodological position was clear and straightforward. He regarded the proper subject matter of sociology as "social facts." These are to be distinguished from both biological (eating, sleeping, for instance) and psychological (reasoning, for instance) facts. They include those aspects of society (for example, a society's religious system, its language, and its system of currency), which have an existence independent of the individual consciousness of society's members and exercise a constraining influence on their behavior. Besides these institutional features, Durkheim mentioned certain "social currents"; for example, "the great movements of enthusiasm, indignation, and pity in a crowd do not originate in any one of the particular individual consciousnesses."[26] Just as the living cell possesses organizational principles different from those of the mineral particles which make it up—and to which it cannot be reduced—so social facts

---

[24] Ibid., p. 54. General discussion of the issue of ethical neutrality is found on pp. 50–63; in Weber, "The Meaning of 'Ethical Neutrality' in Sociology and Economics," in *The Methodology of the Social Sciences,* pp. 1–47; and in Weber, "Science as a Vocation," in *From Max Weber: Essays in Sociology,* ed. and trans. with an introduction by H. H. Gerth and C. Wright Mills (London: Routledge and Kegan Paul, 1970), pp. 129–56.

[25] Durkheim's definition was as follows: "One considers as a normal moral fact for a given social type, at a determinate phase of its development, every rule of conduct to which a repressive diffuse sanction is attached in the average society of this type, considered at the same period of evolution; secondly, the same qualification applies to every rule, which, without precisely presenting this criterion, is, however, analogous to certain of the preceding rules; that is to say, serves the same ends, and depends upon the same causes." Emile Durkheim, "Appendix" to Emile Durkheim, *The Division of Labor in Society,* trans. George Simpson (Glencoe, Ill.: The Free Press, 1949), p. 435. See also his general discussion of the normal and pathological social facts, in Durkheim, *Rules,* pp. 47–75.

[26] Durkheim, *Rules,* p. 4.

"cannot be reduced to their elements without contradiction in terms, since, by definition, they presuppose something different from the properties of these elements."[27] The existence of social facts is (1) to be defined independently of individual consciousness, (2) to be expected to manifest regularities peculiar to themselves and not expressible in psychological terms,[28] and (3) to be expected to impose their influence on the individual's behavior—"[a] social fact is to be recognized by the power of external coercion which it exercises or is capable of exercising over individuals, and the presence of this power may be recognized in its turn either by the existence of some specific sanction or by the resistance offered against every individual effort that tends to violate it."[29]

Thus Durkheim was concerned to set the social level apart from the psychological, and to insist on their independence. In the introduction to the second edition of *The Rules of Sociological Method,* he asserted that social facts differ from psychological facts in quality, in substratum, and in milieu, and he reiterated that the substance of social life cannot be explained by purely psychological factors.[30] The same insistence permeates the pages of *Suicide.* At one point he acknowledged that conditions affecting individual suicides are "obviously quite distinct" from those affecting the social suicide rate, and "have no social repercussions."[31] He emphatically rejected explanations of the social suicide rates based on abnormal or normal psychological states.[32] And in concluding his case, he reasserted that "the regularity of statistical data . . . implies the existence of collective tendencies exterior to the individual, and . . . we can directly establish this exterior character in a considerable number of cases."[33] He acknowledged that individuals differ in their vulnerability to suicide, but the factors that make them so do not *"cause a definite number to kill themselves in each society in a definite period of time."*[34] As we shall see, Durkheim's reference to psychological factors in his own comparative sociology was much more complex and subtle than his methodological observations suggest. In principle, however, he was unequivocally hostile both to the reduction of social to psychological phenomena and to the explanation of social by psychological phenomena.

[27] Ibid., p. xlix.
[28] Ibid., p. 1.
[29] Ibid., p. 10.
[30] Ibid., p. xlix. See also Durkheim, *The Division of Labor in Society,* pp. 279–80.
[31] Emile Durkheim, *Suicide,* ed. with an introduction by George Simpson; trans. John A. Spaulding (Glencoe, Ill.: The Free Press, 1951), p. 51.
[32] Ibid., pp. 57–103.
[33] Ibid., p. 318.
[34] Ibid., p. 324. Emphasis in original.

Weber differed significantly from Durkheim in his starting point for sociological analysis. He incorporated a distinctively psychological level into his definition of the basic substance of sociology and social action. Action is defined as such "insofar as the acting individual attaches a *subjective meaning* to his behavior—be it overt or covert, omission or acquiescence." Action is "social" insofar as "its *subjective meaning* takes account of the behavior of others and is thereby oriented in its course."[35] Weber's concern with subjective meaning implies that he regarded the individual as motivated, assessing his environment in terms of its significance for him, and organizing his behavior accordingly; furthermore, social action cannot be understood, described, or analyzed without reference to this subjective meaning. Durkheim may have agreed, but would have insisted that such meaning is relevant for psychology but not for sociology.

Weber qualified his emphasis on subjective meaning in a variety of ways. First, not all behavior is subjectively meaningful; some is merely reactive, though the distinction between the two is subtle.[36] The meaning of action as rendered by the actor must be taken into account in explaining his behavior, but it is not to be regarded as constituting a valid scientific explanation of his behavior. Not all of his motives and perceptions may be conscious; and, in any event, various "non-meaningful" stimuli (for example, environmental or biological events) condition a person's behavior by acting to favor or hinder circumstances.[37] He asserted, furthermore—in reasoning akin to Durkheim's—that the "subjective meaning-complex of action" had to stand on its own level, and could not be decomposed without loss into bio-chemical reactions.[38] And he was careful to avoid confusing the analysis of subjectively meaningful experience with psychology in general, thus giving the former a distinctive conceptual independence.[39] Again, I shall have more to say about the particular role of psychological factors in Weber's work when I review his strategies for explaining social phenomena and his actual empirical work. At present I only wish to contrast his view of sociological data with that of Durkheim's.

These divergent starting points propelled Durkheim and Weber in different directions with respect to their approach to empirical data. Durkheim focused upon the observable and the measurable. A social fact such as social solidarity, he noted, "is a completely moral phenomenon which, taken by itself, does not lend itself to exact observation nor indeed to

[35] Weber, *Economy and Society*, 1:4. Emphasis supplied in both quotations.
[36] Ibid., pp. 4–5.
[37] Ibid., pp. 7–10.
[38] Ibid., p. 13.
[39] Ibid., p. 19.

measurement." Therefore, he added, "we must substitute for this internal fact which escapes us an external index which symbolizes it and study the former in the light of the latter."[40] He was drawn to study various observable kinds of statistics, which record "the currents of daily life" (for example, market statistics); costumes, which record fashions; and works of art, which record taste.[41] Psychology suffered on this count, Durkheim added, because psychological facts are "internal by definition," and therefore inaccessible; "it seems that they can be treated as external only by doing violence to their nature."[42] Weber, because he focused on subjective meaning, was less prepared to treat sociocultural phenomena as "things." The phenomena of the social sciences involve "a problem of a specifically different type from those which the schemes of the exact natural sciences in general can or seek to solve."[43] These phenomena are "psychological and intellectual" and call for "empathetic understanding." Accordingly, Weber devoted a considerable proportion of his methodological statement in *Economy and Society* to a discussion of different types of understanding, the ways in which meaning can be sensitively and accurately grasped.[44] Weber was also interested in statistical uniformities, but only in so far as they "can be regarded as manifestations of the understandable subjective meaning of a course of social action," as in the case of crime rates or occupational distributions.[45] Furthermore, the two scholars leaned toward a different approach to their data. For Durkheim, the preference would be to regard statistical series as standardized expressions of definite "things" distinct from any meaning that individuals attached to them; for Weber a statistic would be reflective of the subjective-meaning complex of an actor, and would derive its significance from that complex rather than from any "external" or "superficial" characteristic.[46]

At this moment let me pause and attempt to represent formally the different paradigms for the generation of knowledge emerging from Durkheim's and Weber's methodology. Most of the significant contrasts between the two theorists, as reviewed up to this point, may be understood in terms

[40] Durkheim, *The Division of Labor in Society,* p. 64.
[41] Durkheim, *Rules,* p. 30.
[42] Ibid.
[43] Weber, *The Methodology of the Social Sciences,* p. 74.
[44] Weber, *Economy and Society,* 1:5–12.
[45] Ibid., 1:12.
[46] "Processes of action which seem to an observer to be the same or similar may fit into exceedingly various complexes of motive in the case of the individual actor. Then even though the situations appear superficially to be very similar, we must actually understand them or interpret them as very different, perhaps, in terms of meaning, directly opposed." Ibid., p. 10.

of how each conceptualized the role of the investigator (observer) and the role of the actor (observed) in the generation of knowledge. Durkheim assigned a passive role to both. In his insistence that facts are "things" he held that they cannot be modified by a "simple act of the [observer's] will"; in his insistence that the observer free himself of all previous preoccupations, he called on him not to attempt to influence empirical facts, but to let them impress themselves upon his mind according to their inherent properties. In these ways the observer is regarded as passive. And because facts are "social," they enjoy an existence independent from the individual, work their influence upon him despite his efforts to resist, and are governed by laws specific to the social level. In these senses, actors as individuals contribute little to sociological knowledge. Such are the key ingredients of sociological positivism as presented by Durkheim.

Weber contrasts with Durkheim on both counts. By insisting on the impossibility of a "presuppositionless" sociology, he afforded the observer a more active role in the generation of scientific knowledge. The precise role of the observer, moreover, is guided toward empirical data and problems which are significant to him from a cultural point of view. And by insisting on the centrality of subjective meaning as the basic ingredient of action, including social action, Weber gave both the actor and the investigator a more active role. In regarding the actor as meaningfully oriented to his environment, Weber insisted that a significant portion of the variables that "explain" human behavior had to be found in the pattern of meanings given to his environment and behaving in accord with these meanings. The actor's own definition of the situation, in short, contributes to explaining his behavior. (Durkheim might have acknowledged the importance of these meaning-complexes, but would have argued that they have no import for sociological knowledge.) Also, by insisting on the importance of subjective meaning, Weber saw the task of the observer—that of empathetic understanding—as calling for a more active effort than observing and recording the phenomena that nature produces.

Figure 3-1 locates the positions of Durkheim and Weber according to the dimensions of activity and passivity of the observer and the actor, and indicates their general opposition to one another. The differences among them, moreover, are philosophical—or paradigmatic, if you will—in that they deal with first assumptions about the nature and source of empirical knowledge, assumptions that are rooted in articles of conviction or faith and are not easily settled on empirical grounds. Furthermore, the other two "cells" of figure 3-1 indicate two other variants of paradigms for the generation of scientific sociological knowledge. Those who regard the observer as passive in this process, and who insist upon the importance (and the integrity) of the actor as a source of knowledge have assumed

	Actor as passive	Actor as active
Observer as passive	Sociological positivism (Durkheim)	Phenomenology; relativism; historicism
Observer as active	Sociological nominalism	Interpretative sociology (Weber)

FIG. 3–1   Four Paradigms for Generating Sociological Knowledge

many guises, among which phenomenology, relativism, and historicism are the most conspicuous; each regards valid knowledge as emanating from the experience, world-view, or way of life of the people under study. The fourth cell might be termed "sociological nominalism" (for lack of a better term) which acknowledges the independent role of the investigator in formulating categories, constructs, and theories, but does not take into account the meaning-states of the actors being studied.[47] The approach of the self-conscious "model-building" of many contemporary comparative analysts fits into this category.

Because each of these four[48] paradigms rests on different epistemological assumptions, each produces a distinctive kind of knowledge. In addition, theorists of each persuasion create distinctive strengths and vulnerabilities for themselves in generating knowledge that can be assessed as adequate according to the canons of scientific investigation. For example, positivistic approaches to the analysis of dissimilar systems encourage quantitative comparisons (a strength) but tend to become involved in comparing incomparable data; and relativistic or phenomenological ap-

[47] The term is not entirely satisfactory, but it is meant to convey that nominalistic concepts do not mean to reflect "real" states in the empirical world—of which subjective-meaning states would be one—but rather are seen as helpful devices for organizing thinking about the empirical world. See Robert Bierstedt, "Nominal and Real Definitions in Sociological Theory," in Llewellyn Gross, ed., *Symposium on Sociological Theory* (Evanston, Ill.: Row, Peterson & Co., 1959), pp. 121–44.

[48] In no way do I mean to claim that this representation of different paradigms exhausts the approach to sociological knowledge; it is the first of several distinctions I shall introduce to clarify the issues and strategies of comparative analysis in the social sciences.

proaches are more likely to remain faithful to the perspectives of those who have produced the data but have difficulty in generating categories by which those data can be compared. In the sections that follow we shall focus on the vulnerabilities associated with the paradigms generated by Durkheim and Weber, and note their efforts—though not necessarily designed as such—to come to terms with these sources of difficulty.

Classification in Sociological Investigation

Both Durkheim and Weber were committed to the principle that sociology should be a generalizing science, as contrasted, for example, with history.[49] Because of this commitment, they were concerned with generating statements that could deal with many cases (many individuals, many societies). A necessary preliminary to such statements, moreover, is to develop concepts which apply to more than one case. How did Weber and Durkheim come to terms with the necessity of generating general descriptive and classificatory categories, and how did their efforts square with the paradigmatic assumptions each embraced?

One way Durkheim assessed the general significance of social facts was to relate them to a conception of "normal" or "pathological." In characteristic manner, however, he rejected any "premature attempt to grasp the essence" of normality and abnormality, and attempted instead to "seek some external and perceptible characteristic which will enable us merely to distinguish these two orders of facts."[50] In this enterprise he closely followed the reasoning of biology:

> All sociological phenomena (as well as all biological phenomena) can assume different forms in different cases while still conserving their essential characteristics. We can distinguish two kinds of such forms. Some are distributed in the entire range of species; they are to be found, if not in all individuals, at least in the majority of them. If they are not found to be identical in all the cases in question, but vary in different persons, these variations do occur within narrow limits. . . . We shall call "normal" these social conditions that are the most generally distributed, and the others "morbid" or "pathological."[51]

Traits as such cannot be generally assumed to be normal or pathological;

[49] For example, Durkheim, *Suicide,* pp. 35–39; Weber, *Economy and Society,* 1:19.

[50] Durkheim, *Rules,* pp. 54–55.

[51] Ibid., p. 55.

they must be "defined . . . only in relation to a given species" and "only in relation to a given phase of its development."[52] What is normal for a simple, preliterate society is certainly not normal for an advanced, complex society. For any given species it is the statistical generality of a social fact that gives it its normality. But in addition, Durkheim wished to explain normality in another way—not only a "normality of fact" but also a "normality of logical necessity." He proposed to do this by referring to what we now might term the "functional significance" of the social fact for the species:

> The normality of the phenomenon is to be explained by the mere fact that it is bound up with the conditions of existence of the species under consideration, either as a mechanically necessary effect of these conditions or as a means permitting the organisms to adapt themselves.[53]

If a phenomenon persists, for example, throughout a long period of social change when, in fact, the conditions for its existence are no longer present, it may be regarded as "pathological."[54]

The conception of the normal and abnormal in statistical terms, however qualified, is open to severe criticisms. Rather than dwell on these, however, I should like to point out how Durkheim's effort to assess the functional significance of social facts led him directly into the comparative analysis of social systems. The significance of a social fact—that is, whether it is normal or pathological—is to be assessed not by some intrinsic feature of the fact but by the societal context of the fact, viz., the requirements of the species at its level of development. Such a formulation calls immediately for a classification of species and of levels of development, since without it the investigator could not make the necessary assessments.

Durkheim was aware of this pressure to classify that arose from his formulation.[55] And in proposing to classify, he tried, much like Weber, to steer a course between "the nominalism of the historian and the extreme realism of the philosopher":

> For the historian, societies represent just so many heterogeneous individualities, not comparable among themselves. Each people has its own physiognomy, its special constitution, its law, its morality, its economic organiza-

---

[52] Ibid., pp. 57–58.
[53] Ibid., p. 60.
[54] Ibid., pp. 62–63.
[55] "Since a social fact can be construed as normal or abnormal only relatively to a given species, it is implied that one branch of sociology must be devoted to the constitution and classification of these species." Ibid., p. 76.

tion, appropriate only to itself; and all generalizations are well-nigh impossible. For the philosopher, on the contrary, all these individual groupings, called tribes, city-states, and nations, are only contingent and provisional aggregations with no exclusive and separate reality. Only humanity is real, and it is from the general attributes of human nature that all social evolution flows.

For the former, consequently, history is but a sequence of events which follow without repeating one another; for the latter, these same events have value and interest only as illustrating the general laws inherent in the constitution of man and dominating all historical development. For the former, what is good for one society cannot be applied to others. The conditions of the state of health vary from one people to the next and cannot be theoretically determined; it is a matter of practical experience and of cautious research. For the latter, they can be calculated once and for all and for the entire human species. It seems, then, that social reality must be merely subject matter of an abstract and vague philosophy or for purely descriptive monographs.[56]

To avoid these two extremes, Durkheim proposed to approach social reality by classifying it into *social species*. Such a procedure seemed to incorporate "both the unity that all truly scientific research demands and the diversity that is given in the facts, since the species is the same for all the individual units that make it up, and since, on the other hand, the species differ among themselves."[57]

In proceeding, however, Durkheim departed from his general methodological position to a certain degree. On the one hand, he argued that "science can . . . establish classes only after having described, in their entirety, the individuals they comprise."[58] But rather than proceed inductively, he felt it possible to identify certain *decisive* or *crucial* facts—the most essential characteristics of social types—"without entering . . . too far into the study of the facts."[59] In particular, he focused on the fact "that societies are composed in various parts in combination" and that they may be arrayed according to their complexity of parts.[60] Accordingly, he defined a simple society as "[one] which does not include others more simple than itself, and which not only at present contains but a single segment but also presents no trace of previous segmentation," and applied this definition to a "horde."[61] When the horde becomes a segment of a

[56] Ibid., pp. 76–77.
[57] Ibid., p. 77.
[58] Ibid., p. 79.
[59] Ibid., p. 80.
[60] Ibid., pp. 81–82.
[61] Ibid., p. 82.

society, rather than a society itself, however, a more complex type of society presents itself, a "clan society." And, as societies combine, give birth to new societies, which themselves combine, a typology of societies based on the degree of differentiation of their parts emerges.[62]

At one point Durkheim noted, almost in passing, that "[it] is true, perhaps, that no historical society corresponds exactly to [the] description [of a horde]."[63] Shortly thereafter, he noted that the notion of the horde may be "conceived as a historic reality or as a hypothesis of science."[64] By venturing these observations—and, indeed, by proceeding as he did in proposing his scheme for classification—Durkheim made several crucial departures from his paradigmatic insistence on the passivity of the investigator who could not produce changes in positive facts by an act of will. Not only did he acknowledge the necessity—even desirability—of proceeding to some degree in an a priori way in classifying societies. He also stressed the need to *select* decisive or crucial facts as the basis of classification. Furthermore, he acknowledged the legitimacy of the investigator's distorting empirical reality by creating a hypothetically pure type not found in empirical reality for purposes of building a classificatory scheme. In making these departures, moreover, Durkheim moved significantly in the direction of Weber's formulation of the role of the investigator, and—as we shall see presently—in the direction of Weber's view of the nature and purposes of classification.

Weber, too, was aware of the tension between nominalism and realism, though it took a somewhat different form than it did for Durkheim. On the one hand, he rejected any position that social reality could be regarded as a manifestation of general social laws; "the reality of which . . . laws apply always remains equally *individual,* equally *undeducible* from laws."[65] Because he focused on the concrete individual, and, perhaps more important, because he gave the individual's subjective meaning such salience in the definition of social action, he seemed to be flirting with an extreme historical nominalist position. How could individuals, who vary so greatly in their subjective assessment of social reality, be compared with one another? How is it possible to move to the level of social institutions and social structures, which are presumably among the main foci of interest of the sociologist? Weber rejected the idea that the sociologist could "deduce . . . institutions from psychological laws or explain them by elementary psychological phenomena."[66] How then to proceed, simultaneously hold-

[62] Ibid., pp. 82–83.
[63] Ibid., p. 83.
[64] Ibid., p. 84.
[65] Weber, " 'Objectivity' in Social Science and Social Policy," p. 73.
[66] Ibid., p. 89.

ing both his view of social reality and his commitment to sociology as a generalizing science?

It is in the context of this tension that Weber's famous "ideal type" becomes significant. An ideal type is a device employed by an investigator to facilitate empirical analysis. It is not a description of reality; it is not an hypothesis. Rather, according to Weber's somewhat cumbersome definition, it is "formed by the one-sided *accentuation* of one or more points of view and by the synthesis of a great many diffuse, discrete, more or less present and occasionally absent *concrete individual* phenomena, which are arranged according to those one-sidedly emphasized viewpoints into a unified *analytical* construct."[67] The ideal type is not derived from empirical reality; rather, it is the selection of the essential—indeed, one might say "decisive," as did Durkheim—features of a complex historical situation and molding them into a simplified picture. By drawing out type-elements from the myriad unique historical experiences of concrete acting individuals, the investigator *makes them comparable with one another.* By constructing an ideal-typical capitalistic system of pricing and marketing, the investigator characterizes in general terms the orientation of numerous actors, who may differ in detail in their concrete subjective orientations to the market. Description in terms of the ideal type selects from those orientations and makes them similar.

It is apparent from Weber's illustrations of ideal-type concepts that they differ in level of generality. In his commentary he mentioned such varying possibilities as "church" and "sect," "capitalistic culture," "city-economy," "handicraft," "liberalism," "Methodism," "socialism," and "Christianity." In addition to these "abstract concepts of relationships which are conceived by us as stable in the flux of events,"[68] he noted that developmental sequences could also be represented in ideal-typical form— for example, the "typical" shift from handicraft to capitalistic economic organization, or, more generally, the historical sweeps envisioned in Marxian theory.[69]

In *Economy and Society* Weber discussed and illustrated the notion of the ideal type in terms more similar to the way we would currently describe a scientific "model" or "theoretical framework." Constructing a type involves first hypothesizing what course action would take if the actors in a situation were motivated consistently by a single orientation:

> For example a panic on the stock exchange can be most conveniently analysed by attempting to determine first what the course of action would

[67] Ibid., p. 90.
[68] Ibid., p. 101.
[69] Ibid., pp. 101–3.

have been if it had not been influenced by irrational affects; it is then possible to introduce the irrational components as accounting for the observed deviations from this hypothetical course. Similarly, in analysing a political or military campaign it is convenient to determine in the first place what would have been a rational course, given the ends of the participants and adequate knowledge of all the circumstances. Only in this way is it possible to assess the causal significance of irrational factors as accounting for deviations from this type.[70]

Weber regarded the laws of economic theory (including the postulate of maximization) as a representation of "the meaning appropriate to a scientifically formulated pure type (an ideal type) of a common phenomenon."[71] Most sociological laws involve building up hypothetical constructs "on the basis of such rational assumptions."[72]

Weber insisted that the ideal type was a *generalizing* device, to be applied to a variety of instances of action. In this way he was moving away from the historicism which he felt could not produce general statements. In fact, he regarded the use of general types as inevitable in any kind of historical analysis. If the historian rejects such general theoretical constructs, "the inevitable consequence is either that he consciously or unconsciously uses other similar concepts without formulating them verbally and elaborating them logically or that he remains stuck in the realm of the vaguely 'felt.' "[73] Nevertheless, because Weber laid down no rules for *how general* an ideal type should be—ideal types could include anything from general economic models to historical phenomena such as "Methodism" and presumably even subvarieties of "Methodism"—his own conception ran the risks of manifesting a kind of theoretical indeterminacy, an endless creation of types depending on the historical research at hand, and, indeed, a reversion to historical particularism on a slightly higher level of abstraction.[74]

What are the functions of ideal-type concepts from the standpoint of scientific inquiry? Weber stressed several heuristic uses. They "are of great value for research and of high systematic value for expository purposes when they are used as conceptual instruments for *comparison* with and the *measurement* of reality."[75] This would include, as I have mentioned, comparing otherwise different individuals with unique subjective-

[70] Weber, *Economy and Society*, 1:6.

[71] Ibid., p. 9.

[72] Ibid., p. 19.

[73] Durkheim, *The Methodology of the Social Sciences*, p. 94.

[74] This is one of the thrusts of Talcott Parsons' critique of Weber's sociology as producing a sort of "type atomism." See Talcott Parsons, *The Structure of Social Action* (New York: McGraw-Hill, 1937), pp. 607, 610.

[75] Weber, *The Methodology of the Social Sciences*, p. 97. Emphasis in original.

meaning complexes. They permit the transition from focusing on the individual, concrete actor to the analysis of institutional action—including the influence of one institutional complex on another—by treating it as having a common ideal-type meaning for actors. And they are of *explanatory* value, particularly those that deal with "laws" or "developmental sequences"; they are themselves compared with some empirical course of events to see to what extent the factors constructed into the ideal type actually account for its regularities. We shall examine Weber's conception of sociological explanation in more detail in the remaining sections.

What are the criteria that guide the selection of those facets of concrete reality that make up any given ideal type? Weber never developed a systematic methodology for this operation—and for this he can be legitimately criticized, since vagueness on this score means that different investigators would undoubtedly come up with different verisons of the ideal type for any given historical situation. Nevertheless, Roth has identified a number of "rules of experience" which informed Weber's own construction of types.[76] These rules mainly involved empirical claims that the chosen aspect—for example, legitimation of authority—is a regularly recurring and an important feature of social action.

Whatever the difficulties in Weber's conceptualization of ideal types, it is clear that by employing this device he was attempting an escape from the "nominalism of the historians," as Durkheim called it, and was creating an order of concepts that enabled him to analyze phenomena at a level closer to that which Durkheim called "social facts." In that respect Durkheim's recognition of the necessity to construct a typology of social species and Weber's strategy of generating ideal types moved the two scholars closer to one another than they were in their original paradigmatic statements. Certain differences between the two remained, however. Durkheim consistently adhered to the primary reality of the social level independent of individual actors, whereas Weber insisted that his ideal-type constructions were inferences rooted ultimately in the substratum of the subjectively meaningful experience of individual actors. Furthermore, because of their different starting points, Durkheim and Weber chose to classify different orders of phenomena. Preoccupied with assessing normality and pathology as a product of societal context, Durkheim was driven to classify *types of societies*. Preoccupied with attaining modest generalizations about typical historical constellations and processes, Weber

---

[76] Guenther Roth, "Max Weber's Comparative Approach and Historical Typology," in Ivan Vallier, ed., *Comparative Methods in Sociology: Essays on Trends and Applications* (Berkeley and Los Angeles: University of California Press, 1971), pp. 83–85.

remained at the level of identifying *typical historical clusters of meaningful action*. Their mode of classification, then, like all investigative strategies, depended in part on their more general theoretical preoccupations.

Sociological Explanation

Durkheim saw the classification of social species as "a means of grouping facts to facilitate their interpretation." It is "only an introduction to the truly explanatory part of the science."[77] Of what does the latter consist?

Durkheim distinguished between the function fulfilled by a phenomenon —that is, its effects, its usefulness—and "the efficient cause which produces it."[78] He argued further that the former does not constitute an explanation.[79] Causal analysis, instead, involves the search for "a correspondence between the fact under consideration and the general needs of the social organism, and in what this correspondence consists, without occupying ourselves with whether it has been intentional [i.e., directed toward a given end] or not."[80] While stressing this priority, Durkheim acknowledged that knowledge of the function was "necessary for the complete explanation of the phenomena," because "it is generally necessary that [a fact] be useful in order that it may maintain itself."[81]

Durkheim also rejected explanations of social phenomena that called on psychological factors. His position followed from his original definition of a social fact; "[since] their essential characteristic is their power of exerting pressure on individual consciousness, it follows that they are not derived from the latter and, consequently, that sociology is not a corollary of individual psychology."[82] The fact that individuals are the ultimate elements of society is not a compelling reason to seek psychological explanations of social phenomena, any more than it is appropriate to seek inorganic explanations for phenomena constituted at an organic level. The

[77] Durkheim, *Rules*, p. 89. These statements seem odd in one respect, since Durkheim created his own classification of social species as an integral part of the "explanation" of the normality or pathology of social facts.

[78] Ibid., p. 95.

[79] For a model in which functional analysis is converted into causal analysis, see Arthur L. Stinchcombe, *Constructing Social Theories* (New York: Harcourt, Brace and World, 1968), ch. 3.

[80] Durkheim, *Rules*, p. 95. Again the insistence seems a bit odd, because of the clearly "functional" explanation generated in his discussion of the normal and the pathological.

[81] Ibid., p. 97.

[82] Ibid., p. 101.

whole is more than the sum of its parts, and explanations appropriate to the whole must be sought: "The group thinks, feels, and acts quite differently from the way in which its members would were they isolated."[83] On the basis of such reasoning, Durkheim concluded that "every time a social phenomenon is directly explained by a psychological phenomenon, we may be sure that the explanation is false."[84] Specifically, the falsity lies in mistaking effect for cause, assuming that the psychological effects produced by collective life are the determinants of that life.[85]

From this follows Durkheim's principle that "[the] determining cause of a social fact should be sought among the social facts preceding it and not among the states of the individual consciousness."[86] The sociologist's main task is to discover features of the social milieu that contribute to the character of social life; Durkheim himself sought to explain the social division of labor by reference to social facts such as the size of society and its dynamic density, and to explain variations in the social suicide rate by reference to the ways in which groups are integrated and regulated. Hostile as his polemic toward psychology was, he nonetheless showed some ambivalence:

> We do not mean to say . . . that the study of psychological facts is not indispensable to the sociologist. If collective life is not derived from individual life, the two are nevertheless closely related; if the latter cannot explain the former, it can at least facilitate its explanation. First . . . it is indisputable that social facts are produced by action on psychological factors. In addition, this very action is similar to that which takes place in each individual consciousness and by which are transformed the primary elements (sensations, reflexes, instincts) of which it is originally constituted.[87]

Psychology can thus provide "useful suggestions" as to the likely effects of the social milieu on individuals, but in this formulation the individual remains a relatively passive vessel. Psychological phenomena have social consequences only when "the action of the psychological and of the social phenomena is necessarily fused," as in the case of the decision of a public official whose behavior can exert a social influence while being determined by psychological causes. Yet Durkheim regarded such cases as being "due to individual accidents and, consequently, cannot affect the constitu-

---

[83] Ibid., p. 104. The wording of this assertion is infelicitous, and probably supplied ammunition for those who criticized Durkheim for reifying the "group mind."
[84] Ibid.
[85] Ibid., p. 107.
[86] Ibid., p. 110.
[87] Ibid., p. 111.

tive traits of the social species which, alone, is the object of science."[88]   In the end, sociological explanations and sociological knowledge can be generated only if the sociologist "[establishes] himself in the very heart of social facts, in order to observe them directly."[89]   In chapter four I shall resume discussion of this formulation, both in connection with observations of how closely Durkheim lived up to his admonitions in his own empirical research and in connection with my own reformulations on the role of social-structural and psychological variables in comparative analysis.

Weber's conception of sociological explanation is rooted in his notions of interpretation and the ideal type. In his general discussion of how subjective meaning can be understood, he spoke of the importance of "explanatory understanding."[90]   In particular this involves grasping the motive of an individual actor, or understanding "what makes him do [something] at precisely this moment and in these circumstances."[91]   The understanding of the act of a man hitting a log with an ax is understood if it is understood that he is working for a wage. "Similarly we understand the motive of a person aiming a gun if we know that he has been commanded to shoot as a member of a firing squad, that he is fighting against an enemy, or that he is doing it for revenge."[92]   Motives are highly diverse, and Weber did not conceive of them in a narrow psychological sense. They might include, for example, an individual's self-interest in a given situation,[93] his inclination to adhere to normative standards,[94] or his belief in the legitimacy of a given set of social relationships.[95]   In any historical situation the investigator should expect to find not single or pure motives, but a number in complex combination.

Weber identified two types of explanatory understanding. The first involves the interpretative grasp of the "actually intended meaning"—that is

[88] Ibid., p. 112.

[89] Ibid.

[90] Weber, *Economy and Society*, 1:8.

[91] Ibid.

[92] Ibid., 1:9.

[93] "Many of the especially notable uniformities in the course of social action are not determined by orientation to any sort of norm which is held to be valid, nor do they rest on custom, but entirely on the fact that the corresponding type of social action is in the nature of the case best adapted to the normal interests of the actors as they themselves are aware of them." Ibid., 1:30.

[94] "The meaningful content which remains relatively constant in a social relationship is capable of formulation in terms of maxims which the parties concerned expect to be adhered to by their partners on the average and approximately." Ibid., 1:28.

[95] "Action, especially social action which involves a social relationship, may be guided by the belief in the existence of a legitimate order." Ibid., 1:31.

to say, meaning for concrete individual action, represented in its historical complexity. (Weber added a sub-type to this, the understanding of the actually intended meaning of numbers of individuals in sociological mass phenomena.) The second, involving a process of abstraction on the part of the observer, is the grasp of "the meaning appropriate to a scientifically formulated pure type (an ideal type) of a common phenomenon."[96] Understanding action from the standpoint of a model of economic rationality would be a case in point; another would be understanding action from the standpoint of being a member of a patrimonial or a bureaucratic staff. In short, it is the identification of a typical complex of motives in a more or less common historical situation.

Even though an ideal-type understanding of motives is an "explanation" of behavior in some sense, Weber insisted that this operation alone, no matter how clear and certain the interpretation, "cannot on this account claim to be the causally valid interpretation."[97] A further operation is necessary; in particular, "verification of subjective interpretation by comparison with the concrete course of events is, as in the case of all hypotheses, indispensable."[98] What is involved in the operation of verification will be taken up in the final section of this chapter. At the moment I stress only Weber's insistence on the distinction between explanatory interpretation and causal verification.

Weber advanced another distinction that made the same point. He referred on the one hand to interpretation of a course of conduct that is "adequate on the level of meaning"—that is to say, a satisfactory account of the motives for the conduct from the subjective standpoint of the actor (or that standpoint as assessed by the observer). A causally adequate interpretation, however, involves a statement of the way in which a sequence of events will unfold, and an effort to confirm that statement empirically. But in his concluding statement on causal adequacy, he insisted that a correct causal interpretation required "that the process which is claimed to be typical is shown to be *both* adequately grasped on the level of meaning *and* at the same time the interpretation is to some degree causally adequate."[99] If the meaningful—that is, motivational—connection between events is not apprehended, then no matter how close their association, it can remain only "an incomprehensible statistical probability." On the other hand, even if the subjective behavior has been fully grasped on

[96] Ibid., 1:9.

[97] Ibid.

[98] Ibid. This statement leads us to question Weber's assertion in his earlier methodological essay that the ideal type is not an hypothesis. It seems to be precisely that, according to his later formulation.

[99] Ibid., 1:12.

the level of meaning, there can be causal significance "only insofar as there is some kind of proof [verification] that action in fact normally takes the course which has been held to be meaningful."[100]

While Weber did not develop his point about the necessity for a meaningful connection further, it seems to be worth elaborating, because it leads to a contrast with Durkheim and points the way toward a reformulation we shall undertake in chapter seven. What Weber seemed to be saying is that statistical regularities between, say, aggregated rates of behavior are meaningless unless reference is made to some kind of subjective or psychological link between them. For example, the facts that various classes in French society were making irregular forward progress (a statistical regularity) and that numerous members of this class showed evidence of dissatisfaction with the French social order (a statistical regularity) bear no intelligible connection with one another until some typical meaningful connection is made (in Tocqueville's case, a postulate of the principle of relative deprivation). Even further, Weber appeared to suggest that the theoretical significance of regularities is to be found in the realm of subjective meaning.

> We can accomplish something which is never attainable in the natural sciences, namely the subjective understanding of the action of the component individuals. The natural sciences on the other hand cannot do this, being limited to the formulation of causal uniformities in objects and events and the explanation of individual facts by applying them. We do not "understand" the behavior of cells, but can only observe the relevant functional relationships and generalize on the basis of these observations. This additional achievement of explanation by interpretive understanding, as distinguished from external observation, is of course attained only at a price— the more hypothetical and fragmentary character of its results. Nevertheless, subjective understanding is the specific characteristic of sociological knowledge.[101]

This statement highlights the difference between Durkheim and Weber on the issue of explanation. Durkheim, embracing a "natural science" model for sociology—at least in his manifesto—envisioned the possibility in sociology of discovering causal uniformities and explaining individual facts by applying them. Sociological theory should emerge at its own level on the basis of observation of social facts. No recourse need be made to that separate realm of psychology except for "useful suggestions." Weber, however, stressing the differences between sociology and what he under-

---

100 Ibid.
101 Ibid., 1:15.

stood to be the natural sciences of his day, found it essential to construct idealized psychological accounts to give theoretical meaning to social regularities.[102] As we shall see presently, Durkheim turned out to be more Weberian than Durkheimian in his own comparative empirical research.

Verification in Sociology

Both Durkheim and Weber addressed themselves to the empirical procedures available in order to lend empirical support to sociological propositions, and both defined this task in terms of linking causes and effects. Durkheim spoke of "establishing relations of causality," whereas Weber spoke of "causal significance" and "causally adequate interpretation." Durkheim regarded the experiment—when causes and effects "can be artificially produced at the will of the observer"—as a potent device for investigation, but found its use limited in sociology, in which "social phenomena evidently escape the control of the experimenter."[103] Weber found experimentation applicable only in "a few very special cases."[104] Accordingly, each addressed the issue of attaining reliable empirical knowledge in the absence of experimentation.

Durkheim's general answer was simple: when the experiment is not available, the only recourse is indirect comparison, or the comparative method. Before characterizing the particular ways in which he suggested employing it, however, he launched a brief polemic against John Stuart Mill's observation that a given event may have different causes under different circumstances, and enunciated the principle that "a given effect has always a single corresponding cause," adding that, for example, "if suicide depends on more than one cause, it is because, in reality, there are several kinds of suicide."[105]

Durkheim was also skeptical about the applicability of the several strategies that Mill had enunciated in his classic systematic exposition of methods of experimental inquiry. He rejected Mill's "method of residues"— establishing cause by removing all known causes with the remainder constituting the cause[106]—noting that it is inappropriate for sociology be-

---

[102] Weber insisted, however, that in positing rational assumptions of the order incorporated into his ideal types, he was not making "any kind of psychology . . . the ultimate foundation of the sociological interpretation of action." He was addressing mainly those branches of psychology which modeled themselves after the procedures of the natural sciences. Ibid., 1:19.

[103] Durkheim, *Rules*, p. 125.

[104] Weber, *Economy and Society*, 1:10.

[105] Durkheim, *Rules*, pp. 128–29.

[106] John Stuart Mill, *A System of Logic, Ratiocinative and Inductive*, 9th ed. (London: Longmans, Green, Reader, and Dyer, 1875), 1:459–60.

cause it presupposes the existence of known laws already and is, in any case, impractical. He also found the methods of agreement and difference wanting for similar reasons. (The method of agreement establishes cause by grouping cases which agree in one circumstance and differ in all others; the method of difference establishes cause by grouping cases which differ in one circumstance and agree in all others.)[107] The conditions for such methods can never be absolutely met even in the experimental sciences, Durkheim argued, and in sociology their application is impossible; no conceivable inventory of facts could permit an investigator to be certain, for example, "that two societies agree or differ in all respects save one."[108]

Durkheim's chosen method to establish cause and effect was the method of concomitant variation or correlation.

> For this method to be reliable, it is not necessary that all the variables differing from those which we are comparing shall have been strictly excluded. The mere parallelism of the series of values presented by the two phenomena, provided that it has been established in a sufficient number and variety of cases, is proof that a relationship exists between them. Its validity is due to the fact that the concomitant variations display the causal relationship not by coincidence . . . but intrinsically. It does not simply show us two facts which accompany or exclude one another externally, so that there is no direct proof that they are united by an internal bond; on the contrary, it shows them as mutually influencing each other in a continuous manner, at least so far as their quality is concerned. This interaction, in itself, suffices to demonstrate that they are not foreign to one another.[109]

Such reasoning shows the necessity for Durkheim's postulate that a given effect has always a single corresponding cause, which, if correct, permits stronger inference from the correlation than might otherwise be the case. He regarded constant concomitance of cause and effect as "a law in itself, whatever may be the condition of the phenomena excluded from the comparison." It is a very powerful method of proof, even though in any given case covariation might be weakened by the action of other causes that produce "exceptions" to the laws established by covariation. Durkheim felt such exceptions should not lead the investigator to "abandon hastily the results of a methodically conducted demonstration."[110]

But how is the investigator to know, for any given correlation, which is cause and which is effect? Durkheim acknowledged that this is not readily apparent from a correlation—the covariation may result from the fact that

[107] Ibid., pp. 449–52.
[108] Durkheim, *Rules,* p. 130.
[109] Ibid., pp. 130–31. For Mill's exposition of the method of concomitant variation, see Mill, *A System of Logic,* pp. 464–66.
[110] Ibid., p. 131.

both are results of the same cause, or that "there exists between them a third phenomenon, interposed but unperceived, which is the effect of the first and the cause of the second."[111] Durkheim proposed to meet this challenge by a combination of "deduction," or inquiry into "how one of the two terms has produced the other," and new comparisons. Durkheim gave an illustration of a finding to appear subsequently in *Suicide:*

> We can establish in the most certain way that the tendency to suicide varies directly with education. But it is impossible to understand how erudition can lead to suicide; such an explanation is in contradiction to the laws of psychology. Education, especially the elementary branches of knowledge, reaches only the more superficial regions of consciousness; the instinct of self-preservation is, on the contrary, one of our fundamental tendencies. It could not, then, be appreciably affected by a phenomenon as far removed and of so feeble an influence. Thus we come to ask if both facts are not the consequence of an identical condition. This common cause is the weakening of religious traditionalism, which reinforces both the need for knowledge and the tendency toward suicide.[112]

The example is revealing. In attempting to render intelligible the connection among the three "social facts"—education, suicide, and religious traditionalism—was Durkheim not engaging in precisely the operation that Weber described as the interpretative grasp of ideal-typical meanings? Is it not an assessment of the different *meanings* of the drive for self-preservation, increasing knowledge, and decline in religious traditions for the typical actor exposed to these phenomena? Was not Durkheim turning to the psychological level—much as Weber did—to seek abstracted statements of the "laws" which dictate the direction of causality in social life? The answers to both these questions are affirmative, and I shall attempt to confirm the observation further in subsequent chapters.

Toward the end of his discussion of establishing sociological proofs, Durkheim ventured a number of observations on the different types of comparisons necessary to explain data comparatively. Some comparative analysis is possible *within* a single society, if "facts are widely distributed" and statistical information is "extensive and varied." As an example Durkheim noted the possibility of arriving at "genuine laws" by examining the differences in suicide rates over time according to provinces, classes, age, sex, and the like. This method cannot suffice when studying "an institution, a legal or moral regulation, or an established custom which func-

---

111 Ibid.
112 Ibid., p. 132.

tions in the same manner over the entire extent of the country and which changes only in time."[113] In such a case the available data would amount to "only a single pair of parallel curves, namely the curve which shows the progression in history of the phenomenon considered and the curve of the supposed cause in this single society."[114] What Durkheim appeared to say is that the latter case does not provide as much *variability* within the society as the former. Or in other words, the latter case yields only an N of 1 because of the uniformity of the association within the society, whereas the former produced a larger N of groups and categories showing variation in suicide rates throughout a society.

In the latter case, then, it is necessary to extend the field of comparison and include "several people of the same species." If a parallelism is observed between, say, the social milieu of Rome, Athens, and Sparta and the family systems of these city-states at corresponding stages of their development, one has increased the number of cases in which the concomitant variation occurs and thus increased the confidence in the presumed causal association. Even more, it becomes essential to compare the phenomenon (for example, family systems) in other species as well, so that the more fundamental character of family life can be established, and so that its step by step evolution can be traced.[115] In so doing not only is the number of societies increased but the presumed effects (types of domestic organization) and causes (social milieu) are permitted to vary over a wider range.

In concluding, Durkheim warned of a possible error in such extended comparisons. The error consists in comparing "what occurs at the decline of each species with what happens at the beginning of the succeeding species,"[116] regarding them as identical phenomena, and thereby drawing erroneous conclusions. For example, a scholar might observe the religious traditionalism of a society in its late stage of development, and note the religious traditionalism of the society succeeding it, and conclude that "decline in religious traditionalism" is always transitory. This would be an error, Durkheim argued, because the *social context* of the traditionalism is different. The religious life of a young society is a function of "the special conditions in which every young society is placed."[117] Thus the explanation of apparent "transitoriness" is superseded by another explanation. On the basis of this reasoning, Durkheim admonished that in order to arrive

---

[113] Ibid., p. 136.
[114] Ibid., pp. 136–37.
[115] Ibid., pp. 137–39.
[116] Ibid., p. 139.
[117] Ibid., p. 140.

at proper comparisons, "it will suffice to consider the societies compared at the same period of their development."[118]

But in thus admonishing, is not Durkheim paying more homage to Mill's canons than he intended? Is not the insistence that societies be "controlled" for stage of development in order to make just comparisons an invocation of a version of Mill's method of difference, in which cases are made to agree in circumstances (in this case youth, or stage of development) *other than* the presumed causal connection to be discovered in the concomitant variation of the suspected social facts? The control is gained not by experimental manipulation, as Mill insisted it should be, but rather by the *conceptual* manipulation of features of similarity and difference among societies in order to rule out stage of development as a causal factor.

Later in his career, Durkheim was even more forceful in enunciating the dependence of "social facts" on social context. Such facts, he argued,

> cannot be understood when detached from [the social system of which they form a part]. This is why two facts which come from two different societies cannot be profitably compared merely because they seem to resemble each other; it is necessary that these societies themselves resemble each other, that is to say, that they be only varieties of the same species. The comparative method would be impossible, if social types did not exist, and it cannot be usefully applied except within a single type.[119]

Lamenting the errors that have been committed by "scattering . . . researches over all the societies possible," Durkheim called for a concentration on a clearly determined type. If one includes "all sorts of societies and civilizations," he draws facts hastily from different contexts, and ends up with "tumultuous and summary comparisons."[120] To Durkheim this signalled the need to limit the number of societies studied so that greater precision could be gained.[121] The methodological significance of this point, however, is that if the similarity or differences among facts is a function of the similarity or difference of social context, then social contexts must be made similar if the facts are to be judged so. Or to put it even more directly, the operation Durkheim suggests *controls*—by means of classifica-

---

[118] Ibid.

[119] Emile Durkheim, *The Elementary Forms of the Religious Life,* trans. Joseph Ward Swain (Glencoe, Ill.: The Free Press, 1947), p. 94. Note Weber's identical comment regarding the context of motives in establishing the similarity or difference between individual actions.

[120] Ibid., pp. 94–95.

[121] Ibid., p. 95.

tion into types—unwanted sources of variation in the phenomena under study.

For Weber, it will be recalled, the principal source of sociological explanation lies in the generation of one or more ideal-type constructions of the subjective-meaning complex of actors and the comparison of these expectations with the best available data. In comparing such "models" with historical data, it is possible "to arrive at a causal explanation of the observed deviations [from the course of action specified in the ideal type] which will be attributed to such factors as misinformation, strategical errors, logical fallacies, personal temperament, or considerations outside the realm of [the posited course of action]."[122] Weber remained skeptical about the level of scientific generality that could be attained in sociology on several counts: first, he was suspicious of highly generalized systems of deductive laws in general; second, he was continuously aware of—and reminding the reader of—"historical accidents and the plurality of historical factors [that] make it impossible to predict the actual course of events";[123] and third, he was aware of imperfections in the data with which sociology must deal.

With respect to the latter Weber regarded the empirical verification of hypotheses by experimentation to be very limited in sociology, possible "only in the very few special cases susceptible of psychological experimentation."[124] A second mode of verification is feasible "in the limited number of cases of mass phenomena which can be statistically described and unambiguously interpreted,"[125] no doubt because of the large number of cases and the capacity to treat them by techniques of quantitative analysis. Third, "[for] the rest, there remains only the possibility of comparing the largest possible number of historical or contemporary processes which, while otherwise similar, differ in the one decisive point of their relation to the particular motive or fact the role of which is being investigated."[126] In the end, Weber, like Durkheim, laid the heaviest burden in sociology on the comparative analysis of empirical data generated in the historical process.

The second and third types—statistical and comparative analysis—evidently shade into one another. In certain cases, such as the data that might be available to assess the validity of a principle like Gresham's law, "the

122 Weber, *Economy and Society*, 1:21.
123 Roth, "Max Weber's Comparative Approach and Historical Typology," p. 93.
124 Weber, *Economy and Society*, 1:10.
125 Ibid.
126 Ibid. In this phrasing, Weber is enunciating Mill's method of difference, which he employed in his own empirical comparisons. He utilized variants of the method of agreement as well.

correspondence between the theoretical interpretation of motivation and its empirical verification is entirely satisfactory and the cases are numerous enough so that verification can be considered established."[127] For other analyses the number of historical cases are so few as to reduce confidence in the results. As an example, Weber cited Eduard Meyer's interpretation of the causal significance of the battles of Marathon, Salamis, and Platea in terms of typical attitudes of the Greek oracles and prophets toward the Persians. Because analysis had to rest only on the few cases in which the Persians were victorious, such an interpretation, while plausible, must necessarily remain a hypothesis because of the difficulties of verification.[128]

Weber did not develop even as limited a statement of the strategies of comparative analysis as did Durkheim. Insight may be gained into his reasoning, however, by examining what he described as the "imaginary experiment." Listing this "uncertain procedure" after describing the experimental, statistical, and comparative methods, he characterized it as a process of "thinking away certain elements of a chain of motivation and working out the course of action which would then probably ensue, thus arriving at a causal judgment."[129] What sort of methodology underlies this procedure?

In one of his methodological essays, published in 1905,[130] Weber resumed his polemic against those who argued for a "presuppositionless" approach to history. Rather, he argued, historical explanation—the attribution of effects to causes—involves a series of abstractions. The decisive abstraction occurs when "we *conceive* of one or a few of the actual causal components as modified in a certain direction and then ask ourselves whether under the conditions which have been thus changed, the same effect . . . or some other effect 'would be expected.' "[131] Would the relevant chain of historical events have been otherwise if a given battle had had a different outcome, if a political leader had not been assassinated, and so on? To analyze these possibilities is the essence of the mental experiment. It involves disregarding what actually happened and the "mental construction of a course of events which is altered through modification in one or more 'conditions.' "[132]

Weber further described this process in terms of a series of "isolations"

[127] Ibid., 1:11.

[128] Ibid.

[129] Ibid., 1:10.

[130] Max Weber, "Critical Studies in the Logic of the Cultural Sciences: A Critique of Eduard Meyer's Methodological Views," in *The Methodology of the Social Sciences*, pp. 113–88.

[131] Ibid., p. 171.

[132] Ibid., p. 173.

and "generalizations." The first process is to decompose the given historical situation into components or factors, and then, by an "empirical rule," determine what effects each of these "conditions" could be expected to have. The "generalization" aspect lies in the "empirical rule," by which Weber meant the store of general knowledge we have about the historical process which permits us to assess the effect of the altered conditions. Finally, and also on the basis of our general historical knowledge, it is possible to assign a judgment of the relative probability of different historical outcomes. "We can . . . estimate the relative 'degree' to which [an] outcome is 'favored' by the general rule by a comparison involving the consideration of how other conditions operating differently 'would' have 'favored' it."[133] Thus, while the general mission of social (including historical) science is "to understand on the one hand the relationship and the cultural significance of individual events in their contemporary manifestations and on the other the causes of their being historically *so* and not *otherwise*,"[134] much knowledge can be gained by a systematic analysis of the "otherwise" through a series of mental experiments.

From a methodological standpoint, the "imaginary experiment" is a species of comparative analysis. It involves increasing the number of cases under consideration, though in this particular instance the new case or cases are invented rather than observed. Furthermore, by decomposing the historical situation into factors and systematically varying one and then another, Weber was in effect making a conceptual effort to realize the conditions set forth in Mill's method of difference—that is to say, comparing cases that are similar in all respects except one, and attempting to trace the effects of this one difference. The reasons why Weber correctly regarded this procedure as "uncertain" are (1) because the manipulation of the factor is imaginary (not rooted in empirical variation), no actual historical data or variations are produced; and (2) as a result, the imagined "otherwise" data must be posited on the investigator's general knowledge of "laws" and "principles," which are not sufficiently developed in the social sciences to permit the assumption of particular results from certain imaginary situations. Despite the fragile status of the imaginary experiment, however, its logical structure and its strategic significance place it on a continuum with the other methods of generating knowledge in the social sciences.

Durkheim's and Weber's discussion of the logic of verification and proof differ a great deal from one another, because their general programs for sociology differ. Durkheim, approaching social science more from a model

---

[133] Ibid., p. 131.
[134] Ibid., p. 72. Emphasis in original.

of natural science, attempted to modify and adapt the logic and procedures of the natural sciences to sociological inquiry; Weber, approaching social science in a manner which allowed him to escape the pitfalls of historicism, attempted to devise procedures to permit more generalizable inferences than historians typically permitted themselves. Yet the two also approximated one another in significant ways. Both settled on the centrality of comparative sociology—the comparative analysis of similarities and differences in as many empirical instances as could be assembled. Both were sensitive, moreover, to the problems of taking into account—controlling, if you will—sources of empirical variation that could "contaminate" suspected causal associations, though neither produced anything like a systematic strategy designed to overcome these problems.

Conclusion

Rather than reiterate in condensed form the comparisons and contrasts between Durkheim and Weber on the methodology of the social sciences, let me instead indicate, in summary form, the issues that emerged in the thought of each as they turned their minds to considering fundamental principles and how they ought to guide scientific inquiry.

1. What are the respective roles of the actor and observer in the generation of sociological knowledge? To what extent does the outlook of the actor have to be taken into account? In what ways does—and should—the observer influence the concepts and data with which he deals?

2. At what level of generality should sociological explanations be pitched—statements of laws, statements of probabilistic tendencies, or the explanation of historically unique constellations and events?

3. What kinds of data should the investigator consult in the generation of sociological knowledge? In particular, should he seek for quantifiable indices to be standardized for all cases studied, or should he rely on data that somehow reflect the "uniqueness" of each case being studied? Or should he attempt some compromise between these two strategies?

4. At what conceptual level should knowledge be generated—the psychological, the social, in some way that relates the two, or at some other level?

5. How does the investigator deal with the complexity of his subject matter, particularly when he does not control the recording of that data? What are the major methods that are available to isolate, control, and manipulate variables? What are the relations of these methods to one another?

6. With respect to the comparative method as such—the comparison of limited numbers of cases that differ from one another in some respects—

what are the available strategies for isolating, controlling, and manipulating variables? What is the relative effectiveness of these methods in terms of generating valid inferences?

7. What is the role of abstract "models" in empirical investigation?

As we have seen, Durkheim and Weber faced all these questions in one way or another, though they occurred to them often in quite different form than I have phrased them, and they differed from one another both in the *degree* to which they attempted solutions to all and in the *kind* of solutions they generated. In particular, we observed that both had the habit of proposing a definite, sometimes polemical solution that showed them to be in extreme opposition to one another; then, as they elaborated, qualified, or equivocated, they would gradually move toward a position on each issue that emphasized points of agreement more than opposition.

As we shall see, these issues are far from resolved to the present day, and, in fact, they continue—though often in different form—to dominate the concerns of those currently engaged in comparative analysis. And despite the diversity of solutions generated in the past decades, the same issues arise and re-arise. We shall observe this in our reference to more contemporary developments in the last two chapters. Before undertaking that, however, I should like to look at some of the substantive work of Durkheim and Weber, to see what kind of comparative methodology emerged in their own practice of sociology, as contrasted, perhaps, to how they argued the sociologist should practice.

4

Durkheim's Comparative Sociology

Having traced the preachings of Durkheim and Weber on the proper methods for sociology—including the comparative method—I turn now to examine how each of these scholars "practiced" in their own comparative sociological research. The scholarship of both covered an enormous range of sociological issues that are very much alive in contemporary times—alive partly because of the forcefulness with which Durkheim and Weber posed them. In dealing with the work of both, I shall attempt to place their strategies of comparative analysis in the context of their substantive preoccupations since, as in the case of Tocqueville, the latter determined in large part the comparative data they chose and the methods they employed to analyze these data.

I begin with Durkheim. I shall first indicate in general terms the substantive emphases of his major empirical monographs—*The Division of Labor in Society, Suicide,* and *The Elementary Forms of Religious Life.* Next I shall examine his method of defining, describing, classifying, and measuring some of the major variables he studied. Then, returning to his substantive sociological preoccupations, I shall sketch the network of causal relations he developed in each work. And finally, I shall evaluate critically the comparative strategies he devised and employed in an effort to establish those causal relations.

Durkheim's Substantive
Preoccupations

The connecting thread running through Durkheim's empirical research is the salience he gave to the sources, nature, and consequences of *social solidarity*. In *The Division of Labor in Society* he argued that as societies grow more complex, they develop not only a greater degree of social solidarity, but a different kind of solidarity, one directed at harmonizing and reconciling the diversity of interests associated with a more complex organization of society. By the same token, increasing complexity occasions a decline in the kind of solidarity that is directed at reproducing likenesses among individuals and groups. In the same work Durkheim identified certain pathological developments associated with an increasing division of labor, particularly the development of anomie, the forced division of labor, and maldistributions of functions. Turning finally to the conditions affecting the rise of a more complex division of labor, he singled out the adaptive significance of specialization in relation to the heightened struggle for existence associated with the increasing volume and density of social life.

In *Suicide* Durkheim analyzed another series of consequences of social solidarity—its power to protect individuals from or to impel them to self-destruction through suicide. He developed several theses, each demonstrating the master proposition that extremes of solidarity give rise to extremes in the social suicide rate. For example, when individuals and groups are overly integrated into the cultural system of a society, they tend to take their own lives in greater number out of subordination to that system (altruistic suicide). At the other extreme, when individuals and groups are set free to an extreme degree from the constraints of societal integration, the result—an increase in the social rate of suicide—is the same, though the cause in this case is the opposite (egoistic suicide). When conditions of anomie prevail, individuals and groups find their lives unregulated, are confused by a discrepancy between their expectations and their life experiences, and tend toward greater self-destruction out of a sense of disorientation (anomic suicide). Armed with such propositions, Durkheim attempted to account for the different suicide rates observable among different societies, as well as among social groups and categories within societies.

Finally, in *The Elementary Forms of Religious Life* Durkheim undertook to generate a sociological theory of belief and knowledge, arguing that society's power over individuals becomes objectified in the categories of thought that constitute the society's cultural heritage. In particular, using the Australian religions as the simplest form of religion, he argued that the conception of the totem arises from the clan organization of those societies, and that the worship of the totem is, in effect, the worship of society itself. More generally, Durkheim treated the idea of the sacred as the objectification of society and interpreted its various manifestations—in religious beliefs, in the idea of the soul, in celebrations, in rituals—as so many foci of the impingement of society on its members. Society and religion, in short, reinforce one another mutually.

So much for the general themes, now familiar to students of society. On what procedures did Durkheim rely for their demonstration?

Definition, Description, Classification, and Measurement

Durkheim from the beginning insisted on the need for precision in scientific work. Not only must an investigator "observe [facts] carefully, to describe and classify them," but, what is more difficult, he must find *"the way in which they are scientific,* that is to say, to discover in them some objective element that allows an exact determination, and, if possible, measurement."[1] Accordingly, Durkheim was sensitized to the need for clear definition and description of—as well as the identification of what we now call indices for—his major variables.

Durkheim's program for defining social facts is consistent with his positivistic methodology. He saw the need for defining a phenomenon as an absolute pre-requisite for its study.[2] In proceeding to define a phenomenon, such as religion, moreover, "it is necessary to begin by freeing the mind of every preconceived idea,"[3] such as a priori notions of the essence of religion in general. Similarly, in approaching the definition of

[1] Emile Durkheim, *The Division of Labor in Society,* trans. George Simpson (Glencoe, Ill.: The Free Press, 1949), p. 37. Emphasis in original.

[2] "If we are going to look for the most primitive and simple religion which we can observe, it is necessary to begin by defining what is meant by a religion; for without this, we would run the risk of giving the name to a system of ideas and practices which has nothing at all religious about it, or else of leaving to one side many religious facts, without perceiving their true nature." Emile Durkheim, *The Elementary Forms of the Religious Life,* trans. Joseph Ward Swain (Glencoe, Ill.: The Free Press, 1947), p. 23.

[3] Ibid.

suicide, he was skeptical of relying on "the words of everyday language"
—which can be regarded as preconceived ideas of a sort—because of the
multiplicity of meanings they have. If we follow common use, "we risk
distinguishing what should be combined, or combining what should be
distinguished, thus mistaking the real affinities of things, and accordingly
misapprehending their nature."[4] The scholar must shun "roughly assembled groups of facts corresponding to words of common usage."[5] Instead,
and also consistent with his program, Durkheim argued for an inductive
approach. To discover the nature of religion, "let us consider the various
religions in their concrete reality, and attempt to disengage that which they
have in common; for religion cannot be defined except by the characteristics which are found wherever religion itself is found."[6] The definition
of suicide, similarly, should be based on "a category of objects . . . which
are objectively established, that is, correspond to a definite aspect of
things."[7] Yet at the same time he revealed a certain ambivalence about
"common usage"; he argued for the definition of suicide to be based on
facts "sufficiently kin to those commonly called suicides for us to retain
the same term without breaking with common usage."[8] And later, in
rejecting the idea that suicide is caused by individual pathology, he argued
that "[not] every suicide can . . . be considered insane, without doing
violence to language."[9] For the moment I simply note this ambivalence;
presently I shall enumerate some reasons why common usage *must* be
taken into account.

For all his insistence on precise definitions, Durkheim did not define all
his basic categories with equal precision. In particular, the concept of
social solidarity, salient as it was in all of his work, never received a definition that would measure up to his criteria; as we shall see, this vagueness
makes for difficulties in interpreting some of his empirical results. For
some other variables, however—notably suicide and religion—he ventured
very careful definitions. Let us examine the procedures involved, the
functions provided by these definitions, and some of their problematic
elements.

What constitutes the definition of a phenomenon? At bottom it is the
invocation of one or more generic (class) terms that indicate what is to be
included and what is to be excluded under that phenomenon's rubric.

[4] Emile Durkheim, *Suicide*, ed. with an introduction by George Simpson; trans.
John A. Spaulding and George Simpson (Glencoe, Ill.: The Free Press, 1951), p. 41.
[5] Ibid.
[6] Durkheim, *The Elementary Forms of the Religious Life*, p. 24.
[7] Durkheim, *Suicide*, p. 42.
[8] Ibid.
[9] Ibid., p. 66.

Durkheim's procedure in working up a definition of religion demonstrates this. Initially he argued that religion is to be defined by the presence neither of a notion of "supernatural" nor of a notion of "divinity";[10] that is to say, these are not necessary conditions for designating a phenomenon as religious. By contrast, however, all beliefs that involve a distinction between the sacred and the profane are to be included under the heading, religious:

> The real characteristic of religious phenomena is that they always suppose a bipartite division of the whole universe, known and knowable, into two classes which embrace all that exists, but which radically exclude each other. Sacred things are those which the interdictions protect and isolate; profane things, those to which these interdictions are applied and which must remain at a distance from the first.[11]

Similarly, Durkheim excluded magic as a defining characteristic, but argued, instead, that religion, properly defined, consists of a "group leading a common life"—a church—that magic does not have.[12]

Though not quite so systematically developed as his definition of religion, Durkheim's definition of suicide has the same characteristics. The formal definition is as follows: "the term suicide is applied to all cases of death resulting directly or indirectly from a positive or negative act of the victim himself, which he knows will produce this result."[13] The phenomenon thus falls in the general category of "deaths," but is only a sub-class of these, as indicated by qualifying phrases, such as "which he knows will produce this result." By using this definition Durkheim avoided defining suicide in a way that would entail a search for "[ends] sought by the actor" and permitted him to exclude phenomena, such as suicide by animals, since, by definition, they cannot have "an understanding anticipatory to their death nor, especially, of the means to accomplish it."[14]

In approaching definitions in this way, Durkheim was forced to be somewhat untrue to the positivistic, inductionist principles he formally enunciated. By calling on the observer to examine "religions in their concrete reality," he in fact revealed a kind of preconceived category of religion, for, without it, the investigator would not know where to begin to look for religions. And in rejecting the idea of the supernatural as the basis for defining religion, he presented the argument that "this idea does not appear until late in the history of religions,"[15] implying once again a prior

---

[10] Durkheim, *The Elementary Forms of the Religious Life*, pp. 24–35.
[11] Ibid., pp. 40–41.
[12] Ibid., p. 44.
[13] Durkheim, *Suicide*, p. 44.
[14] Ibid., pp. 43, 44.
[15] Durkheim, *The Elementary Forms of the Religious Life*, p. 25.

criterion for identifying religions above and beyond merely inspecting them for the presence or absence of the notion of the supernatural. In other passages Durkheim clearly called for something more than an inductionist recording. He cited the necessity, for example, in the study of religion, of going "underneath the symbol to the reality which it represents and which gives it its meaning," a strategy not inherent in a strict inductionist approach.[16] And in the study of suicide, he argued that "[the scholar] himself must establish the groups he wishes to study in order to give them the homogeneity and the specific meaning necessary for them to be susceptible of scientific treatment."[17] Surely, then, it is more nearly accurate to represent Durkheim's definition of religion, for example, as follows: "That category of beliefs I classify as 'religious beliefs' invariably distinguishes between the profane and the sacred."

However reasoned, a definition is the invocation of a series of rules of inclusion and exclusion. It indicates the sense in which certain phenomena are categorically different from the phenomenon in question (and thus are *not* the objects of study). At the same time, a definition proclaims phenomena as *identical* to one another with respect to the central defining characteristic or characteristics, however they may differ in other respects. Durkheim recognized this function of a definition when he was wrestling with the advisability of comparing the simplest religions with the most advanced. Despite their differences, he argued, "they are not sufficient to place the corresponding religions in different classes."[18] They have, he argued, "a number of fundamental representations or conceptions . . . of ritual attitudes"—of which the distinction between sacred and profane is most fundamental—that justify placing them in the same category.[19] By placing all religions in a single class, moreover, they are rendered comparable to one another. Durkheim noted that ". . . all religions can be compared to each other, and . . . all are species of the same class";[20] he might have added that the former is possible only because of the latter. To establish a class of phenomena that are identical with respect to the defining characteristic, then, is the first requisite for comparative study.

It is appropriate, then, to regard the contribution of Durkheim's definition of religion not so much as an inductive discovery of that which is "essential" in religion but rather to view it as a classification—and a rendering comparable—of religious phenomena on a new basis. Some

[16] Ibid., p. 2.
[17] Durkheim, *Suicide*, p. 41.
[18] Durkheim, *The Elementary Forms of the Religious Life*, p. 3.
[19] Ibid., p. 5.
[20] Ibid., p. 4.

phenomena considered to be religion under other definitions are excluded, and some phenomena not considered religion under other definitions are included. The power of such a contribution should not be underestimated. Instances of the new category (that is, religious beliefs involving the distinction between sacred and profane) while identical from the standpoint of the defining characteristic, resemble and differ from one another with respect to their *other* characteristics, for example, whether a personal god is represented, whether human sacrifice is performed, and so on. Furthermore, the patterns of associations among these other characteristics differ according to the criterion by which the phenomenon (religion) is originally defined, because the invocation of other criteria would yield different classes. The pattern and strength of subsequent correlations, then, is in part a function of the original definition of the class of phenomena to be compared.

As indicated, Durkheim was also concerned at all times with the location of empirical indicators ("external indices") through which generally defined variables may be studied. Accordingly, in *The Division of Labor in Society* he identified law codes as "the visible symbol" of social solidarity; in *Suicide* he turned to available statistics on suicide from many countries, as well as descriptive monographs on suicide without recorded statistics to secure an empirical representation of the social suicide rate; and in *The Elementary Forms of Religious Life* he relied for his empirical indices mainly on the observations of anthropologists and historians regarding the characteristics of religions they had studied.

Just as a formal definition is an invocation of rules for inclusion and exclusion, so is an "operational definition." The latter specifies, for any datum, whether it should be included under or excluded from the general category it is intended to represent. Of all legal codes that might be thought to represent social solidarity, which ought to be included for empirical study? Of all deaths that occur, which of those ought to be categorized as suicides, thus yielding an empirical representation of the social fact of suicide? Durkheim worried over such questions. In relating social solidarity to law he reasoned thus: When social solidarity is strong, "it leads men strongly to one another, frequently puts them in contact, multiplies the occasions when they find themselves related."[21] Furthermore, the number of these relations "is directly proportional to that of the juridical rules which determine them."[22] But is not this index an incomplete one? Should not measures of more informal regulation, such as customs, be included? Durkheim thought not; by a series of arguments we

21 Durkheim, *The Division of Labor in Society,* p. 64.
22 Ibid., pp. 64–65.

need not review here, he concluded that if there are types of solidarity that custom alone manifests, these are secondary, and that "law produces those which are essential and they are the only ones we need to know."[23] Many parts of Durkheim's reasoning are open to objection; but it is clear that he actively concerned himself with the question of the adequacy of his chosen index.

One way of ascertaining the adequacy of an index is to ask the following question: are the results obtained by applying the rules and procedures contained in a formal definition of a phenomenon the same as those attained by applying the rules and procedures for recording instances of the phenomenon? Consider Durkheim's definition of suicide again: "all cases of death resulting directly or indirectly from a positive or negative act of the victim himself, which he knows will produce this result." As indicated, part of his aim in putting forth this definition was to avoid any "motivational" classification of suicide; indeed, he found the conventional "reasons"—reasons such as "family troubles," "remorse," or "unhappy love" —to be unsatisfactory in a variety of ways.[24] He remarked sarcastically that "what are called statistics of the motives of suicides are actually statistics of the opinions concerning such motives of officials, often of lower officials, in charge of this information service," and for this reason are defective.[25] A more important observation, however, is that insofar as a judgment of motive plays a role in an official's recording an event as a suicide—as it undoubtedly does—it becomes a statistic that owes its existence to a *different* classificatory criterion than that envisioned by the scholar's formal definition. The same might be said for acts of suicide that are *not* recorded because of, say, the influence of a wealthy family who wishes not to have the death of one of its members recorded as a suicide. Or, again, the procedures of recording statistics may vary from country to country, either as a result of differences in administrative practice or as the result of, say, the reluctance of officials to record events as suicide in societies with strong taboos against suicide. To put the point in general terms: insofar as the results obtained from the "logic" of recording differ from those obtained from applying a formal definition, the index is correspondingly inadequate. This is the reason, furthermore, that Durkheim *had* to take into account "common usage" in his definition of suicide, for it is by applying the logic of common usage of the term, suicide, that records are compiled. To ignore that logic is to endanger the validity of the empirical index. This is also the reason—though not explicitly averred

23 Ibid., p. 66.
24 Durkheim, *Suicide*, pp. 149–51.
25 Ibid., p. 148.

—that led Durkheim to venture the comforting assertion that "the vast majority of occurrences customarily [called suicide] belong" to the group designated by the formal definition.[26]

As a first approximation, then, we may observe that the "problem of comparability" in social investigation has three distinct facets: (a) the requirement that a generic concept or concepts be provided in a definition in order to specify a basis for identity—or comparability—of a range of phenomena and to exclude those phenomena not so designated; (b) the requirement that as nearly identical results as possible be obtained in applying the logic of the definition and in ascertaining the "logic" by which the phenomena are recorded empirically; and (c) the requirement that the procedures of recording do not differ from empirical case to empirical case.

Causal Networks in
Durkheim's Sociology

In each of his major empirical monographs Durkheim took some sort of social solidarity as a central point of reference and traced its origins and ramifications in a variety of directions. It is essential to sketch these causal connections—as I did with Tocqueville—since they dictate in large part the kinds of social data Durkheim sought and the strategies he used to organize and manipulate these data. Because my aim is to elucidate Durkheim's method, the substantive summaries will necessarily be incomplete; Durkheim's works are quite dense and complex, and adequate representation would require much more space than I have. In addition, I shall emphasize those causal relations on which Durkheim himself attempted to bring empirical data to bear; many of his other causal assertions were ventured but neither defended nor demonstrated, and these are of less interest and will be treated more cursorily.

The division of labor

Durkheim outlined his purposes in *The Division of Labor in Society* as follows: to determine the functions of the division of labor, or what social need it satisfies; to determine the conditions which give rise to the division of labor; and to identify some of its abnormal consequences.[27] The first treats the division of labor as an independent variable, that is, asking after its consequences; the second as dependent; and the third as independent again.

[26] Ibid., p. 42.
[27] Durkheim, *The Division of Labor in Society*, p. 45.

Proceeding according to his dictum that a single cause gives rise to a single effect, Durkheim identified two social tendencies and two corresponding types of social solidarity produced by these tendencies. The tendencies, respectively, are social likeness and social diversity among people. The former, resting on a simple social division of labor (and the corresponding homogeneity of individuals in society) is constituted by "the totality of beliefs and sentiments common to average citizens of the same society."[28] This common conscience insists upon preserving sameness, and the kind of solidarity it produces is mechanical, involving, that is, an automatic, passionate punishment of any deviation from the sameness. This type of solidarity is made visible in repressive, or penal law. The force that this law manifests

> is a product of the most essential social likenesses, and it has for its effect the maintenance of the social cohesion which results from these likenesses. It is this force which penal law protects against all enfeeblement, both in demanding from each of us a minimum of resemblances without which the individual would be a menace to the unity of the social body, and in imposing upon us the respect for the symbol which expresses and summarizes these resemblances at the same time that it guarantees them.[29]

An increase in the division of labor and its accompanying individuation of the consciences of society's members creates a different sort of solidarity, one which takes cognizance of the heterogeneity of interests bred by specialized roles, and binds society together through moderation, regulation, and control. Why should this form of solidarity arise? Largely because it is necessary to retain a relationship of complementarity and cooperation among diversified people—a relationship not required if all individuals in the society were alike in activity and for that reason, less dependent on one another. The visible symbol of this solidarity arising from heterogeneity—what Durkheim called organic solidarity—is restitutive law, which acknowledges the legitimacy of individual differences and operates to maintain and restore balance among parts potentially uncoordinated or in conflict.

Since each type of solidarity depends on the extent of the division of labor and since each type of solidarity is manifested in a particular form of law, these several characteristics should cluster as follows:

> If the two types of solidarity . . . really have the juridical expression we have suggested, the preponderance of repressive law over co-operative law ought to be just as great as the collective type is more pronounced and as

[28] Ibid., p. 79.
[29] Ibid., p. 106.

the division of labor is more rudimentary. Inversely, commensurate with the development of individual types and the specialization of tasks, the proportion between the two types of law ought to become reversed.[30]

These clusters are not universal, however. Durkheim noted in particular that certain pathological or abnormal forms arise from the division of labor. The first, the anomic division of labor, is best characterized as a discrepancy involving a great division of labor but an insufficient organic solidarity to regulate it. Under this condition society experiences dislocations (such as business crises), unregulated conflict (as between capital and labor), and the isolation of individuals and groups. In the second abnormal form, the forced division of labor, individuals are allocated to social functions that do not fit their individual talents and abilities. And a third form of pathology arises when social functions are allocated in a way that underemploys individual talents. While Durkheim insisted upon the abnormality of these forms, he did not enumerate the conditions under which abnormal rather than normal forms arise, or the conditions under which one rather than another abnormal form arises. Thus the causal relations between the division of labor and the abnormal forms remain vague, and few empirical propositions emerge from Durkheim's analysis. Furthermore, since he did not provide a precise definition of social health, and since he made no effort to demonstrate that the pathological forms occur less frequently than the normal form, it remains difficult to ascertain in what senses the former can be unequivocally regarded as abnormal.

In book two, Durkheim turned to the principal causes and conditions of the division of labor. Because this analysis is less developed and more causally documented, I can be briefer in sketching the main causal relations. Basically, Durkheim felt that the main cause of an increase in the division of labor lies in some kind of quantitative increase in the interaction among peoples. "The division of labor develops," he asserted, "as there are more individuals sufficiently in contact to be able to act and react upon one another."[31] He called this factor dynamic or moral density, and argued simply that "the progress of the division of labor is in direct ratio to the moral or dynamic density of society."[32] Density arises with the concentration of populations, the rise of cities, and the development of systems of transportation and communication. He considered these phenomena to be the "visible and measurable symbol" of moral density, and argued that aside from exceptional cases, material density (concentration

[30] Ibid., p. 133.
[31] Ibid., p. 257.
[32] Ibid.

and interaction among populations) and moral density coincide.[33] In addition, he cited another population variable, "social volume," which refers to
size of population—as opposed strictly to density—and which also works
to increase the division of labor.

Why should increasing density and volume produce an increase in the
division of labor? Durkheim argued that as societies become denser and
more voluminous, the "struggle for existence is more acute."[34] Competition for resources is greater if men struggle for them in the same way. He
regarded the increasing differentiation of social roles as analogous to the
differentiation of species in nature. Being different in activity, men can
better provide for one another's needs. The division of labor thus emerges
as a kind of adaptive device in man's struggle for survival in a world of
scarce resources.

Durkheim viewed the common conscience as opposed to the advancing
division of labor; it "holds us back and prevents us from deviating from
the collective type."[35] He also identified a number of factors that weaken
the common conscience, thus contributing indirectly to an increase in the
division of labor. Among these he cited the tendency for the common
conscience to become "more general" as the size and diversity of society
increases, thus allowing for more "individual variations"; the increasing
mobility of individuals, which takes them from their places of origin and
weakens the influence of traditions imparted by their elders; and the decreasing incidence of occupational heredity.[36] Finally, Durkheim identified
a kind of feedback mechanism in asserting that an increased division of
labor, by enhancing interaction among individuals, "in its turn, increases
the concentration of society," thus leading to a positive spiral of development of the division of labor.[37]

The various causal relations I have sketched—treating the division of labor
both as an independent and a dependent variable—are represented graphically in figure 4-1.[38] The diagram may be interpreted in the following
way. When the degree of competition for existence is low, similarity of
consciences is high, homogeneity is high, and the extent of division of
labor is low. As a consequence, societal complexity is low and, under
ordinary conditions, the mode of integration is mechanical and the mode
of legal control is repressive law. On the other hand, when the competition
for existence intensifies, similarity of consciences is lowered, homogeneity

[33] Ibid., p. 260.
[34] Ibid., p. 266.
[35] Ibid., p. 283.
[36] Ibid., bk. 2, chs. 3, 4.
[37] Ibid., p. 260.
[38] Herbert Coster made some helpful suggestions on constructing this diagram.

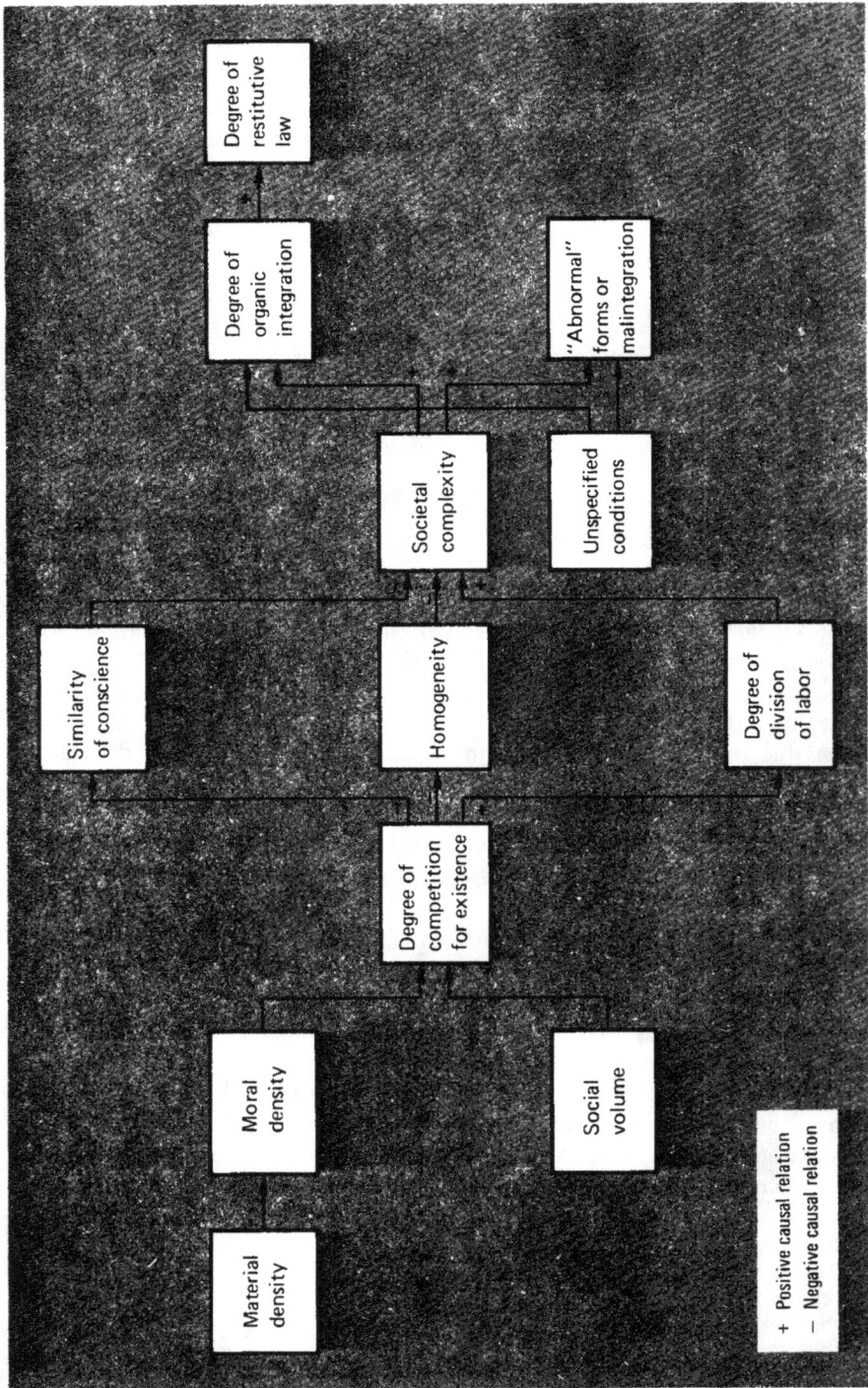

FIG. 4–1 Causal Structure Represented in *The Division of Labor in Society*

is lowered, and a greater division of labor develops. These, in turn, make for high societal complexity and, again under ordinary but unspecified conditions, the mode of integration is then organic and the mode of legal control is restitutive law. Under other but also unspecified conditions, a high level of societal complexity produces the various abnormal forms.

Suicide

Among the complex of changes that an increasing division of labor generates Durkheim mentioned a change in the psychic constitution of individual personalities:

> In so far as societies do not reach certain dimensions nor a certain degree of concentration, the only psychic life which may be truly developed is that which is common to all members of the group, which is found identical in each. But, as societies become more vast and, particularly, more condensed, a psychic life of a new sort appears. Individual diversities, at first lost and confused amidst the mass of social likenesses, become disengaged, become conspicuous, and multiply. A multitude of things which use [*sic*] to remain outside because they did not affect the collective being become objects of representations. Whereas individuals use [*sic*] to act only by involving one another, except in cases where their conduct was determined by physical needs, each of them becomes a source of spontaneous activity. Particular personalities become constituted, take conscience of themselves. Moreover, this growth of psychic life in the individual does not obliterate the psychic life of society, but only transforms it. It becomes freer, more extensive, and as it has, after all, no other bases than individual consciences, these extend, become complex, and thus become flexible.[39]

These remarks give a clue to the substantive preoccupations that informed his next monograph, *Suicide,* published four years after *The Division of Labor in Society.* One of the former's major themes is that the greater individuation of personalities associated with the advance of civilization—as well as their greater exposure to anomic conditions—contributes to a rise in the incidence of self-destruction of individuals and groups thus affected. In *Suicide,* then, the independent variables are a variety of types of social integration and regulation, and the dependent variables are the social rates of suicide.

Durkheim also introduced a methodological modification in his study of suicide. In *The Division of Labor* he was concerned about the elusive nature of social solidarity as an identifiable variable. Because such a fact "escapes us," he proposed to study it through the external index of legal

[39] Durkheim, *The Division of Labor in Society,* pp. 347–48.

codes. Solidarity is a social fact, he said, which "we can know only through the intermediary of its social effects."[40] Thus the proper method to study the effects is "to classify the different types of law to find therefrom the different types of social solidarity which correspond to it."[41] These forms of social solidarity, in their turn, are a result of the extent of the division of labor in society.

In *Suicide* Durkheim adopted a strategy which was in some respects the reverse of that just described. Again invoking his maxim that a specific effect has a specific cause,[42] he proposed to study the social types of suicide not "directly by their preliminarily described characteristics," but rather "by the causes which produce them."

> Without asking why they differ from one another, we will first seek the social conditions responsible for them; then group these conditions in a number of separate classes by their resemblances and differences, and we shall be sure that a specific type of suicide will correspond to each of these classes. In a word, instead of being morphological, our classification will from the start be aetiological. Nor is this a sign of inferiority, for the nature of a phenomenon is much more profoundly got at by knowing its cause than by knowing its characteristics only, even the essential ones.[43]

Sensing, however, that such an approach contains a defect—"to assume the diversity of types [effects] without being able to identify them"[44]— Durkheim promised, after concluding his aetiological analysis, to turn to some data on the morphology of suicide to show that "the deductively established species may be shown not to be imaginary."[45]

Durkheim's classification of causes is familiar and need be only sketched. The first, egoistic suicide, results when individuals and groups become individuated from and lose cohesiveness from their received traditions, and consequently become insufficiently supported by a collective life. Durkheim cited the differences between Protestantism and Catholicism— with Protestants showing a consistent proclivity to a higher rate of suicide because of their religion's less cohesive character—as empirical evidence for the strength of egoism. He also argued that a more cohesive involvement in familial society (for example, married versus single, large family versus small family) produced a moderating effect on suicide, as does the increased integration of society during periods of political crisis (wars,

[40] Ibid., p. 66.
[41] Ibid., p. 68.
[42] Durkheim, *Suicide,* p. 146.
[43] Ibid., p. 147.
[44] Ibid.
[45] Ibid.

revolutionary upheavals, election crises, and the like). All these conditions constitute variations in the strength of integration of social groups. Durkheim's general conclusion is that "suicide varies inversely with the degree of integration of the social groups of which the individual forms a part," and egoistic suicide in particular arises from "excessive individuation."[46]

Egoism, however, is only one side of social integration. The inverse correlation between integration and suicide holds only up to a point, where it reverses itself to produce a new type of suicide. That type, the altruistic, results from "insufficient individuation."[47] Thus Durkheim argued that in primitive societies, suicide takes the form of fulfilling a social duty, preserving honor, or social renunciation. His most extensive empirical evidence of altruistic suicide was drawn from the military. Involvement in the military life, he argued, exposes the individual to a strict code of honor and subordinates his individuality. During military experience the individual's protection against self-destruction is diminished because of society's burdensome demands on him. Evidently, the distinction between egoistic and altruistic suicide corresponds to the distinction between organic solidarity (which establishes a social equilibrium among individuated personalities) and mechanical solidarity (which guarantees sameness through repressive punishment).

The third major cause of suicide lies in conditions of anomie, or the advance of specialization in society without the corresponding development of regulative mechanisms. Under these conditions individuals find their experiences disorienting, because they cannot be assimilated to any consistent set of expectations. Accordingly, Durkheim argued, suicide rates should be high at times of intensive crisis—for example, a business crisis or a domestic crisis such as widowhood or divorce—because such events constitute a breakdown in regulation through institutions, such as the market or marriage. Also, those parts of society least subject to traditional forms of regulation—particularly the industrial and commercial sectors—should also produce higher suicide rates.[48]

To complete his catalogue of types, Durkheim mentioned a fourth form, fatalistic suicide, which is the opposite of the anomic. It results from "excessive regulation, . . . [and is committed by] persons with futures pitilessly blocked and violently choked by oppressive discipline."[49] He asked whether the suicide of slaves, of those suffering from physical or moral despotism, of young husbands, and of the childless married woman

---

[46] Ibid., p. 209.
[47] Ibid., p. 217.
[48] Ibid., bk. 2, ch. 5.
[49] Ibid., p. 276.

are not instances of this type. In any event, its inclusion completes Durkheim's master proposition that suicide results from the four extremes obtained by taking into account the dimensions of social integration and social regulation.

This summary reveals that, while officially designating the causes—the aetiology—of suicide, Durkheim also included a number of observations about the effects of these causes on individual persons. The reason why anomic conditions are disorienting, for example, is that they confuse an individual's sense of the relations between means and ends, and "[no] living being can be happy or even exist unless his needs are sufficiently proportioned to his means."[50] Such a statement involves a psychological generalization; it also reveals the *reason why* the sense of limitlessness of means produced by anomie is disorienting rather than, say, gratifying or exhilarating.

Durkheim was even more explicit about the mediation of psychological variables in his discussion of morphology, even though he maintained a consistent hostility to psychological explanations of suicide. He was careful not to press an oversimple sociologistic determination of the individual suicide. For one thing, more than one social cause may be operating in any individual case. In the suicide of a soldier, for example, the fact that he is in a military environment is naturally salient, but not sufficient as an explanation. The soldier brings influences from his previous life with him and, indeed, "the suicide he commits may . . . sometimes be civilian in its character and causes."[51] More generally, not all peculiarities of individual suicides can be deduced from the social causes:

> Each victim of suicide gives his act a personal stamp which expresses his temperament, the special conditions in which he is involved, and which, consequently, cannot be explained by the social and general causes of the phenomenon.[52]

Despite these qualifications, Durkheim insisted that social causes left their "collective mark" on individuals. He realized that to ascertain this mark is difficult because of the lack of adequate data, and that he had to rely mainly on outlining the logical implications of the social causes.

Egoistic suicide, for example, frequently results from "a condition of melancholic languor which relaxes all the springs of action."[53] It involves the contemplation of non-existence—indeed a fascination with it—so that

[50] Ibid., p. 246.
[51] Ibid., p. 238.
[52] Ibid., pp. 277–78.
[53] Ibid., p. 278.

"one's inclination can be completely satisfied only by completely ceasing to exist."[54] This melancholy detachment, Durkheim argued, springs from excessive individuation. Altruistic suicide, by contrast, is more violent, since the "individual kills himself at the command of his conscience;"[55] whereas the typical psychological states associated with anomic suicide are "anger and all the emotions customarily associated with disappointment."[56] I need not criticize the soundness of Durkheim's psychological observations —some of which appear to be strained—nor examine his speculations about the combination of different types, such as the egoistic-anomic suicide.[57] What is most salient is that in his reflections Durkheim clearly located the individual as an *intervening variable* between the social facts of integration and regulation and the social fact of suicide. Figure 4-2 shows these variations graphically. True, he was reluctant to permit this variable to change much, emphasizing as he did the force of social conditions. But he did in principle grant the importance of the "personal stamp." Even more, his special assumptions about why certain social conditions are disturbing—or otherwise affect—individuals "make sense" of the causal link between, say, anomie and the tendency toward self-destruction. The connection between those two social facts alone is not given in their description as social facts, and behavioral responses other than suicide would be expected if the special psychological assumptions employed by Durkheim were modified. A hedonistic model of man, for example, would certainly reverse the positive association between anomic limitlessness and the tendency toward self-destruction, as contrasted with Durkheim's model of man who cannot tolerate unrestraint. What Durkheim did in his discussion of morphology, in the end, is nothing more than to attribute an ideal-type subjective meaning of certain social conditions for the actor, along with a probability statement that he would respond in a certain way. In this respect Durkheim's method corresponds precisely to Weber's methodological dictates, though he arrived at this method by a very different avenue than that envisioned by Weber.

The sociology of religion

Durkheim's purposes in *The Elementary Forms of Religious Life* differed from those in his other two monographs, and the causal structure of his analysis and his use of comparative materials also differ accordingly.

[54] Ibid.
[55] Ibid., p. 283.
[56] Ibid., p. 284.
[57] Ibid., pp. 287–90.

Social Integration		Social Regulation	
Low	High	Low	High
(Apathy)	(Energy of passion or will)	(Irritation, disgust)	(Resignation?)
Egoistic suicide	Altruistic suicide	Anomic suicide	Fatalistic suicide

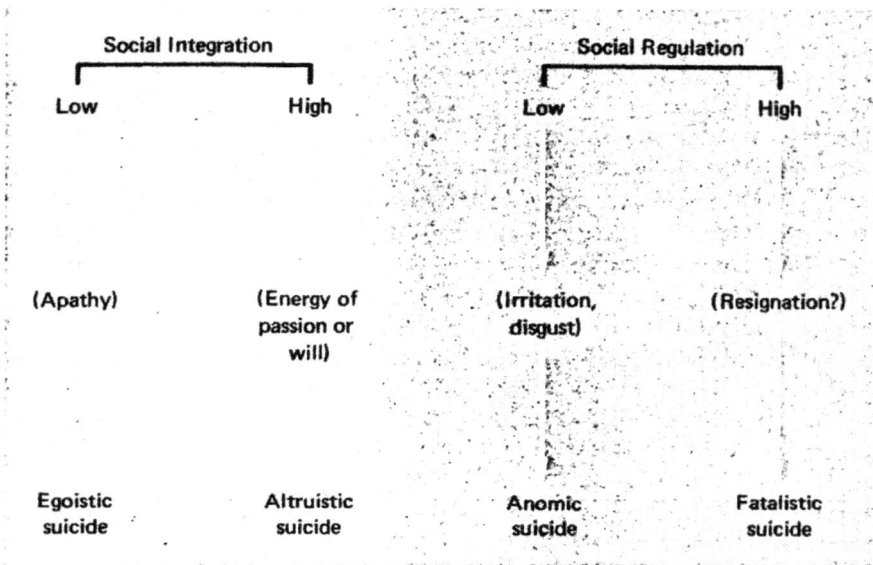

FIG. 4–2   Causal Structure Represented in *Suicide*

The work is in part a special study in the sociology of knowledge; Durkheim wished to inquire into the social bases of common notions that make up language and culture (notions such as number, class, and cause). He was impatient with both the a priori and empiricist theories of the origins of these categories of thought, and proposed, consistent with his general approach, that the fundamental determinants of human knowledge are *social* in character and can not be found in the individual alone—either by power of inborn reason or by the operation of empirical objects on the mind:

> If . . . the categories [number, class, cause, and so on] are . . . essentially collective representations, before all else, they should show the mental states of the group; they should depend upon the way in which this is founded and organized, upon its morphology, upon its religious, moral and economic institutions, etc.[58]

The first and most fundamental link, then, is between the structure of society and the structure of thought, with the former causally prior.

Durkheim's particular strategy of demonstration was an experiment, as

[58] Durkheim, *The Elementary Forms of the Religious Life,* pp. 15–16.

he called it—a selection of the most primitive societies and religions for study.[59] Such systems are simpler and more homogeneous than complex societies,[60] and permit the direct observation of the constituent elements of religion. Furthermore, "[since] the facts are simpler, the relations between them are more apparent. The reasons with which men account for their acts have not yet been elaborated and denatured by studied reflections; they are nearer and more closely related to the motives that have really determined these acts."[61] For his laboratory Durkheim chose the totemic religions of the Australian tribes whose social organization "is the most primitive and simple which is actually known."[62] For comparative purposes he also referred to certain North American Indian tribes, whose social organization was basically similar but in some respects more advanced than that of the Australian tribes.

In analyzing totemic religion, Durkheim attempted to demonstrate—again and again, and in ever more complex ways—the parallels between the structure of Australian tribal societies and the structure of religious beliefs and rituals in these societies. Thus totems, the basic objects of worship in these religions, correspond to and designate the clans, which are the fundamental social units of these societies. The totem serves as a coat of arms, a symbol of collective unity for the clan. Above all, the totem "is the very type of sacred thing."[63] It is worshipped, and it is subject to numerous ritual prohibitions—for example, it may not be eaten except under carefully circumscribed conditions. Furthermore, every member of the clan that worships it partakes of its sacred character.

The key point Durkheim wished to make is that certain logical categories that dominate the thinking of members of these societies arise from their social organization. Thus, the notion of class and subclass is closely parallel to the social organization of primitive societies into phatries (principles of division of clans) and clans, as well as the various objects belonging to each clan.

> These systematic classifications are the first we meet with in history, and . . . they are modelled upon the social organization, or rather . . . they have taken the forms of society as their framework. It is the phatries which have served as classes, and the clans as species. It is because men were

[59] Ibid., p. 415.
[60] "The slighter development of individuality, the small extension of the group, the homogeneity of external circumstances, all contribute to reducing the differences and variations [in the lower societies] to a minimum." Ibid., p. 5.
[61] Ibid., p. 7.
[62] Ibid., p. 96.
[63] Ibid., p. 119.

organized that they have been able to organize things, for in classifying these latter, they limited themselves to giving them places in the groups they formed themselves. And if these different classes of things are not merely put next to each other, but are arranged according to a unified plan, it is because the social groups with which they commingle themselves are unified and, through their union, form an organic whole, the tribe. The unity of these first logical systems merely reproduces the unity of the society.[64]

From totemism Durkheim moved to the analysis of *mana,* the undifferentiated force that endows representations of the totem animals or vegetables whose name the clan bears, as well as the members of the clan itself, their quality of sacredness. Most primitive religions have some notion of this physical and moral force, Durkheim observed, but it differs in degree of generalization. For example, in some North American tribes "mana is diffused into the whole universe" whereas in the Australian tribes "the totemic principle is localized in the more limited circle of beings and things of certain species."[65] The sociological basis for this difference, moreover, is found in the more comprehensive social organization of the North American tribes:

> The idea of a single and universal mana could be born only at the moment when the tribal religion developed above that of the clans and absorbed them more or less completely. It is along with the feeling of the tribal unity that the feeling of the substantial unity of the world awakens.[66]

Arguing that the totem is simultaneously the material symbol of the totemic principle (mana, force, god), and at the same time the symbol of the society called the clan, Durkheim asked, "is that not because the god and the society are only one?"[67] This led him to ask further how society can awaken in the individual the sensation of the divine. The question is important, for its answer provides a psychological mechanism to link the structure of society with the structure of social thought (in this case, religious belief), and, in so doing, to indicate how the parallel between the two is generated and sustained.

In general terms, Durkheim argued, society creates a feeling of the individual's perpetual dependence on it by continually demanding submission. It exercises moral authority. In addition, the collective force of society becomes part of individual consciousnesses; it "must also penetrate

[64] Ibid., pp. 144–45.
[65] Ibid., p. 195.
[66] Ibid., p. 196.
[67] Ibid., p. 206.

us and organize itself within us."[68] Durkheim pointed to moments of ceremony and crisis when the "strengthening and vivifying action of society is especially apparent";[69] but, in addition, the very process of daily interaction among people invokes the power of society and its moral conscience.

The following passage is representative of Durkheim's reasoning:

> We speak a language that we did not make; we use instruments that we did not invent; we invoke rights that we did not found; a treasury of knowledge is transmitted to each generation that it did not gather itself, etc. It is to society that we owe these varied benefits of civilization, and if we do not ordinarily see the source from which we get them, we at least know that they are not our own work. Now it is these things that give man his own place among things; a man is a man only because he is civilized. So he could not escape the feeling that outside of him there are active causes from which he gets the characteristic attributes of his nature and which, as benevolent powers, assist him, protect him, and assure him of a privileged fate. And of course he must attribute to these powers a dignity corresponding to the great value of the good things he attributes to them.[70]

Durkheim's strategy in this passage—as in many other passages devoted to demonstrating the capacity of society to awaken a sense of the divine—is to appeal to that which is psychologically plausible: *if* society is so strong, *if* it operates so continuously on men, and *if* it provides its citizens with traditions not of their own making, then man *must* stand in awe of it. He extended this kind of reasoning further in arguing that since "[the forces of society] exercise over us a pressure of which we are conscious, we are forced to localize them outside ourselves, just as we do for the objective causes of our sensations."[71] Or again, after describing vividly the effervescent quality of an Australian celebration, Durkheim observed that "[one] can readily conceive how, when arrived at this state of exaltation, a man does not recognize himself any longer. Feeling himself dominated and carried away by some sort of an external power which makes him think and act differently than in normal times, he naturally has the impression of being himself no longer."[72]

Durkheim also asked why the forces exercised by the clan assume the form of animal or plant totems. Again, as a matter of psychological principle, he argued that "it is a well-known law that the sentiments aroused

[68] Ibid., p. 209.
[69] Ibid.
[70] Ibid., p. 212.
[71] Ibid.
[72] Ibid., p. 218.

in us by something spontaneously attach themselves to a symbol which represents them." Following on this law of symbolic association, he added that this association is more nearly complete when "the symbol is something simple, definite and easily representable, while the thing itself, owing to its dimensions, the number of its parts, and the complexity of their arrangement, is difficult to hold in the mind." And since the totem is the symbol of the clan,

> it is therefore natural that the impressions aroused by the clan in individual minds—impressions of dependence and of increased vitality—should fix selves to the idea of the totem rather than that of the clan: for the clan is too complex a reality to be represented clearly in all its complex unity by such rudimentary intelligences. More than that, the primitive does not even see that these impressions come to him from the group. He does not know that the coming together of a number of men associated in the same life results in disengaging new energies, which transform each of them. All that he knows is that he is raised above himself and that he sees a different life from the one he ordinarily leads. However, he must connect these sensations to some external object as their cause. Now what does he see about him? On every side those things which appeal to his senses and strike his imagination are the numerous images of the totem. They are the waninga and the nurtunja, which are symbols of the sacred being. They are churinga and bull-roarers, upon which are generally carved combinations of lines having the same significance. They are decorations covering the different parts of his body, which are totemic marks. How could this image, repeated everywhere and in all sorts of forms, fail to stand out with exceptional relief in his mind? Placed thus in the centre of the scene, it becomes representative.[73]

Illustrations of this mode of reasoning could be multiplied, but those cited demonstrate the point that the causal link between the two social facts of social organization and religious belief is established by an appeal to a set of psychological principles, in this case a sort of learning theory.

Durkheim completed his study of religion with an analysis of religious rites, which are fixed patterns of behavior oriented toward the sacred—designed in various ways to prevent the mixing of sacred and profane, not to offend the sacred, and to gain access to and partake of the sacred. His analysis is complex and extended and need not concern us in detail. His general interpretation of the complex patterns of rites associated with religion is that they are moral in significance—that they periodically reaffirm the moral unity of the group, and that, more particularly, they act as implements of social control. In Durkheim's words,

[73] Ibid., pp. 220–21.

howsoever complex the outward manifestations of the religious life may be, at bottom it is one and simple. It responds everywhere to one and the same need, and is everywhere derived from one and the same mental state. In all its forms, its object is to raise man above himself and to make him lead a life superior to that which he would lead, if he followed only his own individual whims: beliefs express this life in representations; rites organize it and regulate its working.[74]

This sketch of Durkheim's sociology of religion reveals a causal chain that is in one respect a circular one. Society (social organization) stands at the beginning and end. It impresses itself with extraordinary force on the human mind and determines the organization of its experience. By a process of externalizing or "objectifying"[75] this influence, people generate a variety of religious beliefs, whose structure parallels the structure of society that gave rise to them. Then, in the name of these beliefs, people organize rites and practices, the main functions of which are to reaffirm the group and its religious beliefs, control the pattern of life of the individual, and thus reinforce the same society from which the religious impulse emanated originally. The lines of this causal structure are indicated in figure 4-3.

Durkheim's Comparative Methods

The division of labor

One of Durkheim's central assertions in *The Division of Labor in Society* is that four sets of variables—social structure (that is, level of the division of labor), degree of individual similarities or dissimilarities, type of solidarity, and type of legal code—are closely correlated. More particularly, a simple division of labor (segmentary society) is associated with a common conscience, mechanical solidarity, and reliance on repressive law; an advanced division of labor (complex society) is associated with individuated consciences, organic solidarity, and reliance on restitutive law. In this formulation he tended to rely on dichotomies. He distinguished between only two types of law and two types of solidarity; and accordingly, "there ought to be two social types which correspond to these two types of solidarity."[76] While Durkheim recognized that these two

---

[74] Ibid., p. 414.

[75] The word is Durkheim's. "Religious force is only the sentiment inspired by the group in its members, but projected outside of the consciousness that experience them, and objectified." Ibid., p. 229.

[76] Durkheim, *The Division of Labor in Society*, p. 174.

Society

Organization of
individual's
beliefs

Social control

Externalization

Rites relating to
the sacred

Religious
beliefs

(collective
representation)

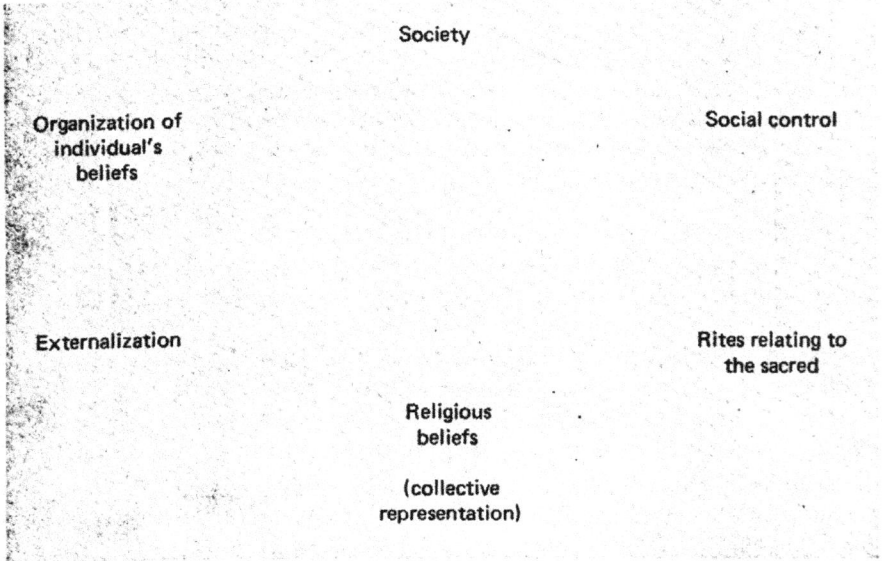

FIG. 4–3 Causal Structure Represented in *The Elementary Forms of Religious Life*

types of society were hypothetical constructs that did not exist in pure form empirically,[77] and while he acknowledged that any given society is a mixture of the two, he never specified a series of intermediate types between the segmental and the complex; consequently, many of his observations take the form of dichotomous contrasts between simple and complex, or lower and higher societies.

How did Durkheim attempt to demonstrate the validity of his causal assertions? In *The Division of Labor in Society* he relied almost exclusively on his chosen method for sociology: the method of concomitant variations.[78] This method consists in establishing positive empirical associations among the four sets of variables in question. In fact, Durkheim's empirical demonstrations—found in chapters four through seven of book one—con-

[77] Of the horde (segmentary society), for example, he acknowledged what was later repeated in *The Rules of the Sociological Method:* "We have not yet, in any completely authentic fashion, observed societies which, in all respects, complied with this definition." Durkheim, *The Division of Labor in Society,* p. 174.

[78] See pp. 63–64. In this respect, as in a number of others, *Rules* can be read in substantial part as a methodological gloss on the procedures that Durkheim had himself adopted in his monograph on the division of labor, published two years before the *Rules.*

sist of descriptions of primitive and advanced societies according to the relevant characteristics.

With respect to the types of conscience, for example, Durkheim argued that "[the] more primitive societies are, the more resemblances there are among the individuals who compose them,"[79] citing a variety of historical and anthropological sources. Contemporary societies, however, while diminishing national and regional differences, have increased in internal diversity; "[there] is now less distance than heretofore between the Frenchman and the Englishman, generally speaking, but that does not stop the contemporary Frenchmen from differing from themselves more than the Frenchmen of yesteryear."[80] Needless to say, Durkheim's arguments are far from compelling, not only because of the possibly questionable scholarship of his sources, but also because he failed to identify the specific dimensions of similarity and difference to which he might have been referring.

As for law, the index of mechanical solidarity, Durkheim stated flatly that "it appears to be entirely repressive"[81] in primitive societies, not only documenting this extensively by direct reference to these societies, but also tracing the decline of repressive law—by a kind of crude "content analysis" of law codes—in Roman and Christian law. Correspondingly, he noted an analogous increase over time in the areas of domestic law, contract law, commercial law, and so on.[82] Likewise, basing his case on anthropological sources, he characterized the segmental society in terms of its simplicity of structure, the functional independence of kinship units (that is, their lack of organic solidarity), the pervasiveness of religion and communality, and so on; this contrasts on every score with his description of societies in which organic solidarity is preponderant—societies with "a system of different organs each of which has a special role, and which are themselves formed of differentiated parts."[83] He attempted to demonstrate that as the differentiation of complex structures advances, the homogeneous ones recede, again making reference to primitive society, Roman society, and more modern societies.[84]

So much for Durkheim's use of the method of concomitant variation— his most utilized comparative strategy in *The Division of Labor in Society*. (His attempt to demonstrate the causes—density and volume—of the division of labor rested on the same method, but is limited to scattered empirical observations.) In many respects the use of this method is open

[79] Durkheim, *The Division of Labor in Society*, p. 133.
[80] Ibid., p. 136.
[81] Ibid., p. 140.
[82] Ibid., chs. 5, 7.
[83] Ibid., p. 181.
[84] Ibid., pp. 183ff.

to serious criticism. Many of the data are inadequate to qualify as compelling demonstrations; much of the analysis rests on simplified dichotomous comparisons between lower and higher societies, and an almost-explicit scheme of simple evolution informs the contrasts. The most telling criticism, however, lies in the fact that Durkheim restricted himself to the method of citing simple correlations. As he noted, this method provides no certainty of causal association among the variables. Why, for instance, should the division of labor be causally *prior* to the development of restitutive law? Could it not be the other way around? Could not the gradual erosion of criminal punishment for a diverse range of activities (for example, money-lending) have constituted a condition that freed people to strike out into new, specialized lines of activity? Or could not both have resulted from a third cause, such as a general cultural impulse toward rationalization of the social order, which affected the occupational structure and the legal system alike? Concomitant variations alone, particularly when applied in the dichotomous way Durkheim applied them, cannot answer these questions, because no effort can be made systematically to *control* the influence of either the main variables or other possibly operative variables.

Despite the impossibility of demonstrating the posited causal relations empirically, Durkheim insisted on their validity. He attempted to bolster his case, moreover, by relying on a variety of strategies other than concomitant variation—logical deduction, further comparisons, analogy, imaginary experiments, and appeal to "what is generally known." Let me illustrate:

Why should a division of labor produce social solidarity? In addition to attempting to demonstrate that social complexity and reliance on restitutive law occur together, Durkheim resorted to a number of other lines of reasoning. Early in his exposition, he undertook to question the overriding importance of the economic functions (for example, higher productivity) of the division of labor and to emphasize the solidary functions. His first line of appeal was to "what is generally known." "Everybody knows," he said, "that we like those who resemble us, those who think and feel as we do. But the opposite is no less true."[85] After citing Aristotle on friendship and Bain on the attraction of opposites, Durkheim suggested that the "true function [of the division of labor] is to create in two or more persons a feeling of solidarity."[86] Next, turning to the institution of marriage, he argued that women and men have become more differentiated, both physiologically and functionally, in the evolution from lower to higher societies and

85 Ibid., p. 54.
86 Ibid., p. 56.

that the marital union has become stronger and more solidary because of this differentiation.[87] (This procedure is a "further comparison" to bolster his observation that dissimilarity gives rise to solidarity.) Subsequently Durkheim invoked other arguments to demonstrate the strength of organic solidarity in complex societies. For example, he noted that complex societies are difficult to separate into parts because of their solidarity and interdependence. Citing Spencer's illustration,

> if we separated from Middlesex its surrounding district, all operations would cease in a few days, due to shortage of materials. Separate the district where cotton is manufactured from Liverpool and other centres, and industry ceases, since the population will perish. Separate the mining populations from the neighboring populations which found metal or make clothing by machinery and they would die socially, since they would die individually.[88]

To reason thus is to invoke Weber's imaginary experiment, which is, as we saw, a species of comparative analysis in which two cases (the current, functioning British economy on the one hand, and the imaginary situation in which industries were cut off from one another) differ in one crucial respect; this, in turn, would lead to a different outcome than is historically the case. Durkheim bolstered this argument by pointing to evidence that primitive societies may be divided into separate parts more easily than complex societies and that they are more easily permeated by foreign elements, thus invoking a "further comparison" to supplement the imaginary experiment.

To close his case, he noted a biological analogy:

> Today, to detach a province from a country is to detach one or several organs from an organism. The life of the annexed region is profoundly troubled, separated as it is from the essential organs upon which it depends; but such mutilations and such troubles necessarily determine durable grief whose memory is not effaceable.[89]

He used such analogies frequently in *The Division of Labor in Society*. He cited organismic parallels to the mechanisms posited for mechanical and organic solidarity at the social level,[90] and he even invoked Spencer's own biological analogy to refute Spencer's conceptualization of regulation:

> [Spencer] compares, as we have done, economic functions to the visceral life

[87] Ibid., pp. 56–63.
[88] Ibid., pp. 149–50.
[89] Ibid., p. 150.
[90] Ibid., pp. 190–92.

of the individual organism, and remarks that the latter does not directly depend upon the cerebro-spinal system, but upon a special system whose principal branches are the great sympathetic and the pneumo-gastric. But from this comparison he is permitted to induce, with some probability, that economic functions are not of a kind to be placed under the immediate influence of the social brain, it does not follow that they can be freed of all regulative influences, for, if the great sympathetic is, in certain measure, independent of the brain, it dominates the movements of the visceral system just as the brain does those of the muscles. If, then, there is in society a system of the same kind, it must have an analogous action over the organs subject to it.[91]

To reason by analogy thus is also to engage in a species of comparative analysis, though the nature of the comparison differs from that of the imaginary experiment. To note an analogy is to expand the number of cases by including a case represented by a different type of species of system than the one under consideration. The argument by analogy is that because the systems resemble one another formally in all significant respects (except in type of system), cause-effect relations in one will prevail, in corresponding form, in the other. The dangers of arguing by analogy, of course, lie in the fact that if principles of systemic organization differ among types of system, this negates the requirement for formal resemblance in all respects.

Thus in attempting to establish a causal link between the division of labor and organic solidarity, Durkheim relied on a battery of ancillary devices with varying degrees of compellingness. He used similar kinds of devices in his effort to establish a causal relation between segmental social structure and mechanical solidarity, though the pattern of his argument differed in detail. He analysis began with a discussion of crime. Crime cannot be defined, he argued, by any intrinsic quality of criminal acts, because they are so diverse in character. What crimes have in common, instead, is that they are "acts universally disapproved by members of each society"; crime shocks sentiments which "are found in all healthy consciences."[92] (Note that Durkheim never attempted to establish empirically what was implied by the terms "universally" and "all"; this level of empirical generality seems to have been simply assumed.) These sentiments are deeply engraved in all consciences in society and, taken together, they constitute the collective conscience. Durkheim further bolstered his case for the strength of these sentiments by noting that punishments for crimes are passionate, violent, and vengeful. In this line of reasoning he was rely-

---

[91] Ibid., p. 217.
[92] Ibid., p. 73.

ing on the "generally known" psychological principle that strong feelings produce violent actions. From his discussion of repressive law Durkheim concluded:

> Everybody knows that there is a social cohesion whose cause lies in a certain conformity of all particular consciences to a common type which is none other than the psychic type of society. In these conditions, not only are all the members of the group individually attracted to one another because they resemble one another, but also because they are joined to what is the condition of existence of this collective type; that is to say, to the society that they form by their union.[93]

But why should simplicity of social structure be logically prior to mechanical solidarity? Durkheim's main demonstration was based on the method of concomitant variation—that societies with a clan structure also show characteristics associated with mechanical solidarity, such as reliance on repressive law, pervasiveness of religious beliefs, and the like. But in an aside, Durkheim observed—after characterizing the simplicity of structure of the politico-family organization of the Iroquois and early Jews—that "this organization, just as the horde, of which it is only an extension, carries with it no other solidarity than that derived from likenesses, since the society is formed of similar segments and these in their turn enclose only homogeneous elements."[94] Here Durkheim was invoking a variant of Mill's method of residues—subtract the effects of other possible causes, and the effect (mechanical solidarity) is the result of that which remains (likeness, simplicity of structure).[95] The argument strikes me as weak, largely because its force—however great—derived in large part from Durkheim's own earlier restriction of the types of solidarity (and their causes) to two, thus producing an oversimple formula: if diversity (complex division of labor) is not present, then likeness (simple division of labor) must be the cause.

Suicide

In this critical examination of methods in *The Division of Labor in Society* I have suggested that the "design" of this study—resting on dichotomous principles and limited largely to the method of concomitant methods—severely restricted Durkheim's ability to establish causal rela-

[93] Ibid., p. 105.
[94] Ibid., pp. 176–77.
[95] In *Rules* Durkheim expressed skepticism about the usefulness of the method of residues in sociology.

tions among the major phenomena under study. This forced him, as it were, to rely on a battery of ancillary arguments to demonstrate that causality. Had he been able to gain direct *control* over some of the possibly operative causes other than the division of labor—control not attainable by the use of simple concomitant variation and the ancillary devices he employed—he would have been able to establish a stronger case for his preferred causal relations. In this regard *Suicide* stands in contrast to *The Division of Labor in Society;* while its empirical results may not be more valid in the end, Durkheim framed his study in a way that permitted him to employ a wider array of methods and thus build a more sophisticated diagnosis of social causality.

To be sure, Durkheim used the method of concomitant variation extensively in *Suicide*. Most of his empirical demonstrations attempted to establish that the social suicide rate of one social group or category differs from that of another in the expected direction; that Protestants have higher suicide rates than Catholics, that military personnel have higher suicide rates than civilians, that industrial and commercial occupational groups have higher suicide rates than other groups, and so on. On the side of the independent variable the relevant variation is the degree to which groups and categories differ on the egoism-altruism and the anomie-fatalism dimensions; on the side of the dependent variable are the differences in suicide rates among the various groups and categories. Durkheim also used a variant of concomitant variation to establish the general importance of the social factor. He argued that suicide statistics vary consistently among different societies and concluded that "[suicide] is peculiar to each social group where it can be considered as a characteristic index."[96] In addition, for any given society the social suicide rate is relatively invariant over time, certainly more so than other demographic indices; from this fact he drew the same conclusion affirming the distinctively social nature of suicide. Durkheim also made "negative" use of the method of concomitant variation—rejecting other possible explanations of suicide by noting the absence of concomitant variation or the reversal of a line of variation expected on the basis of some other theory. Rejecting "neurasthenia" as a causal explanation, Durkheim observed that if it were a genuine cause, women would commit suicide at a higher rate than men, since they suffered more from that mental condition than men; but the reverse ratio between sexes is often observed.[97] Similarly, he argued that statistics on insanity show a rank-order of Protestants, Catholics, and Jews, whereas the suicide rates among these groups rank in precisely the opposite order.[98]

[96] Durkheim, *Suicide*, p. 50.
[97] Ibid., p. 71.
[98] Ibid., p. 72.

Durkheim's use of concomitant variation is unsatisfactory on several counts. In some cases the poor quality of the data raises doubts as to the possible validity of any comparisons—for example, treating the number of inmates of various categories (sex, religious faith, age) in insane asylums as an index of the incidence of insanity among those categories. In other cases the degree of concomitant variation is so slight as to resist any conclusions whatsoever—for example, the small differences among suicides on different days of the week, which Durkheim took to signify variations in the intensity of the collective life.[99] Aside from these illustrations—which could be multiplied—Durkheim's analysis suffers from his inconsistent handling of two sets of problems: (1) the problem of controlling for third, possibly causal variables in interpreting concomitant variation between two variables; and (2) the problem of the degree to which an established correlation at one analytic level (for example, the aggregate social level) is to be considered valid or meaningful at another level (for example, the psychological level). I shall subsume the remaining discussion of methodological problems in *Suicide* under these two headings.

The use of third variables. Durkheim was very sensitive to the possibility of alternative explanations of suicide rates than his own favored social explanation. Indeed, he dedicated almost one-quarter of the book to discrediting a wide range of psychological, racial, and cosmic theories of social suicide rates. And in his own social analysis of suicide he frequently considered the possibility of other causes of the correlations he observed. Yet his method of dealing with these other causes was inconsistent and sometimes cavalier, and his interpretations are weakened accordingly.

Perhaps the most effective use Durkheim made of potential third variables was in ascertaining whether his preferred associations held while varying or in other ways correcting for other possible explanatory variables. For example, he assigned the differences between the suicide rates of Protestants and Catholics to differences in the integration of their collective lives. On examining the countries on which his religious data were available, however, he noticed that the Catholics were in the minority in every case. Could it not be, he asked, that minority status rather than religious tradition is the operative variable in the genesis of lower suicide rates among Catholics?[100] To throw light on this question, he examined regions, such as Austria and Bavaria, where Catholics were in the majority; in such regions he discovered some diminution of the differences between Protestants and Catholics, but Protestant rates were still higher. On the basis of this examination, he concluded that "Catholicism does not owe

---

[99] Ibid., p. 118.

[100] Durkheim did give minority status an important role in explaining the low suicide rates for Jews. Ibid., pp. 159–60.

[its protective influence] solely to its minority status."[101] Durkheim repeated this procedure on a number of occasions. For example, he compared the suicide rates of different marital categories according to age groupings instead of comparing differences among gross marital categories, which would reflect the simultaneous influence of age and marital status; in this way he controlled for age. He did the same for age and marital status in comparing military and civilian suicides in different European countries. Though the effectiveness of these procedures varied greatly according to the kinds of data available, in general such analyses strengthen the presumption in favor of the suspected variable. The strength derives, moreover, from the fact that by such procedures Durkheim was approximating the norm enunciated in Mill's method of difference—to render the cases compared identical in all respects except for a single antecedent, which may then be regarded as the cause. Durkheim certainly did not accomplish this; in most instances his efforts to control were limited to a single third variable and a limited number of cases. Nevertheless he moved in the direction of meeting the requirement of the method of difference.

On other occasions, however, Durkheim *was* prepared to invoke third variables, particularly when the concomitant variations he observed apparently *did not* confirm his theoretical expectations, or when they apparently *did* confirm those of a competing theory. Return, for example, to the data on religious differences. For all the countries on which he had data, "Protestants show far more suicides than the followers of other confessions." The only apparent exceptions were Norway and Sweden which, "though Protestant, have only an average number of suicides."[102] Durkheim first discarded the exception, arguing that international comparisons are not reliable, except for those involving large numbers of cases. Nevertheless, he attempted to account for the exception within the context of his own favored explanation based on religion:

> There are sufficiently great differences between the peoples of the Scandinavian peninsula and those of Central Europe for it to be reasonable that Protestantism does not produce exactly the same effects on both. But furthermore, if the suicide-rate is not in itself very high in these two countries, it seems relatively so if one considers their modest rank among the civilized peoples of Europe. There is no reason to suppose that they have reached an intellectual level above Italy, to say the least, yet self-destruction occurs from twice to three times as often (90 to 100 suicides per million

[101] Ibid., p. 157.
[102] Ibid., pp. 154, 155.

inhabitants as against 40). May Protestantism not be the cause of this higher figure relatively?[103]

The invoked third cause was "level of civilization," which contrived to keep the Scandinavian rate low, but which was not so low as to overwhelm the influence of Protestantism. The reasoning is ingenious; in effect, however, it provided Durkheim with an interpretative formula with which he could be "correct every time." That is to say, with both "religion" and "level of civilization" invoked as independent variables, but without specifying the principles of their interaction—when one overwhelms the other, when one reinforces the other, and so on—either one can be appealed to freely to interpret any given set of empirical results. For example, if the suicide rates of Scandinavian countries had been even lower, Durkheim could simply have given more weight to the "level of civilization" factor; if higher, less weight. The unsystematic appeal to third causes, in short, is a scientific variant of having one's cake and eating it too.

As we have seen, Durkheim was highly skeptical of psychological explanations of suicide. He rejected theories based on both psychopathic and normal psychological factors, and repeatedly characterized psychological influences as random, not decisive, or otherwise irrelevant to the social suicide rate.[104] But as we have also observed, he relied on psychological generalizations to construct meaningful theoretical links between various social states of integration and regulation and social suicide rates.[105] As such, these generalizations constitute "third causes," since, if altered, they would change the significance of the observed empirical associations. On occasion Durkheim indirectly acknowledged this. Among the theories of suicide he wished to reject was one advanced by Ferri and Morselli that high temperatures produce excess energy and a condition of excitability in the organism, one result of which is a heightened predisposition to suicide. Durkheim acknowledged that certain statistics—namely the increase of the social suicide rate in the warm seasons of the year—appeared consistent with such an explanation.[106] But he discarded the cosmic theory by the following logic:

> This theory implies a most debatable conception of suicide. It assumes that its constant psychological antecedent is a state of over-excitement, that it consists in a violent act and is only possible by a great exertion of energy. On the contrary, it very often results from extreme depression. Granted

[103] Ibid., p. 155.
[104] See ibid., bk. 1, chs. 1, 2, esp. pp. 51, 140, 318–25.
[105] See pp. 88–89.
[106] Durkheim, *Suicide*, pp. 105–9.

that excited or exasperated suicide occurs, suicide from unhappiness is as frequent; . . . But heat cannot possibly act in the same way on both; if it stimulates the former, it must make the latter less frequent. Its possibly aggravating influence on certain persons would be offset and discounted by its moderating influence on others; hence it could not appear through the data of statistics, especially in any perceptible fashion.[107]

From this Durkheim concluded that "[the] seasonal variations shown by the statistics must have another cause," and proceeded to locate this cause in heightened social interaction, also correlated with the seasons of the year.[108] Let us disregard the substance of the polemic, which seems forced in any case. From a formal standpoint Durkheim was implicitly invoking a third variable—the intervening psychological mechanism—to reject one theory and bolster another. By the manipulation of assumptions about such intervening mechanisms, an investigator is able to render certain empirical associations meaningless, change the meaning of others, and breathe new meaning into still others. Such is the considerable power of intervening assumptions in interpreting empirical results.

One source of weakness of the case developed in *Suicide* is the apparent arbitrariness in Durkheim's willingness to entertain the possibility of the operation of third variables. In discussing the possible influence of insanity on suicide, he noted one association that might support such a notion—the fact that both suicide and insanity are more frequent in cities than in the country. Yet he judged this relation to be not one of cause and effect but probably "a mere coincidence." The reason for such an association is that "the social causes of suicide are . . . themselves closely related to urban civilization and are most intense in these great centers."[109] Here he invoked a third cause to cast doubt on an association that apparently supported another theory. Citing evidence *against* the insanity theory of suicide, however, he noted that "idiocy seems . . . a safeguard against [suicide]; for idiots are much more numerous in the country than in the city, while suicides are much rarer in the country," without suggesting that third causes might be responsible for this association as well.[110]

Finally, the structure of Durkheim's theoretical framework encouraged unsystematic appeal to third variables in cases of possibly embarrassing empirical associations. Noting the generally low rate of suicides among Jews, Durkheim attributed this mainly to the solidarity developed by an

[107] Ibid., p. 109.
[108] Ibid., pp. 109, 116–20.
[109] Ibid., p. 70.
[110] Ibid., p. 75. Both associations—insanity and suicide and idiocy and suicide—are suspect on grounds that they may involve the so-called ecological fallacy.

oppressed minority. But in addition, specifically Jewish beliefs play a role: "Judaism . . . like all early religions, consists basically of a body of practices minutely governing all the details of life and leaving little free room to individual judgment."[111] Yet, in the treatment of altruistic suicide Durkheim cited primitive religions as among the primary forces that discipline individuals and call forth sacrificial suicide of different sorts.[112] Why should not Judaism, an "early religion," manifest this tendency to augment the social suicide rate as well? The question points to a fundamental weakness in Durkheim's formulation. He regarded high suicide rates as the products of extremes of integration or regulation—either too much or too little. Such a formulation is satisfactory, however, only if some sort of scale is also provided, a scale which indicates the point at which integration and regulation are to be regarded as extreme, and—more important— which indicates the point at which the decline in egoism (and a corresponding decline in suicide rate) becomes significant as an increase in altruism (and an increase in suicide rate). Without such a scale an investigator can interpret *any* change in the suicide rate (up or down) associated with *any* change in social integration, depending on whether this change is read as a decline of egoism or an increase in altruism. In this sense the possibility of continuous, unsystematic appeal to a third variable was built into the logic of Durkheim's theory.

Generalizability of findings to different analytic levels. One strategy that Durkheim employed frequently in *Suicide* was to move to a different level of analysis to see whether some regularity which prevailed in the gross also prevailed in the fine. For example, in assessing racial theories of suicide, he noted that the racial groups generally recognized in Europe in his time —the Germanic, the Celto-Romans, and the Slavs—ranked in that order in terms of aptitude for suicide. He was reluctant to impute race as a cause, however, for the reason—among others—that this relationship does not persist when smaller social units are compared. For example, he cited "the greatest differences . . . between nations of the same race."[113] And within countries like Austria, he found little apparent trace of German influence among provinces varying by size of Germanic minority. In Switzerland, he cross-tabulated French and Germans according to whether they were Protestant or Catholic, and found that religious differences in suicide rate were much more pronounced than ethnic differences. From these data he concluded that "Germans commit suicide more than other peoples not because of their blood but because of the civilization in which they are

111 Ibid., p. 160.
112 Ibid., pp. 217–28.
113 Ibid., p. 85.

reared."[114] More generally, he suggested that the gross racial correlations "may well be a mere encounter of independent factors."[115] In reasoning thus Durkheim revealed the possibility that different confluences of causal factors can occur at different analytical levels; regularities holding between units can be nullified or reversed within units if they come into combination with other causal factors, and vice-versa.

On other occasions Durkheim used replication at different levels to fortify his own preferred explanations. He considered the gross differences in social suicide rates among "Protestant states," "Mixed states," and "Catholic states"—while in the expected direction—to be "too summary" a comparison, and turned to within-nation religious differences between Protestant and Catholics for the bulk of his demonstration.[116] The most extensive series of replications at different levels, however, is found in his treatment of military suicide. After establishing to his satisfaction that military suicides (altruistic) are higher than civilian and that this relationship is free from the influence of age and marital status, Durkheim cited various intra-military differences: the longer the military service, the higher the rate of suicide; officers and non-commissioned officers show higher suicide rates than private soldiers; and those who choose the military as a vocation (volunteers and re-enlisted men) apparently show a higher rate of suicide than conscripts; and elite troops show higher rates of suicide than regulars.[117] Finally, he argued that military suicide had been decreasing in all countries, attributing this to the fact that "a decline in the old military spirit has occurred in all these countries at the same time."[118] Durkheim's figures are crude and in some cases—as in the last assertion—his arguments remain altogether undocumented. But the logic of his demonstration is clear: those more intimately associated with military life —that is, closer to the "spirit of abnegation and military renunciation"[119]— are more inclined to suicide, and this relationship holds at a variety of levels and in a variety of contexts. In effect, Durkheim multiplied the number of comparative cases by moving from level to level.

This strategy is not without its potential methodological problems, however, for the reason hinted at by Durkheim in the racial example—that different combinations of causal forces may prevail at the different levels, thus giving different significance to empirical associations. One of Durkheim's points about military suicides illustrates these problems. He noted

[114] Ibid., p. 89.
[115] Ibid., p. 91.
[116] Ibid., pp. 152–55.
[117] Ibid., pp. 231–37.
[118] Ibid., p. 238.
[119] Ibid., p. 237.

an apparent regularity: the higher the suicide rate of the civilian population in a given country or region, the lower the apparent influence of the military on the suicide rate—that is, the lower the "coefficient of aggravation" by the military. Durkheim interpreted these figures as follows. Those societies in Europe with low civilian suicide rates are "among the least advanced, those whose customs most resemble the customs observed in lower societies";[120] that is to say, they are already moving in the altruistic direction, and their populations are guarded against egoistic suicide. These are the societies, however, in which the aggravation contributed by the military is relatively great. Durkheim argued that "in countries where there is sufficient altruism to protect the population as a whole to a degree, it is easily carried by the army to a point where it becomes the cause of considerable aggravation."[121] However, in countries where "the military spirit is steadily and strongly opposed by [an egoistic] public morality," the aggravating effect of the military is not so strong.[122] Thus, in Denmark, "the classical country for [civilian] suicides," there is no difference between military and civilian suicide, whereas in Italy the difference is great.[123] Durkheim's reasoning reveals again the kinds of interpretative gymnastics that are possible when the relations between egoism and altruism are left unclear.[124] The point to be stressed, however, is that at different levels of analysis and under different circumstances a certain relation (in this case the relation between military and civilian suicides) may grow stronger, grow weaker, disappear, or reverse. Furthermore, the discovery of similar associations at different analytical levels may not constitute a replication of a single causal relation but the uncovering of a different causal pattern; similarly, the failure to discover such a relationship may signify that it is overwhelmed by other causes rather than that it is simply disconfirmed. The problems involved in assessing the relations between inter-unit and intra-unit associations—or, more generally, associations at different levels of analysis—are subtle and profound, and I shall have to return to them in greater detail later.

The difficulties in inferring relations at one level from associations at another is revealed in Durkheim's transition from the aetiological to the morphological analysis of suicide. Most of the former involved the citation of concomitant variations between different categories or groups (representing different states of social integration or regulation) on the one hand

---

[120] Ibid., p. 236.

[121] Ibid.

[122] Ibid.

[123] Ibid., p. 235.

[124] See pp. 106–7 for the methodological problems that were created by not scaling or grading the egoism-altruism dimension.

and different rates of suicide on the other, sometimes supplementing this with an attempt to approximate Mill's method of difference by controlling for other variables. These were associations of aggregated data at the social level. When he turned to the morphology of suicide, however, he argued that the social variables (egoism, altruism, anomie) were correlated with suicide at the *individual* level as well. Admittedly Durkheim had access to little direct data, and mainly reasoned "deductively," tracing the logical implications of the "respective [social] causes from which they seem to spring,"[125] and bringing direct psychological evidence to bear only in the form of casual literary and clinical references. It has been shown, however, that to move directly from associations obtained in the aggregate to a claim of individual correlation is under certain circumstances illegitimate, and that, in particular, Durkheim's interpretations in *Suicide* suffer on this count.[126] I shall also return to this kind of fallacy in more general terms after covering a wider sample of comparative social science literature.

The sociology of religion

I can be briefer in assessing Durkheim's comparative strategies in *The Elementary Forms of Religious Life,* because it is less a comparative study than the other two empirical monographs. It is, rather, a case study, since Durkheim concentrated on the Australian tribal religions, and while noting varieties among them, felt it legitimate to treat them as "one common type."[127] The only comparative data he incorporated were from the religions of the North American Indian tribes, which he considered to be slightly more advanced than the Australian tribes, and which afforded instructive comparisons and contrasts as "two successive moments of a single evolution."[128] Nevertheless, since Durkheim considered his results both comparative and generalizable,[129] it is worth examining his comparative data, his procedures, and his claims.

When Durkheim did refer to the North American tribes, he mainly pointed out general parallels in social structure and religion between the two, but also noted minor differences associated with the more advanced status of the Indian societies. For example, after outlining the characteristics of Australian totems, Durkheim observed that "[all] that has been

125 Durkheim, *Suicide*, p. 278.

126 For a discussion of difficulties of this sort in *Suicide,* see Hanan C. Selvin, "Durkheim's *Suicide* and Problems of Empirical Research," *American Journal of Sociology* 63(1957–58):607–19.

127 Durkheim, *The Elementary Forms of the Religious Life*, p. 95.

128 Ibid., p. 96.

129 Ibid., p. 415.

said of the totem in Australian societies is equally applicable to the Indian tribes of North America."[130] The major difference is that in America, "the totemic system has better defined forms," which is, in turn, related to the greater clarity of its clan organization.[131] Durkheim also found conceptions of *mana*—the generalized religious force—in North American as well as Australian tribal religions, but found it "abstracted and generalized to a higher degree" in the former. This difference, moreover, he traced to the greater unity of the American tribes.[132] These observations represent the method of concomitant variations of cause (social organization) and effect (religious belief) so characteristically employed by Durkheim.

Durkheim used the same method, though less explicitly and systematically, in noting the continuity between religious and scientific thought. The former is diffuse and multifunctional, but contains the ingredients— for example, the idea of *mana* as religious force—that later become the more precise formulations of causality in science. Science is a more highly differentiated system of thought, born of religion and systematizing the speculative aspect of religious thought.[133] In fact, religion was regarded by Durkheim as the undifferentiated parent of all succeeding cultural forms.[134] Implicit in this characterization is the corollary that these specialized cultural traditions arise from structural changes in society, though Durkheim did not identify any exact parallels.

Most of *The Elementary Forms of Religious Life* is not devoted to analyzing *variation* at all, but rather to delineating the patterned relation among stable ingredients of a single system—Australian society and its religious beliefs and practices. In fact, Durkheim's major aim was to demonstrate a fixed and *invariant* set of relations between social organization on the one hand and the components of primitive religion—"the division of things into sacred and profane, the notions of the soul, of spirits, of mythical personalities, and of a national and even international divinity, a negative cult with ascetic practices which are its exaggerated form, rites of oblation and communion, imitative rites, commemorative rites and expiatory rites."[135] He viewed these as varying with social organization, but his analysis of empirical variations from society to society was minimal and unsystematic.

What are the methodological implications of undertaking a study of a

---

130 Ibid., p. 111.

131 Ibid.

132 Ibid., p. 196.

133 Ibid., pp. 203–4, 239, 428–30.

134 "It may be said that nearly all great social institutions have been born in religion." Ibid., pp. 418–19.

135 Ibid., p. 415.

system with unvarying parts? The main implication is that most of the methods for establishing causation become *unavailable* to the investigator, because such methods require variation over time with regard to one case or simple variation with regard to a number of cases. Durkheim himself noted the difficulty of establishing sociological proofs when studying "an institution, a legal or moral regulation, or an established custom which functions in the same manner over the entire extent of the country and which changes only in time."[136] With one exception, however, this was what he faced in studying the Australian religions, which he treated as "one common type"; the exception was that he did not even treat changes in these religions over time, thus making causal inferences even more difficult. The method of concomitant variation was not available, since the Australian societies represented no variation, only patterned relations among social structure and religion. Likewise, the several approximations to the method of difference he employed in *Suicide* were not available, because these typically involve holding constant some variation among a number of cases to determine whether an expected association persists or not. In short, the lack of variation restricted Durkheim's ability to establish associations and draw causal inferences.

Consequently most of the efforts to demonstrate connections among phenomena in *The Elementary Forms of Religious Life* rest not on the manipulation of suspected sources of variation but rather on different grounds—logical demonstration, construction of plausible causal chains linking two sets of phenomena, appeal to "what is generally known," and so on. As we have seen, Durkheim's attempt to link the social structure causally to the fundamental categories of religious and logical thought rested on psychological mechanisms posited by him. Much of his rejection of competing animistic and naturistic explanations rested not on empirical refutation but rather on the *implausibility* of putting forth a theory of religion that was based on the dependence of the ideas of the sacred and the supernatural on biological or physical sensations:

> It is inadmissible that systems of ideas like religions, which have held so considerable a place in history, and to which, in all times, men have come to receive the energy which they must have to live, should be made up of a tissue of illusions. . . . It is hard to understand how men have continued to do certain things for centuries without any object.[137]

[136] See pp. 64–65.
[137] Durkheim, *The Elementary Forms of the Religious Life*, pp. 69, 82. For the presentation of empirical data, however, that cast doubt on animistic conceptions, see pp. 60–65.

And much of his discussion of ritual attempts to show the *logical* consistency between his conception of ritual and his conception of the sacred and profane. "By definition," he said, "sacred beings are separated beings [that is, separated from profane things]." And rites have "the object of realizing this state of separation which is essential." Following on these formulations, Durkheim cited a range of ritualistic practices which appear to be consistent with the formulations.[138] A final example: after attempting to establish by empirical illustration that asceticism is "one of [the] essential elements of the religious life," Durkheim argued that this phenomenon is logically consistent with his general perspective on religion and society:

> Asceticism does not serve religious ends only. Here, as elsewhere, religious interests are only the symbolic form of social and moral interests. The ideal beings to whom the cults are addressed are not the only ones who demand of their followers a certain disdain for suffering: society itself is possible only at this price. Though exalting the strength of man, it is frequently rude to individuals; it necessarily demands perpetual sacrifices from them; it is constantly doing violence to our natural appetites, just because it raises us above ourselves. If we are going to fulfil our duties towards it, then we must be prepared to do violence to our instincts sometimes and to ascend the decline of nature when it is necessary.[139]

In examining Durkheim's comparative strategies in *The Division of Labor in Society* and *Suicide* I noted that his causal explanation of social facts rested on two types of assertion: (1) the assertion that two orders of social fact co-vary consistently with one another; this co-variation is established by various measures of association, as well as procedures designed to demonstrate that the association is not the product of some other cause; and (2) the assertion that the association is causal, because some posited intervening mechanism—usually psychological—"makes sense" of the association. Because Durkheim's study of primitive religion was essentially a case study, he could point to the co-existence but not the co-variation of social facts. Not having recourse to systematic comparative procedures to establish the presumed causal relations between associated characteristics, Durkheim built the case for his sociological theory of religion almost entirely on the basis of plausible arguments.

138 Ibid., pp. 299–308.
139 Ibid., p. 316.

5

Weber's Comparative Sociology

I turn now to a substantial portion of Weber's comparative historical analyses. Though his substantive interests and his comparative strategies differed from those of Durkheim, it is possible to treat his comparative sociology in parallel manner. Accordingly, I shall begin by mentioning the substantive concerns of Weber that will command most of my attention. Next I shall examine how Weber treated issues of definition, description, classification, and measurement of some of the variables he studied. Then, returning to his substantive preoccupations, I shall outline the kinds of causal models he employed—to the degree that these are explicit in his work—and his explanatory strategies. Finally, I shall ask how he assembled and manipulated comparative data to elucidate his historical explanations and theories of change. At the end of the chapter I shall present a general summary assessment of Durkheim and Weber as comparative analysts.

Some of Weber's Substantive
Preoccupations

The number of substantive areas that Weber touched in his lifetime of scholarship is enormous, and any effort to comprehend all his comparative work would run the risk of superficiality. Accordingly, I shall concentrate on three major areas in which he conducted extensive comparative scholarship—his sociology of religion, his sociology of political authority, and his economic sociology. To select these areas still includes many of Weber's works—most of his massive *Economy and Society,* his comparative work on Protestantism, Judaism, Confucianism, and Hinduism, his *General Economic History,* and some of his essays. At the same time it omits his sociology of law, his sociology of the city, his sociology of music, and his historical works on ancient and medieval economies and societies.

The three substantive areas I shall emphasize are linked by certain common preoccupations. In his sociology of religion Weber was interested in the factors that condition the rise, propagation, development, and spread of religious doctrines. Among the factors he singled out were the predilections of different social groups—warriors, peasants, ruling elites, for example—to accept different religious beliefs; the tensions and accommodations among prophets, priests, and laity; and the tensions and accommodations between the tendencies to monopolize and proselytize among religious groups. His comparative interests in religion were marked, moreover, by a concern with the degree to which religious doctrines become *rationalized*—that is to say, the degree to which they divest themselves of magical elements and develop a universal ethic emanating from a conception of man's relation to a diety. Furthermore, he was consistently preoccupied with the implication of different patterns of religious rationalization (or lack of it) for the rationalization of life in other spheres, particularly the economic.[1] Weber's interest in the sociology of economic forms was quite diverse, but here, too, he showed a recurring preoccupation with ration-

---

[1] For his statement of explicit concern between the relation of the major world religions and their implications for the development of the ethic and structures of industrial capitalism, see Max Weber, *The Protestant Ethic and the Spirit of Capitalism,* trans. Talcott Parsons (New York: Charles Scribner's Sons, 1958), p. 27; Max Weber, *The Religion of India,* ed. and trans. Hans H. Gerth and Don Martindale (Glencoe, Ill.: The Free Press, 1958), p. 4; Max Weber, *The Religion of China,* ed. and trans. Hans H. Gerth (Glencoe, Ill.: The Free Press, 1951), p. 104; Max Weber, *Economy and Society,* ed. with an introduction by Guenther Roth, co-ed. Claus Wittich (New York: Bedminister Press, 1968), 2:551–56, 611–23.

ality. In particular, he focused on the variety of conditions that contributed to the rise and consolidation of rational bourgeois capitalism —conditions such as a stable monetary system, a rationally administered system of law, and certain patterns of appropriation of human and nonhuman resources.[2] Much of his political sociology rested on the identification of several types of legitimacy—the rational-legal, the traditional, and the charismatic—the conditions of the rise of each, the consequences of each, and the vicissitudes of each. Yet in this line of analysis, too, a preoccupation with rationalization persisted, particularly in his discussion of the efficiency and potency of the rational-legal type and its associated social structure, bureaucracy, as a rationalizing force in society. My concern will not be limited only to Weber's comparative analysis of the fate of different kinds of rationalization, as his comparative concerns ranged much more widely. But because he returned so often to that theme,[3] I shall do so as well.

Definition, Description, Classification, and Measurement

On the whole, Weber took cognizance of the need for careful definition of basic comparative concepts (ideal types), and the need to set off these definitions analytically from one another. The section of *Economy and Society* that follows his initial methodological discussion is a series of careful definitions of "basic sociological terms" such as the general types of social action, social relationship, communal and associative relationships, open and closed relationships, and the like. His general procedure was to define several types analytically; to give an empirical illustration of type; to point up the empirical variability of each type; and meantime, to remind the reader from time to time that the types are not to be found in pure form empirically, but rather are always mixed. For example, he defined a social relationship as "open" to outsiders "if and insofar as its system of order does not deny participation to anyone who wishes to join and is actually in a position to do so." A relationship is "closed" against out-

---

[2] Especially in Weber, *Economy and Society*, vol. 1, pt. 1, ch. 2, pt. 2, ch. 1; Weber, *The Protestant Ethic and the Spirit of Capitalism*, pp. 21–28; and Weber, *General Economic History*, trans. Frank H. Knight (Glencoe, Ill.: The Free Press, 1950), pt. 4.

[3] The concern with rationalization was certainly one of the central preoccupations —though not the only one—that guided Weber in his preparation of *Economy and Society*. See Guenther Roth, "Introduction" to Weber, *Economy and Society*, 1:lvii–lviii.

siders insofar as "according to its subjective meaning and its binding rules, participation of certain persons is excluded, limited, or subjected to conditions."[4] Such a definition appears to meet the criteria of mutual exclusiveness—that is, as between "open" and "closed"—requisite for a definition. Then Weber indicated that "closedness" may be based on a number of grounds, such as emotional (an erotic relationship), value-rational (a group sharing religious beliefs), or rational (an economic monopoly), indicating further that all these may assume the most varied forms.[5] Weber's effort to define phenomena and variables clearly at the outset is consistent with his methodological positions that social science investigation cannot be "presuppositionless," that a degree of selectivity is involved in all analysis, and that the investigator should be as explicit as possible in identifying his own principles of selection. On occasion Weber deviated from his practice of establishing clear, rigorous definitions in advance:

> To define "religion," to say what it *is* is not possible at the start of a presentation such as this. Definition can be attempted, if at all, only at the conclusion of the study. The essence of religion is not even our concern, as we make it our task to study the conditions and effects of a particular type of social action.[6]

But to proceed to identify and analyze religious phenomena without such a definition means that Weber was in fact operating with an implicit definition or definitions in the nature of the case.

Comparative description that uses ideal types involves a number of historical judgments by the investigator. Does a given historical case have a sufficient number of requisite empirical characteristics to be classified as an instance of the ideal type? What empirical characteristics are decisive for excluding a phenomenon as an instance of an ideal type? What distinctive patterns of similarities and differences justify regarding an historical instance as a formally identified subtype? Weber made such judgments thousands of times in carrying out his enterprise of comparative sociology. But because his criteria for making them remained largely implicit, his comparative descriptions have an element of arbitrariness; that is, there are few assurances that an investigator other than Weber undertaking the same task would emerge with the same assignments of historical situations to the same ideal types.

Three additional kinds of ambiguity appear in the procedures that Weber employed to define ideal types:

4 Weber, *Economy and Society,* 1:43.
5 Ibid., pp. 44–45.
6 Ibid., 2:399.

1. Whether the definition of a series of types is intended to be logically systematic and exhaustive or whether it is intended as an enumerative "list" is unclear. In the initial definition of his four general types of action —instrumentally rational, value-rational, affectual, and traditional—Weber said, simply, that "[social] action, like all action, may be oriented in four ways,"[7] leaving unspecified whether he meant four *and only four*. In a subsequent qualifying remark, however, he explicitly denied this possibility:

> This classification of the modes of orientation of action is in no sense meant to exhaust the possibilities of the field, but only to formulate in conceptually pure form certain sociologically important types to which actual action is more or less closely approximated or, in the more common case, which constitute its elements.[8]

This classificatory status is further confirmed by observing that, except for the first two types of rational action, no over-arching dimensions evidently relate the four types, and that "affectual" and "traditional" are somewhat vague residuals in relation to the first two.[9] On other occasions as well it is apparent that Weber's listing of "types" is not meant to be systematically exhaustive, but rather is intended as a list of empirical illustrations he recorded in his extensive scanning of historical cases—for example, the identification of the modes of designating a successor to a charismatic leader.[10] And Weber qualified his classification of the world's "great religions" by adding that "taken all together, they exhaust only a few of the possible combinations that could conceivably be framed from the very numerous individual factors to be considered in such historical combinations."[11]

Sometimes, however, Weber's claims seem stronger. Speaking of ultimate principles of legitimacy to justify a relationship of domination, Weber said "there are only three"—rational-legal, traditional, and charismatic— and that three types of domination correspond to "these three possible types of legitimation."[12] Such language clearly implies the logical exhaustion of types of legitimation and types of authority. Furthermore, the three

[7] Ibid., 1:24.

[8] Ibid., 1:26.

[9] Talcott Parsons, *The Structure of Social Action* (New York: McGraw-Hill, 1937), pp. 646–49.

[10] Weber, *Economy and Society*, 1:246–49.

[11] *From Max Weber: Essays in Sociology*, ed. and trans. with an introduction by H. H. Gerth and C. Wright Mills (London: Routledge and Kegan Paul, 1970), p. 292.

[12] Weber, *Economy and Society*, 3:954.

types are related systematically to one another. The basic distinction is domination by appeal to norms (rational-legal) or by appeal to personal authority (the other two). The other two are distinguished by whether obedience is demanded in the name of the established and ordinary (traditional) or in the name of the extraordinary (charisma).[13] (The ambiguity of these formulations is heightened by the fact that the types of authority—which are presumably logically exhaustive—stand in rough logical correspondence with the more general types of social action—which are presented as a listing of non-exhaustive "elements" of action.)

This point of ambiguity is a salient one, for one's critical assessment of Weber as a theorist depends on which reading of the possibilities one makes. If the "types" are regarded in their "weak" sense as a number of salient dimensions of social life, then Weber cannot be regarded as a *systematic* theorist, since the types do not represent a determinate and exhaustive range of outcomes requisite for such a theory. Viewed in a balanced fashion, despite the ambiguity, it seems most accurate to regard Weber's definitions and typologies in this "weak" sense, as abstract representations of typical empirical complexes that are helpful in generating generalizations but which do not cohere as a theoretical system.

2. Whether a feature of a definition is to be regarded as necessary for the *definition* of the phenomenon or as an *empirical condition* for it is unclear as well. In introducing *The Protestant Ethic and the Spirit of Capitalism,* Weber defined a capitalist economic action as "one which rests on the expectation of profit by the utilization of opportunities for exchange, that is on (formally) peaceful chances of profit."[14] He went on to identify different types of capitalism, such as adventure capitalism and colonial entrepreneurship. One of these forms, peculiar to the modern Occident, is "the rational capitalistic organization of (formally) free labour."[15] This criterion—a particular type of organization of labor—would seem to be the necessary defining characteristic of modern Western capitalism. But in a subsequent passage, he noted that "[exact] calculation—the basis of everything else—is only possible on a basis of free labour."[16] This wording suggests that free labor is not a necessary defining characteristic of modern capitalism but an empirical condition that must be realized before capitalism can reach certain levels of development. The same ambiguity characterizes Weber's characterization of two other "peculiarities" of Western capitalism—the separation of business from the household and rational

13 Ibid.
14 Weber, *The Protestant Ethic,* p. 17.
15 Ibid., p. 21.
16 Ibid., p. 22.

bookkeeping. On the one hand, the word "peculiarities" suggests an attribute of the phenomenon of capitalism; on the other, the sentence, "[the] modern rational organization of capitalistic enterprise would not have been possible without two other important *factors* [that is, the separation of business from household and rational bookkeeping]," suggests that Weber regarded them as empirical conditions favorable to its development. Such phrasing leaves it unclear whether the ingredients are definitionally necessary, empirically necessary, or empirically facilitative for conditions of modern capitalism.

3. Whether defining an ideal type involves an assumption of unverified associations is the third ambiguity. In his methodological writings Weber envisioned the creation of an ideal type as a procedure whereby an investigator identifies features that are "more or less present and occasionally absent" in historically significant constellations. The ideal types, as abstractions, form the basis for generating hypotheses—that is, how actors typically behave if they follow the pattern of meanings and constraints built into the ideal type. Verification, finally, involves the examination of historical data in the light of a battery of ideal types to determine whether the behavior of actors and the evolution of structures is consistent with the logic of the ideal types. It may be asked, however, whether the *construction* of the ideal type itself involves the same order of empirical assertion as the subsequent *application* of ideal types, but without the requisite empirical procedures.

Let me illustrate this problem. One of Weber's most famous ideal-typical constructs was that of charismatic authority, which he defined as "resting on devotion to the exceptional sanctity, heroism or exemplary character of an individual person, and of the normative patterns or order revealed or ordained by him."[17] In subsequent discussion of this type, Weber explicated a number of its additional features:

1. Basis of followership: "it is the duty of those subject to charismatic authority to recognize its genuineness and to act accordingly."[18]
2. Psychology of followership: "complete personal devotion to the possessor of the [charismatic] quality."[19]
3. Type of group: "an emotional form of communal relationship."[20]
4. Type of administrative staff: "disciples . . . bodyguard . . . agents."[21]

[17] Weber, *Economy and Society,* 1:215.
[18] Ibid., 1:242.
[19] Ibid.
[20] Ibid., 1:243.
[21] Ibid.

5. Basis of recruitment and advancement: no standard procedures; personal conviction, loyalty to the leader, designation by the leader.[22]
6. Relation to the economy: "specifically foreign to economic considerations, . . . charisma rejects as undignified all methodical rational acquisition, in fact, all economic conduct." Relies on booty, gifts, etc.[23]

Such characteristics were contrasted systematically—on the same general dimensions—with traditional and rational-legal authority.

Charismatic authority (as well as the other types), then, is a *cluster* of characteristics that are "more or less present and occasionally absent"— that is to say, positively correlated with one another. Moreover, they cluster because of a "principle of consistency" dictated by the implications of a group of followers subordinated emotionally and dutifully to a leader regarded as sacred. Insofar as these characteristics are *causally* related to one another—for example, insofar as "foreignness to economic considerations" is a function of unquestioned submission to a leader considered as sacred—it would seem to call for an application of the battery of statistical and comparative methods to assess the validity of that causal relation. Yet in constructing his types, Weber relied mainly on "historical judgments" and "rules of experience" which, however insightful, are less rigorous and involve more subjective assessments than standardized research methods. One of the possible vulnerabilities of dealing with ideal types, then, is that the investigator, regarding the construction of types as preliminary to the assessment of causal relations among types, may in fact make a number of correlational and causal assertions in the process of construction itself, without assessing the validity of these assertions in the light of available research methods.[24]

I conclude this section with a few remarks on the relation between abstracted types and "empirical indicators." Durkheim, we saw, distinguished clearly between analytic constructs, such as social integration (he termed them "internal facts") and empirical indicators of these constructs, such as legal codes ("external indices"). The relations among the former, he argued, are established by studying the relations among the latter. Weber also distinguished between a "pure type" and the "verification . . . by comparison with the concrete course of events [empirical data]."[25] But because Weber relied on a certain version of ideal-type constructs, his dis-

[22] Ibid., 3:1112–13.
[23] Ibid., 1:244, 3:1113–14.
[24] For further discussion of "type" concepts as reservoirs of implicit hypotheses, see Reinhard Bendix, "Concepts and Generalizations in Comparative Sociological Studies," *American Sociological Review* 28(1963):533–34.
[25] See, pp. 46–47, 59–61.

tinction could not be as sharp as that proposed by Durkheim. Weber's ideal type is, above all, a general empirical construct generated by a process of inspection, induction, and selection from a number of concrete empirical cases. In attempting to assess the causal relations among historical phenomena by applying ideal types an investigator might well, then, return to some of the very data from which the type concepts were originally constructed. There is certainly nothing illegitimate about this, except that the procedures for establishing causal relations should be independent of the procedures for establishing the type concepts, in order to avoid proof by definition.

In connection with the construction of type concepts, the familiar methodological problem of "validity" arises in Weber's work. It might be asked, for example, whether his reliance on Richard Baxter's writings to characterize the Calvinist economic ethic and on Benjamin Franklin's writings to characterize the capitalist spirit was appropriate, since both writers developed their views well after the Protestant Reformation and the foundation of capitalism.[26] It might also be asked whether these documents represent the "mentality" of the typical capitalist or typical Puritan, or whether formal Confucian documents represented the "mentality" of the typical Chinese bureaucrat. In choosing religious and ethical statements as indicators of the spirit of an epoch, Weber in fact made a number of substantive psychological assumptions about the potency of such beliefs. For example, ". . . an ethic based on religion places certain psychological sanctions (not of an economic character) on the maintenance of the attitude prescribed by it, sanctions which, so long as the religious belief remains alive, are highly effective. . . ."[27] Such an assumption can in principle be assessed empirically, and the validity of his choice of religious and other documents as indicators could be judged in the light of that assessment. The point I wish to stress, however, is that in claiming that an empirical phenomenon is a "valid" indicator for a general concept, an investigator simultaneously makes a number of substantive social and psychological claims.[28]

[26] Weber, *The Protestant Ethic,* pp. 48–50, 155. See Tawney's critical remark on the use of 17th-century Puritan sources, p. 9. In fairness to Weber, it should be pointed out that he observed that "we are not studying the personal views of Calvin, but Calvinism, and that in the form to which it had evolved by the end of the sixteenth and in the seventeenth centuries in the great areas where it had a decisive influence and which were at the same time the home of capitalistic culture." Fn., p. 220. Nevertheless, the question of the "representativeness" of the writers he chose can legitimately be raised.

[27] Ibid., fn., p. 197.

[28] We saw this in Durkheim's effort to maintain that legal codes constitute an indicator of social solidarity. See pp. 78–79. For a more extended discussion of validity, see pp. 185–89.

Weber observed repeatedly that ideal-type constructs do not exhaust empirical reality, and that any historical situation is a mixture of many ideal-type tendencies. For example, "[the] forms of domination occurring in historical reality constitute combinations, mixtures, adaptations, or modifications of [the 'pure' types of bureaucracy, patriarchism, and the charismatic structure of domination]."[29] To choose an example of this close to home, it is possible to find in the American political system elements of the rational-legal (the system of administrative law relating to the civil service bureaucracy), the traditional (reliance on precedents relating to the Constitution in court interpretations), and the charismatic (reference to the "founding fathers"; the charisma of individual presidents). If such an observation is carried no further, however, there is a danger that an investigator simply arms himself with a whole battery of tendencies (ideal types), any one of which can be appealed to residually to interpret any empirical outcome experienced in a given case.[30] For any given interpretation, it is necessary to estimate the relative *primacies* and *strengths* of different tendencies, as well as to account for any "external" influences that might be operating. (This was often Weber's strategy, though as we shall see soon, he carried out such interpretations with varying degrees of thoroughness.) To generate more general theoretical knowledge, it would be essential to develop an abstract statement of the principles of combination of different ideal-type tendencies, specifying the conditions under which one rather than another might predominate, and specifying the general principles of interaction among them. Weber, who preferred not to stray from the comparative analysis of historical cases, did not go far in developing such general principles. However, he frequently compared ideal-type constructs with one another in the abstract, thus generating propositions of a more general order.[31]

Causal Models and Strategies of Explanation

Weber's approach to sociological explanation was simultaneously ambitious and modest. On the one hand, few scholars have undertaken such a massive coverage of comparative historical materials. In dealing with these materials, however, he was cautious about—indeed, hostile to—venturing universal and monocausal explanations. He recognized the centrality of

---

[29] Weber, *Economy and Society*, 3:954, 1:26, 216.

[30] This criticism is identical to that made of Durkheim's unsystematic appeal to third variables. See pp. 103–7.

[31] Some of the most extensive comparisons among types are found in his discussions of types of legitimacy. Weber, *Economy and Society*, 1:212–301, 3:941–1157.

certain dimensions—for example, the economic, the religious, and the dimension of political domination—as particularly crucial in explaining sociological phenomena, but he refused to consider any of these as *the* most decisive, and insisted repeatedly on their mutual interaction.

In his methodological essay of 1904, for example, Weber acknowledged that the *Archiv für Sozialwissenschaft und Sozialpolitik* would concentrate on "socio-economic data," which are related to "the fact that our physical existence and the satisfaction of our most ideal needs are everywhere confronted with the quantitative limits and the qualitative inadequacy of the necessary external means, so that their satisfaction requires planful provision and work, struggle with nature and the association of human beings."[32] While asserting the importance and universality of the economic (scarcity) dimension, however, Weber immediately distinguished among three types of phenomena:

> —*economic* phenomena, "when institutions are involved which were deliberately created or used for economic ends" (for example, banks, the stock exchange).
> —*economically relevant* phenomena, such as legal, religious, and other phenomena which are not primarily economic but which "do acquire significance because under some circumstances they have consequences which are of interest from the economic point of view."
> —*economically conditioned* phenomena, such as the stratification system or the state, which are also not primarily economic, but which are affected in some way by economic phenomena.[33]

Furthermore, he refused to reduce any of the three to one another, called for "freedom from dogmatic restrictions" in studying their relations, and explicitly disassociated his emphasis from the "materialistic conception of history."[34]

A corollary of such a formulation is that any given phenomenon is codetermined by a variety of other phenomena. In introducing *The Protestant Ethic and the Spirit of Capitalism*, Weber identified religion as one among a number of conditions fostering the development of rational bourgeois capitalism.[35] More generally, he argued that

> religion nowhere creates certain economic conditions unless there are also

[32] Max Weber, " 'Objectivity' in Social Science and Social Policy," in *The Methodology of the Social Sciences*, ed. and trans. Edward A. Shils and Henry A. Finch (New York: The Free Press, 1949), pp. 63–64.

[33] Ibid., pp. 64–65.

[34] Ibid., pp. 68–69.

[35] Pp. 21–27.

present in the existing relationships and constellations of interests certain possibilities of, or even powerful drives toward, such an economic transformation. It is not possible to enunciate any general formula that will summarize the comparative substantive powers of the various factors involved in such a transformation or will summarize the manner of their accommodation to one another.[36]

This passage, the spirit of which he repeated many times, typifies Weber's reluctance to move too far in the direction of theoretical generalities.

Another corollary is that the various factors in social life stand in an interactive relation with one another. Factors that are economically relevant are also economically conditioned. Weber acknowledged this in the famous qualification that his interest in the religious origins of capitalism was concerned with only "one side of the causal chain."[37] In his general writings on the sociology of religion, he analyzed the implications of the material and ideal interests of different social groups for their receptiveness to different kinds of religious beliefs.[38] Finally, in his assessment of the relations between economic power and political authority, Weber issued the following, highly qualified, formulation:

As in the case of other forms of power, those who exercise domination do not apply it exclusively, or even usually, to the pursuit of purely economic ends, such as, for example, a plentiful supply of economic goods. It is true, however, that the control over economic goods, i.e., economic power, is a frequent, often purposively willed, consequence of domination as well as one of its most important instruments. Not every position of economic power, however, represents domination in our sense of the word. Nor does domination utilize in every case economic power for its foundation and maintenance. But in the vast majority of cases, and indeed in the most important ones, this is just what happens in one way or another and often to such an extent that the mode of applying economic means for the purpose of maintaining domination, in turn, exercises a determining influence on the structure of domination. Furthermore, the great majority of all economic organizations, among them the most important and modern ones, reveal a structure of dominancy. The crucial characteristics of any form of domination may, it is true, not be correlated in any particular form of economic organization. Yet, the structure of dominancy is in many cases both a factor of great economic importance and, at least to some extent, a result of economic conditions.[39]

36 Weber, *Economy and Society,* 2:577.
37 Weber, *The Protestant Ethic,* p. 27.
38 Weber, *Economy and Society,* 2:468–517.
39 Ibid., 3:942.

Despite the modesty of these formulations, despite the qualifications, despite Weber's insistence on the necessary incompleteness of explanations, and despite his periodic appeal to "accidents," he nevertheless generated several kinds of partial "models" of explanation which provided the bases for his historical and comparative analysis. What kinds of models were these?

Conditions generating a certain ideal type

Weber frequently selected a certain kind of ideal-typical phenomenon which he regarded as significant for one reason or another, and proceeded to develop a statement of the kinds of conditions that determine or facilitate its historical emergence. In his *General Economic History*, for example, he dedicated one brief chapter to the development of the factory system of manufacture, which he regarded as an ideal-typical system of production which "implies separation between household and industry, in contrast with home work."[40] Among the economic prerequisites for the development of this kind of production are both mass demand and steady demand—that is, "a certain organization of the market"; another is "a relatively inexpensive production process"; a third is "the presence of a sufficient supply of free labourers."[41] After noting these general prerequisites, Weber generated a series of "sub-models," mainly based on individual national experiences, indicating how the general prerequisites were or were not realized in any empirical instance. The labor supply in England, for example, was made possible by the eviction of peasants from the land during the enclosures movement, and by the relatively small requirements for manpower for the British armed forces. In Germany shop industries were deliberately established by the state as institutions for relieving and providing work for the poor, whose situation had worsened under the effects of guild monopolization.[42] Demand expanded in Germany because of increased military needs, a new interest in luxuries, and a mass interest in imitations of luxuries.[43] Another facilitating condition for the development of factories was the "technical specialization and organization of work and the simultaneous utilization of non-human sources of power."[44] Finally, Weber cited a number of obstacles to the development of shop production, such as the opposition of the guilds, caste resistances

---

40 Weber, *General Economic History*, p. 162.
41 Ibid., pp. 163, 164.
42 Ibid., pp. 164–65.
43 Ibid., pp. 170–71.
44 Ibid., p. 169.

in India, and clan cohesion in China.[45] In generating his model of the rise of the factory system, then, Weber actually constructed a *series* of models at different levels of historical specificity. On the one hand, he spoke of general requisites for factory production, but he also developed a series of models for his specific historical illustrations, indicating the extent to which and the processes by which the requisites were realized.

Weber also enumerated several conditions for the development of bureaucracy. Among these he cited a money economy, which was "not an indispensable precondition," but did facilitate the continuous supply of revenues.[46] Bureaucracy is also stimulated by various demand factors, such as the quantitative increase of administrative tasks, growing cultural demands (for example, for education), demands for political order and pacification, and demands for systems of transportation and communication.[47] The most decisive reason for the advance of bureaucratization, however, lies on the "supply" side; it is "[bureaucracy's] purely *technical* superiority over any other form of organization."[48] Weber also referred to a number of obstacles which slowed the development of bureaucracy. Among the strongest of these was the resistance of notables and other traditionally privileged groups that opposed "the levelling of the governed in face of the governing and bureaucratically articulated group."[49] In classical China, in fact, the absence of sufficiently strong forces to oppose the bureaucracy helped permit the Chinese bureaucrats to work out an extreme version of practical rationalism.[50] Finally, Weber mentioned a number of conditions that sustain bureaucracy once it is fully established, conditions that make bureaucracy "among those social structures which are the hardest to destroy."[51] Some of these conditions are the superiority of rationally organized and directed action over other kinds of collective action, the indispensability of a bureaucratic apparatus for the ruler and the ruled, the capacity of bureaucratic organization to sustain radical changes of leadership without significant modification of administrative procedures, and its secrecy.[52]

Conditions for the historical appearance of other kinds of ideal-typical phenomena, however, are scarcely analyzed by Weber. His comments on

[45] Ibid., pp. 175–76.
[46] Weber, *Economy and Society*, 3:963–68.
[47] Ibid., 3:969–73.
[48] Ibid., 3:973.
[49] Ibid., 3:985.
[50] Weber, *The Religion of China*, chs. 5, 6, esp. pp. 149–52.
[51] Weber, *Economy and Society*, 3:987.
[52] Ibid., 3:987–94.

the conditions generating and sustaining charismatic authority, for example, are very skimpy. He saw charismatic leadership emerging "in moments of distress—whether psychic, physical, economic, ethical, religious, or political"; or again, it results from "unusual, especially political or economic situations, or from extraordinary psychic, particularly religious states, or from both together."[53] It is likely to be "immediately activated whenever an extraordinary event occurs; a major hunting expedition, a drought or some other danger precipitated by the wrath of the demons, and especially a military threat."[54] In situations of stably-structured domination, it is likely to erupt "only in short-lived mass emotions with unpredictable effects, during elections and similar occasions."[55] Beyond these general and heterogeneous conditions, Weber said little about the activation of charisma, though he developed a more detailed model (which we shall discuss later) of its consequences and its fate.

These examples of models of the rise of ideal-type phenomena could be multiplied, but they suffice to indicate the reasons why it is difficult to represent the logic of Weber's explanations in general terms. First, the ideal-type phenomena themselves vary greatly in level of generality, and call for corresponding differences in level of generality of causal analysis. Second, Weber developed such models with varying degrees of thoroughness. Third, the conditions he assembled to explain the rise of a historical phenomenon are very diverse—various kinds of demands for the phenomenon, various factors that make it superior to alternatives, vested interests that oppose its existence, the unavailability of alternative responses, and various sustaining factors, to name a few. And fourth, these diverse conditions are organized in different patterns from one explanatory model to another. Such are some of the features that justify labeling Weber's explanatory procedure as relatively eclectic.

Autonomous "tendencies" and internal "tensions" of ideal types and their consequences

In considering the historical emergence of different administrative structures, Weber posed a question that was to guide his inquiry: "How far are these administrative structures in their developmental chances subject to economic, political or any other external determinants, or to an 'autonomous' logic inherent in their technical structure?"[56] The question is crucial

---

[53] Ibid., 3:1111–12, 1121.
[54] Ibid., 3:1134.
[55] Ibid., 3:1146.
[56] Ibid., 3:1002.

for understanding Weber's account not only of the development of administrative structures, but also of the emergence of social arrangements generally.

Stated most generally, Weber's explanatory strategy unfolds in the following way. Involvement in a given ideal-typical social or cultural relationship (for example, being a member of a charismatic community or a rational-legal bureaucracy, or believing in a certain kind of religious faith) constitutes a kind of "program" for individual and group action; it orients behavior in certain directions rather than others and imbues this behavior with meaning. For example, involvement in a structure of patriarchical domination orients a follower toward a leader in terms of a personal loyalty; it orients the leader as well, toward norms which derive from received tradition.[57] Weber often traced the fate of the ideal-type phenomenon and the consequences for its social setting *if* actors behaved according to the meaning-system of the ideal type—that is to say, according to its "autonomous logic." The most familiar examples of these analyses are found in Weber's characterization of the impact of the different types of authority. The consequences of rational-legal authority are to foster leveling and recruitment on the basis of technical competence, long periods of technical training, a spirit of impersonality, and the dehumanization of the individual. The financial and administrative practices associated with traditional authority tend to result in the restriction of rational economic activity. Charismatic authority, particularly because of its rejection of the routine, is likely to have revolutionary consequences for the social order.[58] When charisma is transformed in an anti-authoritarian direction, as in plebiscitary democracy, a leader "will attempt to consolidate the loyalty of those he governs either by winning glory and honor in war or by promoting their material welfare, or under certain circumstances, by attempting to combine both. Success in these will be regarded as proof of his charisma."[59] Or again: "Under genuinely charismatic domination, parties are necessarily schismatic sects. Their conflict is essentially over questions of faith and, as such, is basically irreconcilable."[60] The "autonomous logic" that produces such a result is that, because charismatic authority implies social relations based on personal devotion to a sacred leader and his principles, party divisions will reflect this basic orientation.

Not only does the autonomous logic of involvement in certain ideal-type situations produce definite consequences, it rules out others. On this

[57] Ibid., 3:1006.
[58] Ibid., 1:225, 237–41, 244–45.
[59] Ibid., 1:269.
[60] Ibid., 1:287.

point Weber's observations on the relations of religious ethics to rational economic activity are pertinent. The pariah status of Jews, and particularly their double standard in dealing with in-group and out-group members impeded "their participation in the organization of industrial labor," even though other ingredients of their religion—for example, its anti-magical elements—disposed them favorably toward rational economic activity.[61] With respect to ancient Buddhism, "[there] is no path leading from this only really consistent position of world-flight to any economic ethic or to any rational social ethic."[62] Ancient Confucianism, with its toleration of magic, its insistence on adjustment to "the world," and its insistence on filial duty also discouraged any orientation toward the radical transformation of the world.[63]

But the autonomous logic of socio-cultural arrangements is not the only source of determinants that direct social change. The forces set in motion by this logic are continuously deflected, diverted, even blocked by the independent material and ideal interests of individuals and groups, by group conflict, by the unavailability of resources, by the intervention of outside powers, and the like. Many of Weber's explanatory "models"— which again varied in historical specificity—were constructed by specifying different combinations and compromises between the "autonomous logic" of ideal types and such external determinants. These models can be illustrated by Weber's treatment of the vicissitudes of charismatic authority.

By virtue of its "autonomous logic," charismatic authority inevitably promises to fade after a short life, because of its "character specifically foreign to everyday routine structures." In pure form it cannot remain stable.[64] Historically, however, charisma is preserved in the social order by its transformation and incorporation into a community. The forces with which the charismatic impulse combines to effect this consolidation are the following:

(a) The ideal and also the material interests of the followers in the continuation and the continual reactivation of the community, (b) the still stronger ideal and also stronger material interests of the members of the administrative staff, the disciples, the party workers, or others continuing their relationship. Not only this, but they have an interest in continuing it in such a way that both from an ideal and a material point of view, their own position is put on a stable everyday basis. This means, above all, making it possible to participate in normal family relationships or at least to

[61] Ibid., 1:614, 3:1200–4; Weber, *Ancient Judaism*, pp. 343–45.

[62] Weber, *Economy and Society*, 2:628; Weber, *The Religion of India*, ch. 10.

[63] Weber, *The Religion of China*, pp. 226–43.

[64] Weber, *Economy and Society*, 1:246.

enjoy a secure social position in place of the kind of discipleship which is cut off from ordinary worldly connections, notably in the family and in economic relationships.[65]

Specifically, the charismatic community "comes to terms" with these interests and with the socio-economic environment by arranging some sort of succession, necessary if the essence of charisma is to be extended beyond the lifetime of the charismatic leader; by regularizing recruitment and reward for charismatic followers; and by developing "some form of fiscal organization to provide for the needs of the group and hence to the economic conditions necessary for raising taxes and contributions."[66]

Weber listed a number of types of succession, including designation of the successor by the leader, charismatic acclamation, hereditary charisma, and the development of the "charisma of office."[67] These resolutions of the tension between the transitoriness of charisma and the interest in preserving it were listed as "the principal possible types of solution."[68] This language suggests that Weber was presenting a logically exhaustive series of possibilities; but the actual list consists of a number of mechanisms, each illustrated by one or more historical examples, which suggests that Weber simply compiled and organized the empirical instances that his vast research revealed. Furthermore, Weber did not ask under what conditions each type of transformation might occur. His analysis is, on the contrary, somewhat weaker, consisting only of a list of types of succession that *may* develop, and perhaps discussing the likely further consequences if one, rather than another, type of arrangement arises. So while Weber insisted that "[it] is the fate of charisma . . . to recede with the development of permanent institutional structures,"[69] he did not develop detailed causal models of its different lines of recession.

Weber's characterization of the interplay of "material and ideal interests" was more circumstantial, however, in his analysis of the social fate of prophecy. The prophet is the prototype of a charismatic leader, who proclaims a religious doctrine or divine commandment and draws followers to him on the basis of his personal appeal. Prophets, however, like all charismatic leaders, are transitory, and their following is frequently routinized into some form of congregation, or permanent association of laymen. Under some circumstances a class of priests, or carriers of the sacred tradition, becomes consolidated. The behavior of the priests—and

[65] Ibid.
[66] Ibid., 1:246–51.
[67] Ibid., 1:246–48, 3:1121–48.
[68] Ibid., 1:246.
[69] Ibid., 3:1133.

the direction of change of religious doctrine—emerges as a resultant of the accommodations this class makes with reference to (a) the character of the prophecy itself, and the need to relate it to the on-going social life; (b) the traditional interests of the laity; and (c) the intellectual interests of the laity.[70] Weber interpreted the process of systematization of sacred doctrines and the development of preaching and pastoral care as an interplay among these sometimes-opposed forces, plus the priesthood's own interests.

As part of his analysis of the fate of religious doctrines, Weber developed an extended statement of the affinities of different social groups for different religious doctrines. He found peasants

> so strongly tied to nature, so dependent on organic processes and natural events, and economically so little oriented to rational systematization that in general the peasantry will become a carrier of religion only when it is threatened by enslavement or proletarianization, either by domestic forces (financial or seigneurial) or by some external political power.[71]

Likewise, the life patterns of warrior nobles reveal little affinity "with the notion of a benificent providence, or with the systematic ethical demands of a transcendental god." But if prophetic religion "directs its promises to the warrior in the cause of religion," it is more likely to be accepted.[72] Weber also noted the predilection of bureaucrats to treat religion as an instrument of social control, as well as the familiar affinity between capitalist classes and rational, ethical religious beliefs. More generally, he regarded upper strata as inclined to utilize religion to legitimize their own situations, whereas the disprivileged orient themselves differently:

> Their particular need is for release from suffering. They do not always experience this need for salvation in a religious form, as shown by the example of the modern proletariat. Furthermore, their need for religious salvation, where it exists, may assume diverse forms. Most important, it may be combined with a need for just compensation, envisaged in various ways but always involving reward for one's own good deeds and punishment for the unrighteousness of others. This hope for an expectation of just compensation, a fairly calculating attitude, is, next to magic (indeed, not unconnected with it), the most widely diffused form of mass religion all over the world. Even religious prophecies, which rejected the more mechanical forms of this belief, tended as they underwent popularization and routinization to slip back into these expectations of compensation. The type and scope of these hopes for compensation and salvation varied greatly

[70] Ibid., 2:456.
[71] Ibid., 2:468.
[72] Ibid., 2:472–73.

depending on the expectations aroused by the religious promises, especially when these hopes were projected from the earthly existence of the individual into a future life.[73]

These illustrations reveal that Weber's model of social process as an interplay between the "autonomous logic" of typical situations and other social and cultural forces rests solidly on a body of psychological assumptions and generalizations. For example, to attribute "interests" to a social actor is to assert that the actor *values* something about his situation (its round of activities, its rewards, or whatever) and that he is psychologically disposed to protect or augment that which he values. Furthermore, the precise character of the "interests" attributed to actors depends in part on the investigator's judgment of the relative psychological importance of different aspects (economic, political, religious) of his existence. In this sense Weber's concepts of "material and ideal interests" constitute a psychological link between the social situation of individuals or groups, on the one hand, and their behavioral orientations, on the other. His discussion of the affinity of different groups for religion also reveals the intervening role of psychological assumptions. The passage, just quoted, on the religious predilections of the disprivileged rests on the assumptions that an objective social situation (disprivilege) generates feelings of suffering, and that these feelings receive symbolic expression by embracing certain religious and other doctrines. Moreover, the psychological assumptions are those of "absolute deprivation," and contrast with the assumptions employed as intervening variables by both Tocqueville and Durkheim. Despite this substantive difference, however, the formal structure of Weber's explanation—linking an objective social situation with behavioral orientation by means of a psychological generalization—resembles that employed by both those writers.

Consider also the weight carried by intervening psychological variables in Weber's discussion of Calvinism in *The Protestant Ethic and the Spirit of Capitalism*. Weber laid great stress on the doctrine of predestination, particularly as it concerned human salvation. In extreme form the doctrine totally denies the relevance of human striving:

> We know only that a part of humanity is saved, the rest damned. To assume that human merit or guilt play a part in determining this destiny would be to think of God's absolutely free decrees, which have been settled from eternity, as subject to change by human influence, an impossible contradiction. The Father in heaven of the New Testament, so human and

---

[73] Ibid., 2:492. However, Weber rejected the notion that the need for salvation among the disprivileged was "only . . . a product of resentment." P. 498.

understanding, who rejoices over the repentance of a sinner as a woman over the lost piece of silver she has found, is gone. His place has been taken by a transcendental being, beyond the reach of human understanding, who with His quite incomprehensible decrees has decided the fate of every individual and regulated the tiniest details of the cosmos from eternity.[74]

Weber regarded this doctrine as one of "extreme inhumanity." He argued that it "must above all have had one consequence" for its adherents: "a feeling of unprecedented inner loneliness of the single individual."[75] The doctrine also generated a haunting sense of uncertainty. "The question, Am I one of the elect? must sooner or later have arisen for every believer and have forced all other interests into the background."[76] In the context of this religious anxiety arose the emphasis on "intense worldly activity" as the most suitable means of "counteracting feelings of religious anxiety,"[77] and the surest sign of salvation. And in Calvinism, this worldly activity took the form of ascetic, systematic self-control. Finally, Weber found in the emphasis on the methodical organization of life the crucial link to the sober rationalism of the capitalist, so essential for the efficient and profitable conduct of this enterprise.

The link between the doctrine of predestination and a particular economic ethic, then, was built on a series of special psychological generalizations.[78] Weber at least implicitly recognized the special importance of these assumptions when, in a footnote, he attempted to reject a set of alternative assumptions. He acknowledged that "[fatalism] is, of course, the only logical consequence of predestination." On the face of it this acknowledgment was embarrassing for Weber's favored interpretation, since fatalism implies the opposite of activist mastery. But, Weber insisted, "on account of the idea of proof the psychological result was precisely the opposite [of fatalism]." That is to say, the elected "are, on account of their election, proof against fatalism." Their practical interests, he argued, "cut off the fatalistic consequences of logic."[79]

[74] Weber, *The Protestant Ethic,* pp. 103–4.

[75] Ibid., p. 104. Weber adduced various arguments why this should be so. For example, "No one could help him"—no priest, no sacraments, no church, and even no God. He also cited one observation by another author on the "solitary heart" of the Puritan. Ibid., fn., p. 221.

[76] Ibid., p. 110.

[77] Ibid., p. 112.

[78] Weber's effort to demonstrate the lesser potency of other branches of Christianity to develop the ethic of ascetic mastery also rests, in part, on psychological arguments. In Catholicism, for example, "[the] psychological effect of the confessional was everywhere to relieve the individual of responsibility for his own conduct, that is why it was sought, and that weakened the rigorous consistency of the demands of asceticism." Ibid., fn., p. 250.

[79] Ibid., fn., p. 232.

In his comparative analyses of religious beliefs, Weber also leaned on psychological "first principles"; this is vividly seen in his forceful statement of the "problem of theodicy." While not every religion is based on the idea of a transcendental god, Weber noted that "the legitimation of every distinctively ethical prophecy has always required the notion of a god characterized by attributes that set him sublimely above the world, and has normally been based on the rationalization of the god-idea along such lines."[80] He noted, further, that this notion of sublime god is inevitably accompanied by a psychological tension: "how the extraordinary power of such a god may be reconciled with the imperfection of the world that he has created and rules over."[81] This is the problem of theodicy. In one way or another, "this problem belongs everywhere among the factors determining religious evolution and the need for salvation."[82] In fact, the mode of solution of the problem—that is to say, the conception of sin and the mode of salvation—constituted one of the central comparative dimensions for the analysis of religious phenomena. On the basis of this dimension Weber analyzed a number of major solutions—a line of analysis that led him to conclude that the decisive contrast between Oriental and Occidental religion was that between the mystical and the ascetic solutions to the problems of theodicy and salvation, solutions which had very different implications for the tendency to rationalize the conduct of life.[83]

Most of Weber's comparative explanation, then, involves the construction of an ideal type (or a battery of ideal types) with a certain "autonomous logic," which "programs" action in some direction, and creates tensions or "issues" for actors engaged in that type of action. For example, in the patrimonial state—an ideal type involving the development of a sizeable officialdom, but one which remains tied to the leader by essentially traditional bonds—one of the tendencies Weber identified was the disintegration of the state through the appropriation of offices by subordinates: "The ruler endeavors to safeguard the integrity of his domination in various ways and to protect it against the appropriation of offices by the officials and their heirs as well as against other means by which officials can gain independent powers."[84] Using this issue as a comparative yardstick, Weber turned to analyze historical trends in a variety of specific cases—in ancient Egypt, in the Chinese Empire, in various decentralized cases, in the British case, and so on. In each case he concentrated on the issue of the means employed by the ruler to counter the tendencies toward appropriation, but, for each case, he brought other factors to bear—the size

[80] Weber, *Economy and Society*, 2:518.
[81] Ibid., 2:519.
[82] Ibid.
[83] Ibid., 2:541–56.
[84] Ibid., 3:1042.

of the country, the role of the army, the presence or absence of *honoratiores,* the power-balance among significant groups, and the like—that led to diverse resolutions of the issue of preservation or disintegration of the central power.[85] The different historical outcomes themselves become subtypes of patrimonial officialdom. For Weber, in fact, the creation of subtypes is closely related to his comparative historical explanations. What appear to be comparative description and classification of subtypes are actually comparative historical explanations of the course of development of an ideal type with respect to certain tensions arising from its autonomous logic.[86]

A final illustration of an explanatory model: the rise of rational bourgeois capitalism

I could well multiply examples of Weber's mode of explanation with other historical models: Caesero-papism and hierocracy,[87] subtypes of traditional authority,[88] and the transitions among various ideal types of productive arrangements as the West moved toward modern industrial capitalism.[89] Such a multiplication would now be tedious, however, since the major features of Weber's explanations have already been revealed. I shall, however, dwell briefly on Weber's most famous line of analysis—the origins of rational bourgeois capitalism in the West. More than others, this line of analysis reveals how he treated the *structure* of determinants of historical processes.

At the outset I mention two points on which Weber has been frequently misrepresented. First, his theory is in no sense monocausal. Western rational bourgeois capitalism arose from a unique combination of a variety of conditions, of which the religious ethic was only one; his summary statement in *General Economic History* gives evidence enough for this:

> If [rational bourgeois capitalism] took place only in the occident the reason is to be found in the special features of its general cultural evolution which are peculiar to it. Only the occident knows the state in the modern sense, with a professional administration, specialized officialdom, and law based

[85] Ibid., 3:1044–69.

[86] For a similar characterization of Weber's explanatory strategies—which Roth calls the "blueprint" and "battery" approaches—see Guenther Roth, "Max Weber's Comparative Approach and Historical Typology," in Ivan Vallier, ed., *Comparative Methods in Sociology: Essays on Trends and Applications* (Berkeley and Los Angeles: University of California Press, 1971), pp. 91–92.

[87] Weber, *Economy and Society,* vol. 3, ch. 15.

[88] Ibid., 1:226–41, 3:1006–1110.

[89] Weber, *General Economic History,* chs. 8–13.

on the concept of citizenship. Beginnings of this institution in antiquity and the orient were never able to develop. Only the occident knows rational law, made by jurists and rationally interpreted and applied, and only in the occident is found the concept of citizenship . . . because only in the occident again are there cities in the specific sense. Furthermore, only the occident possesses science in the present-day sense of the word. Theology, philosophy, reflection on the ultimate problems of life, were known to the Chinese and the Hindu, perhaps even of a depth unreached by the European; but a rational science and in connection with it a rational technology remained unknown to those civilizations. Finally, western civilization is further distinguished from every other by the presence of men with a rational ethic for the conduct of life. Magic and religion are found everywhere; but a religious basis for the ordering of life which consistently followed out must lead to explicit rationalism is again peculiar to western civilization alone.[90]

Furthermore, the factors that inhibited similar economic developments in other societies were not limited to religious ones. While Weber stressed religious obstacles to economic development of Indian and Chinese societies, he also explored the implications of Indian caste and clan organization for the recruitment of labor, credit, and migration[91] and, in China, the implications of limited opportunities for trade, the fetters of kinship on the economy, and the lack of "a formally guaranteed law, a rational administration and judiciary."[92]

Second, Weber was not solely preoccupied with the Western rationalism, but developed independent models for socio-historical change in non-Western societies. He developed and applied a model of Indian asceticism, which he characterized as "the most rationally developed in the world."[93] He developed a model for the rationalization of patrimonial bureaucracy in China, also an extreme development in that direction.[94] Yet these and other forms of rationalism were based on different premises than that of the Occident, and, as such, constituted different "gyroscopes" that pointed the several societies in different directions of social evolution.[95]

In his comparative analysis of the rise of rational bourgeois capitalism, Weber assigned different causal status to many factors he considered relevant to any explanation. He regarded some factors, such as the accumulation of wealth generated by foreign trade, as "unimportant," largely

[90] Ibid., pp. 313–14.
[91] Weber, *The Religion of India*, pp. 52–53; 102–6; 111–17.
[92] Weber, *The Religion of China*, ch. 4.
[93] Weber, *The Religion of India*, pp. 148–49.
[94] Weber, *The Religion of China*, ch. 6.
[95] Weber, *The Protestant Ethic*, p. 26.

because it did little to further any reorganization of labor, but rested, instead, mainly on the principle of simple exploitation.[96] He considered other factors as facilitative and perhaps even necessary but not as decisive or sufficient conditions—factors such as the growth of population, the increase in the supply of precious metals, and the economic pressure of military requirements. He rejected these as conditions sufficient for economic development largely on comparative grounds—such conditions had been found in other countries in perhaps even more developed form than in the West, yet these countries did not experience the economic development typical in the West. Thus, he pointed to classical India's considerable trade, its urban development, its number system that permitted "calculability," its rational science, its system of justice ("which could have served capitalistic purposes as easily and well as corresponding institutions in our own medieval law"), and the acquisitiveness "of all [its] strata." Yet, he concluded, "modern capitalism did not develop indigenously [in India] before or during the English rule."[97] Likewise, China experienced a "strong increase of wealth in precious metals [which] had unmistakably led to a stronger development of the money economy, especially in state finance," as well as an enormous population growth. But these and other "varied conditions which externally favored the origin of capitalism in China did not suffice to create it."[98] And the Chinese, he argued, were if anything more acquisitive and materialistic than Westerners, but these characteristics did not foster the development of rational capitalistic forms.[99]

Weber made the same point in another way by pointing to obstacles to development that were apparently more salient in the West than elsewhere in order to demonstrate the ultimate indecisiveness of such obstacles:

> Many of the circumstances which could or had to hinder capitalism in China similarly existed in the Occident and assumed definite shape in the period of modern capitalism. Thus, there were the patrimonial traits of occidental rulers, their bureaucracy, and the fact that the money economy was unsettled and undeveloped. The money economy of Ptolemaic Egypt was carried through much more thoroughly than it was in fifteenth or sixteenth century Europe. Circumstances which are usually considered to have been obstacles to capitalist development in the Occident had not existed for thousands of years in China. Such circumstances as the fetters of feudalism, landlordism and, in part also, the guild system were lacking there. Besides, a considerable part of the various trade-restricting monopolies which were characteristic of the Occident did not apparently exist in China. Also, in the past,

[96] Weber, *General Economic History*, p. 300.
[97] Weber, *The Religion of India*, p. 4.
[98] Weber, *The Religion of China*, pp. 12, 248.
[99] Ibid., p. 242.

China knew time and again the political conditions arising out of preparation for war and warfare between competing states.[100]

To point out that certain factors do not constitute sufficient conditions is valuable in discrediting explanations that rely solely or even predominantly on them, but it has limits as a strategy for constructing models. Even if a certain factor—such as extensive internal trade or a monetary system—is positively associated with cases of *non*-development of capitalism, this does not prove that it is not a *necessary* condition for the development of capitalism. In fact, Weber regarded a monetary system with a high degree of formal rationality as a condition "necessary for obtaining a maximum of formal rationality of capital accounting in production enterprises."[101] It became operative as a condition, however, only *in combination with* other necessary and facilitative conditions. Weber's line of reasoning thus established the non-sufficiency but not the non-necessity of such factors.

A more determinate account of the rise of rational bourgeois capitalism would require a more precise delineation of the causal status of the various factors under consideration. Weber did make certain attempts to discriminate among types of causes. He said, for example, that "[in] the last resort the factor which produced capitalism is the rational permanent enterprise, rational accounting, rational technology and rational law, but again not these alone." He listed as "necessary complementary factors . . . the rational spirit, the rationalization of the conduct of life in general, and a rationalistic economic ethic."[102] Weber regarded these as unequivocally necessary because they were unique to the West. He also mentioned certain "favorable" conditions such as the availability of coastal trade, military requirements, and luxury demand.[103] Whether or not these were "necessary" or merely "facilitative" is not always clear from his formulations. Clearly *some* level of demand for products was necessary, but presumably it did not have to take the form it did in the West. Some conditions, furthermore, such as an independent judiciary, were essential for the development of a rational system of law[104]—itself a necessary condition for rational bourgeois capitalism—but would not themselves be regarded as a direct, necessary condition for the rise of capitalism.

Given Weber's theoretical caution and his appreciation of the complexities of historical causation, it is not surprising that he did not press any

[100] Ibid., p. 249.
[101] Weber, *Economy and Society,* 1:161–62, 166–211.
[102] Weber, *General Economic History,* p. 354.
[103] Ibid.
[104] Weber, *The Religion of China,* pp. 102–3.

further than he did to define a fixed causal status and systematic organization of factors. But to make his model of the rise of rational bourgeois capitalism more adequate would require further distinction among and clarification of (a) sufficient, (b) necessary, (c) facilitative, and (d) irrelevant conditions. It would further require a statement of the *context*— that is to say, the presence or absence of other conditions—in which any given condition assumed its assigned causal status. For example, the presence of an extensive market may be non-operative unless combined with other conditions, in which case it becomes a necessary condition for rational economic development. These specifications would, in a word, lend greater *structure* to the model than it has in the form he presented it.

One feature of Weber's formulations of the model for the development of rational bourgeois capitalism, however, suggests an ambiguity with respect to the degree of structure possessed by the various facilitating conditions. On the one hand, his account of the various factors that were critical "in the last resort" for capitalism traced them to the most diverse historical origins, many of which were remote from religious developments. For the development of the rational state, for example, Weber traced the convergence of different strands of Roman law, English judicial history, and other legal traditions. The most salient contribution of Roman law, in particular, was "formal juristic thinking."[105] In another formulation, however, he interpreted *both* the development of capitalism *and* the development of a rational state and rational legal system—as well as developments in science, historical scholarship, art and music, and bureaucratic organization—as manifestations of a pervasive tendency toward rationalization in the modern West.[106] Weber was above all concerned with the "specific and peculiar rationalism of Western culture" which took directions different from the rationalization of other societies—for example, in the direction of mysticism—and as factors in this development he mentioned economic conditions, rational technical knowledge and law, and the "disposition of men to adopt certain types of practical rational conduct."[107] While Weber pressed this line of reasoning no further, it suggests two types of possibilities that are alternatives to the procedure of "enumerating causal conditions" usually employed in Weber's work: (a) the possibility that the peculiar emphasis on rational conduct developed in the Reformation was a *general* emphasis, and affected many spheres of life—economic, legal, political—in a like manner; and (b) the possibility that both the methodical rationalism of certain branches of Protestant religion and the develop-

[105] Weber, *General Economic History*, p. 342.
[106] Weber, *The Protestant Ethic*, pp. 13–17.
[107] Ibid., p. 26.

ment of a rational attitude in numerous other spheres of life were manifestations of a more general change in cultural values.[108]

Weber's Comparative Methods

The essence of Weber's comparative strategy has already been bared: the models of behavior and social process built into the abstracted ideal types should be brought to bear on historical data by tracing the vicissitudes of relevant data that result from the interplay among the tendencies built into the models and the intrusion of additional historical factors. In addition, Weber was concerned with the criteria for the adequate demonstration of hypotheses.[109] In this final section of chapter five I shall analyze his strategies of comparative analysis.

A fundamental contrast with Durkheim

Recall that Durkheim rejected Mill's principle that a given event may have different causes, and embraced the opposing principle that an effect always has a single, corresponding cause. Furthermore, Durkheim rejected Mill's methods of residues, agreement, and difference, largely on the grounds that in sociology the conditions for applying them cannot be met —that is to say, in natural historical settings the suspected conditions cannot be controlled. Under such a limitation, he opted for the method of concomitant variations, or correlation.[110] The power he attributed to this method, moreover, rested in part on his assumption that a single cause produces a single effect. Recall also that Durkheim relied heavily on the method of concomitant variation in his own comparative empirical research.

[108] See R. H. Tawney's phrase in "Introduction" to *The Protestant Ethic and the Spirit of Capitalism:* "Religious beliefs and social institutions as different expressions of a common psychological attitude. . . ." P. 5. See also his observation that ". . . the change of opinion on economic ethics ascribed to Calvinism was by no means confined to it, but was part of a general intellectual movement, which was reflected in the outlook of Catholic, as well as Protestant, writers." P. 9.

[109] As we saw, however, he did not develop a *formal* methodology for the generation of inferences about comparative data.

[110] See pp. 62–63. Mill himself recommended the use of the method of concomitant variation under exactly those circumstances. He said it was particularly relevant in studying "Permanent Causes, or indestructible natural agents, which it is impossible either to exclude or to isolate; which we can neither hinder from being present, nor contrive that they shall be present alone." John Stuart Mill, *A System of Logic, Ratiocinative and Inductive,* 9th ed. (London: Longmans, Green, Reader, and Dyer, 1875), 1:460.

Everything we have observed about Weber's view of historical causation suggests an approach foreign to that of Durkheim. Far from accepting the possibility of discovering laws arising from the association among phenomena, Weber regarded historical situations as always produced by a complex and unique constellation of forces.[111] Furthermore, given Weber's view, it is possible, even probable, that different sets of causes give rise to the same effect. To take only one example, Weber analyzed the premium on worldly asceticism alternatively as (a) a product of the unique Calvinist preoccupation with the doctrine of predestination, (b) a product of the doctrine of the Baptists (who rejected predestination), and (c) a product of the "Church organization" among some groups who differed doctrinally from the Calvinists.[112] He attributed the pervasiveness of the capitalist spirit in its early stages to the religious force of worldly asceticism, and in later times to the established institutional structure and people's needs to adapt to this structure.[113]

Such a view of historical causation raises serious doubts about the utility of the method of concomitant variation as a basis for historical inference. Indeed, as we have seen, to search for positive correlation between the degree of development of a merchant class (or any of several other suspected "factors") with the degree of development of capitalism would yield a relatively low order of correlation, because that condition can be demonstrated to exist in developed form in societies that never witnessed the rise of capitalism, and is at its strongest only a necessary condition for its rise. Those factors held to be decisive "in the last resort" would yield higher correlations with capitalist development, but even these assume significance only in combination with other conditions.

It is not surprising, then, that Weber relied little on the method of concomitant variation—though he did in some instances, to be mentioned later. Moreover, Weber adopted a method of investigation identified by Mill as especially appropriate to situations when "the agency by which we can produce [a] phenomenon is not that of one single antecedent, but *a combination of antecedents,* which we have no power of separating from each other, and exhibiting apart."[114] Mill called this the "indirect method of difference," or the "joint method of agreement and difference." It consists of a twofold application of the method of agreement, as follows: A

[111] Durkheim also acknowledged the existence of idiosyncratic causes and multiple levels of determination, but insisted on the emergence of definite laws at the social level.

[112] Weber, *The Protestant Ethic,* pp. 99–122, 128, 148–49.

[113] Ibid., pp. 72, 181.

[114] Mill, *A System of Logic,* p. 456. Emphasis added.

number of instances having a common effect are also found to share in the same cause (first application); a second number of instances lacking the common effect are also found to lack the cause (second application); the proofs for each application should be established independently from one another. If the two applications yield consistent results, a presumption in favor of the suspected cause is established.[115]

The line of argument adopted by Weber in his comparative studies of religion and capitalism corresponds precisely to the logic of the indirect method of difference, though I found no evidence in Weber's work that he borrowed self-consciously from Mill's logic of inquiry. As we have seen, Weber singled out certain crucial features—rational law, a certain economic ethic, and so on—and argued that these were *unique* to the countries that developed capitalism, and *lacking* in those societies that had not experienced that development. Mill had admonished, however, that such a demonstration lacks power, because the investigator cannot be "quite sure either that the instances affirmative of [the effect] agree in no antecedent whatever but [the cause], or that the instances negative of [the effect] agree in nothing but the negation of [the cause]."[116] As if aware of this admonition, Weber also undertook to note those features which capitalistic (positive) and non-capitalistic (negative) societies *shared* in varying degree, thus attempting to reduce the number of causal factors in which the two sets of cases might fail to agree.

Weber's comparative study of the rationalization of religious belief systems reveals the same procedure. Most of his analysis was grounded in the rich historical detail of the world's major religions, but on one occasion he ventured a general characterization of the nature of religious rationalization:

> To judge the level of rationalization a religion represents we may use two primary yardsticks which are in many ways interrelated. One is the degree to which the religion has divested itself of magic; the other is the degree to which it has systematically unified the relation between God and the world and therewith its own ethical relationship to the world.[117]

On these two yardsticks—each of which contained, in the concrete, several subdimensions—Weber painstakingly compared and contrasted the great religions of the world. Calvinism represented an extreme on both counts, considering "all magic as devilish," developing an extreme doctrine of

115 Ibid., pp. 457–58.
116 Ibid., p. 458.
117 Weber, *The Religion of China*, p. 226.

direct responsibility of man to God, and devising a highly rational and methodical mode of conduct.[118] Judaism shared many characteristics with Calvinism, particularly the aversion to magic and the rationalization of conduct, but was less ascetic in character, and, most decisively distinguishing, it lacked "an integrated relationship to the world from the point of view of the individual's conviction of salvation."[119] Catholicism stressed rationalization only along certain lines—for example, only the clergy is to follow a "methodical ascetic way of life oriented toward a unified goal"—in addition, through confession and its emphasis on the church itself as an agent of salvation, "the church inevitably weakens the believer's motivation for living his worldly and occupational life methodically and exclusively on his own responsibility."[120] Calvinism contrasted with Confucionism on both measures:

> Both [Confucian and Puritan] ethics had their irrational anchorages, the one in magic, the other in the ultimately inscrutable resolves of a supra-mundane God. But from magic there followed the inviolability of tradition as the proven magical means and ultimately all bequeathed forms of life-conduct were unchangeable if the wrath of the spirits were to be avoided. From the relation between the supra-mundane God and the creaturely wicked, ethically irrational world there resulted, however, the absolute un-holiness of tradition and the truly endless task of ethically and rationally subduing and mastering the given world, i.e., rational, objective "progress." Here, the task of the rational transformation of the world stood opposed to the Confucian adjustment to the world. Confucianism demanded constant and vigilant self-control in order to maintain the dignity of the universally accomplished man of the world; Puritan ethics demanded this self-control in order methodically to concentrate man's attitudes on God's will.[121]

Puritanism might share *some* of its ingredients—asceticism (with certain varieties of Indian religion), economic success as a sign of good conduct (with Judaism), and so on. But it was not these "variables," but rather their *combination* with the unique doctrinal differences of religion that made the decisive comparative difference. Following Weber, then, the comparative investigator would not search for correlations (concomitant variations) among religious variables—or between religious and other variables—for, given Weber's substantive and methodological perspective, these correlations would necessarily be modest. Rather he would search

---

[118] Ibid., p. 227; Weber, *Economy and Society*, 3:1198–1200.
[119] Weber, *Economy and Society*, 2:615–23; Weber, *Ancient Judaism*, chs. 15, 16.
[120] Weber, *Economy and Society*, 3:1191.
[121] Weber, *The Religion of China*, p. 240.

for distinctive combinations of variables to explain the crucial comparative differences among religious systems.[122]

Such is the crucial and overriding methodological difference between Durkheim and Weber, a difference which accounts in large part for the different design of their comparative studies, their reliance on different kinds and measures of association, and the different kinds of results they obtained.[123] This methodological difference, moreover, is ultimately traceable to the differences in their conceptions of the scientific mission of sociology, the nature of society and of "social facts," and the nature of social causality.

Other methodological strategies

Elsewhere in his work, Weber supplemented his primary comparative strategy with a variety of ancillary methods that resemble those employed by Durkheim in many respects.

Concomitant variation, the method of difference, and the problem of third causes. In beginning the series of essays that comprise *The Protestant Ethic and the Spirit of Capitalism*, Weber noted several correlations (concomitant variations) between religious affiliation and various economic indices. Protestants, as contrasted with Catholics, are overwhelmingly represented among "business leaders and owners of capital, as well as the higher grades of skilled labour, and even more [among] the higher technically and commercially trained personnel of modern enterprises."[124] Given Weber's main purpose in those essays, this statistic was of great interest, and was consistent with the proposition that motivation bred by religious commitment was of causal significance for patterns of economic behavior.

Yet Weber recognized immediately that that causal significance was not evident from the association alone. Accordingly, he undertook a number of inquiries designed to bolster support for his preferred interpretation.

[122] Herbert Costner in personal correspondence has pointed out that Weber's emphasis on the combination of causal factors can be conceived of as an interaction effect. Regarded as such, Weber's methodological emphasis would not be hostile to the method of concomitant variation but rather to a special variant of that method— less simple than the term "concomitant variation" ordinarily connotes but still entailing concomitant variation of factors.

[123] Other differences in their comparative findings, of course, can be traced to their choice of different substantive dimensions—for example, Durkheim giving such substantive centrality to integrative dimensions, Weber to dimensions such as hierarchical relations, "interests," and religious belief-systems.

[124] Weber, *The Protestant Ethic*, p. 35.

Most of these involved an attempt to hold constant or otherwise neutralize some other possible explanatory factor, and thereby demonstrate that the only critical difference among groups with different occupational fortunes was the religious one. This procedure, we have seen, involves an attempt to approximate Mill's method of difference.

In conducting these further inquiries, Weber envisioned the possibility that the differences in wealth might be explained in terms of inherited wealth and educational advantages among Protestants, rather than any particular motivational factor. To counter this possibility, he turned to "certain other phenomena" which could not be explained in the same way. In certain European localities a higher percentage of Protestants than Catholics receive a higher education; that could be accounted for by differences in inherited wealth. But among those students who complete their course of studies—which would tend to neutralize differences in advantages due to inherited wealth, Weber implied—Catholics study technical, industrial, and commercial subjects less. Also, among workers in the same crafts—and presumably of similar economic circumstance—Protestants more than Catholics tend to be attracted to the factories "to fill the upper ranks of skilled labour and administrative positions."[125] In this operation Weber was attempting to hold inheritance or advantage constant, and demonstrate that correlations between religion and economic behavior persist. Similarly, he attempted to rule out the possibility that minority status accounts for the differences by pointing out that in Germany, where Catholics were in a minority, they showed no evidence of being "driven with peculiar force into economic activity."[126] Even granting the causal importance to religious affiliation, Weber attempted to rule out the possibility that the religious impulse sprang from materialist motives, by pointing to the piety and religiosity of many of the Protestant sects.[127] His skepticism of materialistic explanations of the spirit of capitalism, his argument that laborers are less responsive to material incentives than to a "calling," his argument that the availability of sums of capital was less important than "the development of the spirit of capitalism"[128]—complete the list of "eliminated factors." And while Weber's onslaught on these other possibilities was less painstaking and thorough than Durkheim's rejection of alternative explanations for suicide rates, their objectives were identical, and their principal weapon—to approximate the method of difference—was the same.

[125] Ibid., pp. 38–39.
[126] Ibid., pp. 39–40.
[127] Ibid., pp. 40–45.
[128] Ibid., pp. 55, 61–62, 68.

In one respect, however, Weber was less driven to reject "third factors" than was Durkheim, because of his commitment to the principle that the same effect may emanate from different causes. We have seen that Weber was perfectly comfortable in explaining an attitude of worldly asceticism as emanating here from a preoccupation with predestination, there from another doctrine, and elsewhere from social-organizational factors. Similarly, the capitalist spirit could have diverse historical origins.[129] Weber maintained that his mission was more modest than generating laws explaining the rise of capitalism. "The origin [of the capitalist spirit]," he remarked, "is what really needs explanation,"[130] and by this he meant the historically specific origins in the 16th and 17th centuries. Weber's handling of apparent "exceptions" as simply due to other historical combinations of circumstances was, however, inadmissible for Durkheim, who at the theoretical level remained committed to the notion that specific causes have specific effects; Durkheim would have had to regard apparent exceptions as possible contradictions of his preferred explanation, and he would have dealt with them more aggressively. Once again, the fact that Weber was theoretically more modest accounts in part for differences in what kinds of data he considered either relevant or embarrassing, and the kind of strategy he adopted in relation to these data.

The "imaginary experiment," and reliance on "what is generally known." Weber gave a place in historical investigation to the imaginary experiment as a means—albeit uncertain—of generating knowledge, and on occasion he utilized such a method in his own work. For example, in his discussion of direct democracy as typified by the New England town meeting, he ventured that "[wherever] it exists, direct democratic administration is unstable."[131] He provided no data for this generalization (though no doubt he had some historical cases in mind), but rather, reasoned why it should be so. When economic differentiation arises, he argued, administration falls into the hands of the wealthy, because they have the time and income to carry on the administrative functions. The inevitable transition is toward a "rule by notables."[132] In other cases he applied the mental experiment to quite specific historical situations. Had it not been for the occurrence of World War I, the peasantry, dispossessed as a result of Stolypin's agrarian reform, "would have furnished a new support and 'cudgel guard' for czarism."[133] In both examples Weber's judgments rested on a number of propositions about how people change their behavior and

[129] Ibid., fn. p. 188.
[130] Ibid., p. 55.
[131] Weber, *Economy and Society,* 3:949.
[132] Ibid., 3:949–50.
[133] Weber, *General Economic History,* p. 19.

attitudes in response to changes in economic circumstances. He advanced no direct evidence for these propositions—and hence they can be challenged as weak links in the argument—but nonetheless they are necessary pillars in constructing the explanation or prediction ventured. These propositions occupy the same explanatory status as the intervening psychological variables that lend meaning to Weber's accounts in his sociology of religion. In Weber's and Durkheim's sociology alike, then, knowledge that they were *explicitly* attempting to establish rested on a substructure of additional assumptions and generalizations that bolstered that knowledge. Later I shall generalize this point for comparative sociology as a whole.

Analogy. In one sense the whole of Weber's comparative work rests on analogy, since to assign concrete historical events or situations to a common "type" involves a historical judgment that these events or situations are similar to one another.[134] To take only one of hundreds of possible illustrations, to group the Assyrian kingdoms, certain African kingdoms, Persian satrapies, Japanese daimyos, and the Chinese Empire until modern times as instances of "decentralized patrimonial domination" involved the assertion that these cases are similar with respect to their patterns of political authority and its degrees of concentration, and different from other (presumably less centralized) cases.[135] In many instances these kinds of judgments remain implicit in Weber's comparative work; in other instances his descriptions of the cases reveal some empirical characteristics of a case that presumably led him to assign it to a given type.

Beyond this general use, Weber did not press the method of explanation by analogy. On occasion he explicitly elucidated one historical process by pointing to another analogous one:

> In very important respects German university life is being Americanized, as is German life in general. This development, I am convinced, will engulf those disciplines in which the craftsman personally owns the tools, essentially the library, as is still the case to a large extent in my own field. This development corresponds entirely to what happened to the artisan of the past and it is now fully under way.[136]

In addition, Weber pointed out parallel tendencies toward rationalization in the modern West. The general spirit of offering such analogies was,

[134] See pp. 77–78, 167–74. See also Roth, "Introduction" to Weber, *Economy and Society*, 1:xliii–xliv, and Roth, "Max Weber's Comparative Approach and Historical Typology," in Vallier, ed., *Comparative Methods*, pp. 79–82.

[135] Weber, *Economy and Society*, 3:1051–52.

[136] Weber, "Science as a Vocation," in Gerth and Mills, eds., *From Max Weber*, p. 131.

however, to elucidate rather than prove, and to facilitate the development of type concepts. And finally, Weber almost entirely shunned analogies from other types of systems—especially the biological—that Durkheim frequently employed, especially in his early writings, to bolster his analyses of social facts.

A Concluding Note on Durkheim and Weber

This chapter, along with the preceding two, reveals a complex picture of comparisons and contrasts in the sociologies of two of the most outstanding representatives of comparative scholarship. The comparisons and contrasts emerge, moreover, as a product *both* of tensions between the theoretical and methodological perspectives of the two *and* of tensions that developed as each attempted to square the dictates of his respective theoretical and methodological position with the exigencies of empirical research.

The perspectives of the two differed sharply on a number of dimensions. Durkheim, rooted in a positivist tradition, envisioned the generation of scientific sociological laws on the principles of objectivity and induction he regarded as characteristic of the natural sciences; furthermore, he polemically excluded psychological and other non-sociological bases of explanation, pressing consistently for the analysis of social facts in their own right. Weber, closer to a historicist tradition, regarded social reality as unique, concrete historical configurations, and doubted the possibility of generating objectively-based general laws of sociology; rather he saw the conceptualization of laws as heuristic devices helpful in interpreting and elucidating specific historical processes. In still another way Weber rejected the natural-science model for sociology, insisting on taking the subjective meaning that individuals bring to their social situations into account in all sociological explanations.

Yet as each attempted to come to terms with the study of social reality, their perspectives converged in certain respects. In principle an inductionist, Durkheim nevertheless acknowledged the necessity for self-conscious selection, even distortion in the development of typological constructs; Weber, committed to sociology as a generalizing science, invoked the method of creating general "ideal types" which involved the same sorts of procedures on the part of the investigator. Both were aware of the limits of the experimental method in sociology, and both assigned a central place to the comparative study of societies. Despite their very different theoretical perspectives on the place of psychology in sociological explanation, they made parallel use of psychological assumptions in their construction of sociological explanations. And the methods they employed to bolster their hypotheses overlapped considerably.

At the same time, differences between the two persisted on all these counts. Durkheim was comfortable in comparing types of societies and types of general social integration; except for his general comparisons among ideal types, Weber tended to take more concrete historical clusterings of phenomena for his comparisons. Durkheim developed causal theories of society and social processes that were abstract and general; he attempted to interpret social phenomena *consistently* in terms of these theories, and was thereby forced to rely to some extent on ancillary causal factors. Weber generated his ideal types self-consciously as heuristic devices, and while some were quite general, his interpretations of historical data always self-consciously incorporated causal forces external to the models contained in his type-constructs. And finally, persistent differences between them in causal assumptions led each to adopt a favored method of establishing sociological proofs—Durkheim used the method of concomitant variation and Weber the indirect method of difference—though both employed a battery of similar ancillary methods.

6

Classification, Description, and Measurement

At this point we reach a kind of turning point. I have concluded the analysis of the strengths and weaknesses of some of those who fathered the systematic comparative analysis of societies. I shall now turn to a somewhat more formal treatment of the methodological issues of contemporary comparative research in anthropology, political science, and sociology—and to a lesser extent in economics, history, and psychology. Needless to say, much has happened in the half century since Durkheim and Weber completed their scholarly careers. Modern comparative analysis in the social sciences has taken advantage of a revolutionary increase in the quantity and quality of data, the development of dozens of research techniques unavailable to them, and the proliferation of many new interpretive models and theories. As we shall see, however, the methodological *issues* facing contemporary comparative analysis have changed much less than their data, methods, and theories.

I do not intend to be exhaustive in referring to modern works. For one thing, they are simply too numerous to cover in detail.[1] For another, the

---

[1] In their annotated bibliography relating to comparative survey analysis alone,

literature on the methodological aspects of comparative studies is very repetitive. The same methodological issues have arisen in field after field as investigators included diverse cultures and nations in the scope of their inquiry. Furthermore, those who have discussed these issues have made the same arguments repeatedly under headings such as validity, reliability, equivalence of measures and cross-cultural bias, and it would be pointless to cite these essentially identical arguments simply in the interests of comprehensive coverage. Rather, I shall undertake a selective analysis, concentrating on the most salient methodological issues that arise in the effort to analyze scientifically social systems that are evidently dissimilar from one another.

The first task is to develop a general framework in which to pinpoint these methodological issues, both as they appear in the works of the classics and in their more modern guise.

The Scientific Enterprise as an Effort to Control Variation

For any phenomenon that a social scientist might wish to explain, the number of causal conditions that affect it is, at first sight, discouragingly great. Suppose we wish to explain why individuals differ in their ability to perform a simple task in a small-group setting. In the first instance, this ability is influenced by individuals' different intelligence, training, and motivation. These three immediate factors are further conditioned by their social-class backgrounds, their ordinal positions in their families, the presence or absence of others in the same room while they are performing the task, the behavior of the person assigning them the task, and dozens of other factors. The number of conditions influencing complex social aggregates, such as changes in the divorce rate over the past century in different industrializing societies, appears even more forbidding. The initial picture, then, is one of a *multiplicity* of conditions, a *confounding* of their influences on what is to be explained (the dependent variable) and an *indeterminacy* regarding the effect of any one condition or several conditions in combina-

Rokkan and his collaborators were able to list, in 1969, some 982 references. Stein Rokkan, Sidney Verba, Jean Viet, and Elina Almasy, *Comparative Survey Analysis* (Paris-The Hague: Mouton, 1969). For a lengthy bibliography of comparative studies in sociology, see Robert M. Marsh, *Comparative Sociology* (New York: Harcourt, Brace & World, 1967), pp. 375–496. Another, more selective bibliography is that prepared by Susan Bettelheim Garfin in Ivan Vallier, ed., *Comparative Methods in Sociology: Essays on Trends and Applications* (Berkeley and Los Angeles: University of California Press, 1971), pp. 423–67.

tion. The corresponding problems facing the investigator are to *reduce* the number of conditions, to *isolate* one condition from another, and thereby to *make precise* the role of each condition, both singly and in combination with other conditions. How does the investigator deal with such problems?

The general answer is that he imposes some sort of *organization* on the conditions. One of the simplest ways of organizing conditions is seen in the distinction between independent, intervening, and dependent variables. An example will show the power of this distinction. Examining a great amount of cross-cultural material, Whiting and Child found correlations between types of child-training practices and types of beliefs concerning the genesis of disease; for example, cultures that impose strict and early weaning on children tend, in their belief systems, to attribute disease to "oral" causes such as poisoning.[2] In interpreting this association, Whiting and Child asserted that certain personality variables—such as fixations on traumatic childhood experiences, and typical defenses against the anxiety associated with these fixations—"intervene" between child training and adult beliefs. That is to say, the personality variables are dependent in relation to child-training practices, but independent in relation to adult beliefs. Speculating further, Whiting and Child argued that child-training practices are themselves dependent on a society's "maintenance systems" —"the economic, political, and social organizations of a society . . . surrounding the nourishment, sheltering, and protection of its members."[3] The several classes of variables constitute a chain of independent, intervening, and dependent variables, as follows:

| maintenance systems | $\longrightarrow$ | child-training practices | $\longrightarrow$ | personality variables | $\longrightarrow$ | projective systems |

The relationship among the variables, thus organized, is much simpler than a lengthy list of associations among every combination of variables.

The example also reveals that the distinction among independent, intervening, and dependent variables is relative, and that the status of any given variable may change. For instance, the variable "child-training practices" is dependent with respect to "maintenance systems" and "personality variables." Furthermore, while the variable "projective systems" is dependent in every respect in the example, such beliefs may be important independent variables in shaping the institutionalization of the "maintenance systems." No given variable, then, can be considered as inherently independent, intervening, or dependent.

[2] John W. M. Whiting and Irvin L. Child, *Child Training and Personality: A Cross-Cultural Study* (New Haven: Yale University Press, 1953).

[3] Ibid., p. 310.

The assignment of different causal status to different variables—and the process of building more complex explanatory models and theories by so doing—is a way of gaining *logical* control over sources of variation. It does not regard them as random, but as organized in causal networks.[4] Another way of gaining control in scientific investigation is an *empirical* one—to manipulate the empirical variation of suspected causes, and by so doing, to generate varying degrees of confidence as to their significance (or lack of significance) as causes. Various methodological commentators have stressed this kind of control as the key to scientific explanation,[5] and have pointed to the major difficulties in social-scientific analysis that stem from investigators' inability to isolate and control sources of variation.[6]

The process of gaining empirical control over sources of variation is clarified by referring to the distinction between causal conditions treated as *parameters* and causal conditions treated as *operative variables*. Parameters are conditions that are known or suspected to influence a dependent variable but, in the investigation at hand, are assumed or made not to vary. Operative variables are conditions that are known or suspected to influence the dependent variable and, in the investigation, are allowed or made to vary in order to assess this influence. By converting variables into parameters, most of the potentially operative conditions are made not to vary, so that the influence of one or a few conditions may be isolated and analyzed. As we shall see presently, all methods of scientific inquiry, and those striving to approximate it, rest on the systematic manipulation and control of parameters and variables.

Like the independent-intervening-dependent distinction, the distinction between parameters and operative variables is relative. What is treated as parameter in one investigation may become an operative variable in another. Suppose, for example, it is known that foreign trade is important in the determination of the national income of a society, but that calculation of the impact of foreign trade on the domestic economy is impossible unless certain internal relations—say, between private investment, govern-

---

[4] This facet of obtaining control—that is, theory-construction—will be one focus of analysis in chapter seven.

[5] See Oscar Lewis' comment: "The major difference between common-sense, everyday comparisons by the layman and those by the scientist, is that the latter, in their systematic study of similarities and differences, strive for a greater degree of *control* by utilizing the methods of correlation and co-variation." "Comparisons in Cultural Anthropology," in Frank W. Moore, ed., *Readings in Cross-Cultural Methodology* (New Haven: HRAF Press, 1966), p. 51.

[6] Hubert M. Blalock, Jr., "Theory Building and Causal Inferences," in Hubert M. Blalock, Jr. and Ann B. Blalock, eds., *Methodology in Social Research* (New York: McGraw-Hill, 1968), p. 157.

ment investment, and consumption—are also known. The investigator may begin by assuming that foreign trade is a parameter—that is, that it does not exist, or that it is constant—and, by thus simplifying the determinants of income, may proceed to establish national income as some function of private investment, government investment, and current consumption. Having established these relations, he may then "relax" the restricting assumption about foreign trade and "allow" it to vary, thus tracing its impact on the known relations within the economy. In this final operation he has transformed the parameter into an operative variable. In the same operation he could also have transformed domestic investment into a parameter—that is, assumed that it does not vary—in order to pinpoint the impact of foreign trade more precisely.

By continuously and systematically transforming conditions into parameters and operative variables, and by systematically combining and recombining them, scientific explanation is refined and generalized. Moreover, the several methods of scientific inquiry differ according to the ways in which conditions are converted into parameters and variables, respectively. Consider the following:

1. Situational manipulation, or control over the *creation* of data. This is the defining feature of the experimental method. In a simple, classic experiment in the natural sciences, the investigator wishes to determine the effect of temperature on the boiling point of water. To assess this effect, he must be certain that a number of other conditions—for instance, purity of the water and atmospheric pressure—are treated as parameters, that is, not allowed to vary. If he does not assure this, the precise relation between heat and the changing state of water will be "contaminated" by variations in these other conditions, and the investigator will not be able to determine the precise source of influence. If he does control for purity and atmospheric pressure, the investigator will discover the "principle" that water boils at 212° Fahrenheit at sea level. To illustrate the relativity of the distinction between parameter and operative condition, it might be added that the investigator might well have decided to treat atmospheric pressure as the operative variable and heat and purity as parameters, or purity as the operative variable and heat and pressure as parameters. In each case he would discover another principle linking an independent variable with the changing state of water. In every case the emergent principle (law, prediction) is not a claim of empirical universality, but a conditional statement of regularity, involving a number of assumptions about parametric constants within which and only within which the regularity prevails.

In this example the parameters were created by direct manipulation. In most experimentation in the social sciences it is not possible to gain such direct control over all possible conditions. Instead, the investigator resorts to randomizing conditions in various ways to gain the same objective.[7] Most often experimentation is conducted by establishing two groups—the experimental and the control—that are identical in respect to many known or suspected sources of variation, such as age, sex, intelligence, educational level, and socioeconomic background; these conditions shared by the two groups are treated as parameters—that is, as "cancelled out" in their influence on the dependent variable.[8] Then, with regard to the suspected causal condition, the experimental group is stimulated, the control group not; this condition not shared by the two groups is treated as the operative variable. The experimental method is thus a species of comparison; its distinctive feature is that the social units being compared are deliberately created by the investigator.[9]

Despite the fact that some investigators have intervened in natural situations or treated natural events as "experimental manipulations"—thus attempting to generate laboratory conditions[10]—most data in the social sciences remain "historical" in the sense that they are precipitates from the flow of social life that transpires without controlled experimentation. Furthermore, even if the investigator wishes to establish control groups, he is prevented from doing so for many variables—such as suicide and crime rates—by ethical and practical considerations. The social scientist is therefore presented with given data or with data gathered under relatively uncontrolled conditions (for example, surveys, field observations); he is then obliged to ask why these data are arrayed in a certain way and not in some other way. But the "some other way" usually cannot be concretized experimentally. At the same time, the investigator wishes to observe the

---

[7] Thus Wiggins defined the experimental method as "the experimenter's manipulation of the variation in one or more independent variables and the randomization of other independent variables, followed by the measurement of the variation in one or more dependent variables." James A. Wiggins, "Hypothesis Validity and Experimental Laboratory Methods," in Blalock and Blalock, eds., *Methodology in Social Research*, p. 392.

[8] For discussion of a variety of ways of controlling for variation due to extraneous factors, see ibid., pp. 393–96.

[9] The experiment, as described here, is designed to conform to Mill's method of difference.

[10] For comment on the status of these designs, see Matilda White Riley and Edward E. Nelson, "Research on Stability and Change in Social Systems," in Bernard Barber and Alex Inkeles, eds., *Stability and Social Change* (Boston: Little, Brown, 1971), pp. 423–24. For citation of some methodological difficulties in treating "natural experiments" as true experiments, see Hubert M. Blalock, "Causal Inferences in Natural Experiments: Some Complications in Matching Designs," *Sociometry* 30(1967):300–15.

same methodological canons that govern the experimental method.[11] Because of the character of his data, however, he must rely on one or more approximations. What are these approximations?

2. Conceptual manipulation of data *after they have been created*. This method assumes three forms—which shade into one another—according to the number of cases available for treatment and the corresponding possibility of using formal mathematical techniques.

First, the statistical method involves applying mathematical techniques to populations and to samples of events containing large numbers, in order to achieve the same transformation of potentially operative conditions into parameters as does the experimental method. An example of correcting for variation can be taken from time series analysis. Suppose we wish to trace the influences on the long-term trend of potato prices over several decades. We know that potato prices vary seasonally as well as year by year, but we do not wish to measure the seasonal variation. So we calculate the average seasonal variation for fifty years and cancel out seasonal fluctuations for each individual year by adding or subtracting the average seasonal variation from the actual prices. In this way we "correct for" seasonal fluctuations and presumably obtain a more accurate picture of uncontaminated long-term price trends. Suppose also that over the fifty-year period the economy has experienced a steady inflationary trend. To correct for this trend, we might deflate the potato price series by the rate of general price inflation. By these statistical operations we make *parameters* out of seasonal fluctuation and general inflation, and we are thereby enabled to relate trends in potato prices more precisely to other determinants of price changes. Other methods besides standardization—such as multivariate analysis, path analysis, or matching samples for common background characteristics—are among the social scientist's repertoire of statistical techniques to convert suspected sources of variation into parameters.

Second, when the number of cases does not permit statistical manipulation, the investigator can approximate it—though without the same degree of confidence—by systematic comparative illustration. This method is most often required in the comparative analysis of national units or cultures—where the sample is often small—but it may also be used in comparing regions, cities, communities, and other sub-national units. There is a tendency in the literature to refer to systematic comparative illustration

[11] As Nagel observed, "every branch of inquiry aiming at reliable general laws concerning empirical subject matter must employ a procedure that, if it is not strictly controlled experimentation, has the essential logical functions of experiment in inquiry." Ernst Nagel, *The Structure of Science* (New York: Harcourt, Brace & World, 1961), p. 452.

as *the* comparative method—in contradistinction to the experimental and statistical methods[12]—but this is erroneous, since all three methods do involve comparisons.

Despite its limitations in terms of numbers of cases, the logic of systematic comparative illustration is identical to the methods just reviewed in that it attempts to develop explanations by the systematic manipulation of parameters and operative variables. This logic was evident in the works of Tocqueville, Durkheim, and Weber. In noting that Americans and Englishmen have "their religion, their language, and partially . . . their customs" in common, Tocqueville argued that these conditions, being constant, could not be regarded as causes of the differences in the behavior of these two peoples when abroad, but that causes should be found in their different social conditions.[13] In comparing suicide rates of Protestants and Catholics in countries in which Catholics were both a majority and a minority, Durkheim was attempting to hold minority status constant. And in his comparative studies of religion in the Occident and the Orient, Weber argued, in effect, that those characteristics common to the two (for example, the development of a merchant class) should be treated as parameters, whereas those respects in which they differed should be treated as the operative variables.[14]

Third, when the number of cases is even smaller—as small as one—the method of deviant case analysis can be understood as yet another method to manipulate parameters and operative variables. This method always stands in relation to a more general statistical or comparative association that has been established. The starting point, in fact, for deviant case analysis is "the empirical fact that no statistical relationship, particularly in the social sciences, is a perfect one."[15] In deviant case analysis, the

[12] I did so myself in an earlier formulation of types of research methods. See Neil J. Smelser, "The Methodology of Comparative Analysis," in Donald P. Warwick and Samuel Osherson, eds., *Comparative Research Methods* (Englewood Cliffs, N.J.: Prentice-Hall, 1973), pp. 45–52. The present section is a revision of that classification.

[13] Alexis de Tocqueville, *Democracy in America*, Vintage Book edition (New York: Knopf and Random House, 1945), 2:180.

[14] As we observed, however, Weber's conception of causation was different from Durkheim's (and Tocqueville's, in this instance), so his manipulation of variables tended to approximate Mill's indirect method of difference, whereas the others tended to approximate the method of difference. Nonetheless, he was similarly preoccupied with conditions of similarity (parameters) and difference (operative variables).

[15] Patricia L. Kendall and Paul F. Lazarsfeld, "Problems of Survey Analysis," in Robert K. Merton and Paul F. Lazarsfeld, eds., *Continuities in Social Research: Studies in the Scope and Method of "The American Soldier"* (Glencoe, Ill.: The Free Press, 1950), p. 167.

investigator takes the instance or instances that are exceptions to the general trend and attempts to locate independent variables that set them off from it. Methodologically, the method of deviant case analysis is a crude attempt to approximate the method of difference. The investigator takes two "groups" that differ in outcome (dependent variable) and attempts to locate differences in conditions between them (independent variable). In deviant case analysis, one "group" is comprised of the deviant case itself, and the other by the majority of cases expressing the general finding. The method of deviant case analysis is also a method of "reading backwards" to approximate the experimental situation. In experimentation the independent variable is varied between experimental and control groups to produce different outcomes. In deviant case analysis the starting point is the different outcomes themselves (as between the deviant case and the majority of cases). The main difference between deviant case analysis on the one hand and the methods of statistical analysis and systematic comparative illustration on the other is that the number of deviant cases is always so small that it is difficult to know which of the many respects the deviant case differs from the majority of cases is the crucial one. For this reason, deviant case analysis is not as powerful as the other methods— despite the identity of their logic—and must be regarded more as a method of locating new variables, which can be "established" more or less firmly only by the application of more powerful research methods.

An example of the usefulness of deviant case analysis can be found in a study of cross-cultural associations by Whiting.[16] In a comparative analysis of the incidence of sorcery as a cultural explanation of the onset of disease, she hypothesized that in societies that had a delegated system of authority to mete out sanctions against murder, sorcery would not occur as an explanation of disease, whereas in societies in which murder was settled by retaliatory methods, sorcery would be widespread. Taking fifty societies as a sample, she found that the association between sorcery and the presence of a superordinate system of justice was significant in the predicted direction. Despite this strong association, it became apparent that "Africa was strikingly aberrant, all but three of the nine tribes sampled having sorcery as an important explanation for sickness and not coordinate but superordinate control." Taking the African cases as deviant, she decided to "[analyze the material] in more detail to see if some other variables could be discovered."[17] This is the essence of deviant case method. She discovered that among the Azande, justice is decided by

[16] Beatrice Blyth Whiting, *Paiute Sorcery*, Viking Fund Publications in Anthropology, no. 15 (New York: Viking Press, 1950).

[17] Ibid., p. 85.

oracles and chiefs, but the actual retaliation is executed by relatives of the slain party with permission of the chief. On the basis of this information Whiting "[reclassified] all tribes, distinguishing between superordinate justice and superordinate punishment," and recalculated a number of correlations on the basis of this altered conception of social control.[18] In this case the method of deviant case analysis led to the refinement of the same variable—type of social control—that was important in the original association; it could also have led to the discovery of new variables.

3. Manipulation of suspected sources of variation *by simplified assumptions regarding non-existent data or by appeal to "general knowledge."* This method commonly assumes two forms. First, the method of heuristic assumption is a crude but widely employed method of transforming potentially operative variables into parameters. The most familiar version of this method is the famous explanatory strategy of *ceteris paribus*—"other things being equal." Economists explicitly assume, for instance, that for many purposes of analysis various noneconomic factors—especially institutions and tastes—are "given," that is, to be treated as parameters. Economists have also traditionally assumed some version of the postulate of economic rationality: if an individual is presented with a situation of choice in an economic setting, he will behave so as to maximize his economic position. By extensive use of this method, economic analysts have been able to reduce the number of operative variables and to create relatively simple and elegant models of economic variables; moreover, its use accounts in part for the degree of theoretical sophistication of economics.

Outside economics the method of heuristic assumption is as widely but not normally as explicitly employed. Weber explicitly built it into his conception of the ideal type, which he presented as a series of simplified and hypothetical assumptions regarding the motivation and behavior of individual actors in typical situations. We saw, furthermore, that the analyses of Tocqueville, Durkheim, and Weber rested on largely unexamined but fixed psychological assumptions linking sociocultural conditions with individuals' beliefs and behavior. We also observed that Durkheim attempted to "randomize"—that is, convert to a parameter—psychological causes of suicide by asserting that they have no effect on the social suicide rate. Even in experimental settings the method of heuristic assumption is employed. In a small-group setting, in which the influence of leadership structures on morale is being experimentally studied, the investigator makes use of a number of important and sometimes problematic heuristic assumptions—that the subjects speak the same language, that they share many cultural assumptions, that they are more or less uniformly

[18] Ibid., pp. 86ff.

motivated to participate in the experiment, and so on. All these variables, if treated as operative, would influence the outcome of the experiment, but they are often implicitly assumed to be parametric. To choose yet another example, studies of voting behavior often rest on the assumption that such behavior takes place within an unchanging constitutional, legal, and electoral framework. This framework, if varied, would influence the rates and direction of voting.

Second, the "imaginary experiment," which I considered in examining Weber's comparative work, may be regarded as among the crudest of all efforts to approximate the method of difference by manipulating suspected sources of variation. In this case one "group" is the historical situation actually being analyzed; the other "group" is the imaginary situation—the "experiment"—which resembles the historical situation in all respects except that circumstance imagined to be different by the investigator. This salient difference is then traced to a difference in outcome—one that was observed in the historical situation and the other imagined by the investigator. In this process, the investigator converts (in the imagination) a causal variable that had only one value in a particular historical situation into an operative variable. As Weber indicated, moreover, this particular type of experiment rests on general knowledge of historical processes, and is only as valid as that knowledge.

Every method of gaining scientific knowledge, then, has in common the effort to control suspected sources of variation among causal conditions by means of transforming operative variables into parameters and vice versa.[19] The several methods vary considerably in explanatory power, however, for several different reasons: (a) They vary according to the degree to which the investigator actually exercises empirical control. Experimentation is the most nearly certain, since the investigator himself directs the course of the unfolding events, presumably in accord with the theoretical expectations guiding the research.[20] Statistical manipulation depends on a certain level of mathematical guarantee that the variation has been controlled. The other types of manipulation of data after they have been created— systematic comparative illustration and deviant case analysis—lack such a guarantee. And the methods of heuristic assumption and imaginary experiment—resting on highly variable levels of empirical knowledge and presupposition—often accomplish by "making believe" what the other

[19] Wold defined causation as "the relation between stimulus and response in controlled experiments, real or fictitious." Herman O. A. Wold, "On the Definition and Meaning of Causal Concepts," in Herman O. A. Wold, ed., *Model Building in the Human Sciences* (Monaco: Editions "Sciences Humaines," 1964), p. 270.

[20] The experimenter's own behavior, of course, may constitute a contaminating source of variation.

methods accomplish by situational and formal conceptual manipulation of data. (b) The various methods may be ranked in the same way in that, as greater empirical control is established, it is easier to record that control by some sort of measurement. (c) Finally, and also by the same logic, the methods employing situational controls have a greater capacity to control the variable of time (that is, before-after relations among variables); the methods manipulating existing data a lesser capacity;[21] and the largely hypothetical methods almost none at all.

Any given piece of scientific research employs a variety—though not necessarily all—of the various methods of research, and can be assessed according to the strengths and weaknesses of the pattern of methods of gaining control that have been employed. Furthermore, by referring to the type and degree of control attained, it is possible to elucidate *all* the methodological issues that arise in the comparative analysis of diverse social units, despite the fact that these issues appear in diverse and particularized forms. To raise and review these issues from the standpoint of the effort to control sources of variation is the agenda for this chapter and the next.

The Research Situation in Comparative
Analysis: Units, Concepts, Indicators,
and the Investigator

An underlying assumption of this book is that the comparative analysis of dissimilar social units poses no unique methodological obstacles—the methodological problems are those of all social-scientific investigation. Because of its focus on *dissimilar* units, however, some of these problems are posed in especially complicated and intractable fashion. To identify these special aspects, let me begin by characterizing a simple research situation, then elaborating it to cover the salient features of the comparative analysis of dissimilar units.

The model of the simple research situation I choose is one presented by Costner.[22] He represented the research situation as a one-way causal rela-

---

[21] For a review of efforts to assess temporal priority by nonexperimental methods, see Riley and Nelson, "Research on Stability and Change in Social Systems," in Barber and Inkeles, eds., *Stability and Social Change*, pp. 412–42.

[22] Herbert L. Costner, "Theory, Deduction, and Rules of Correspondence," *American Journal of Sociology* 75(1969–70):245–63. Costner's work builds on that of Blalock and others who have proposed that social research be constructed in two languages—a theoretical language and an operational language—which are themselves related by an auxiliary theory expressing rules of correspondence. See Hubert

FIG. 6–1   A Simple Research Situation

tion between two abstract variables, X and Y, as shown in figure 6-1; for purposes of illustration these variables could be a deficit in social regulation (X) and anomic suicide (Y), respectively.   In addition, each abstract variable is represented by an empirical indicator, x and y; these might be periods of business crisis and the recorded rates of suicide during these periods, respectively.[23]   For purposes of illustration, Costner assumed that the "theory" linking variables with indicators is a simple one: "the indicators are 'reflectors' of the abstract variables, that is, that a change in the abstract variable will lead to a change in its own indicator."[24]   This relationship is shown by the arrows X $\longrightarrow$ x and Y $\longrightarrow$ y in figure 6-1.   (Additional sources of unspecified error are represented by the small diagonal arrows.)   The usual procedure in testing causal models is to calculate a correlation between the observed indicators, and consider this as the correlation between the abstract variables.[25]   But as Costner pointed

M. Blalock Jr., "The Measurement Problem: A Gap between the Languages of Theory and Research," in Hubert M. Blalock, Jr. and Ann B. Blalock, eds., *Methodology in Social Research*, pp. 5–27. For a somewhat different formulation of the same principle, see Neil J. Smelser, "The Optimum Scope of Sociology," *Essays in Sociological Explanation* (Englewood Cliffs, N.J.: Prentice-Hall, 1968), pp. 58–59. Costner also built on the methodological literature that deals with measurement error as resulting from causal processes; Paul M. Siegel and Robert W. Hodge, "A Causal Approach to the Study of Measurement Error," in Blalock and Blalock, eds., *Methodology in Social Research*, pp. 28–59.

[23] See pp. 46–47 for Durkheim's representation of variables and indicators in this way.

[24] Costner, "Theory, Deduction, and Rules of Correspondence," p. 246.

[25] Note how close this formulation is to Durkheim's assertion that "internal facts" are studied by examining "external indices."

out, this procedure assumes that the correlations between X and x and between Y and y are "[a unity] or else very high and subject only to minor
random errors."[26] If this is not the case, the correlation between X and Y
cannot be read simply as corresponding to the correlation between x and y,
for it is "contaminated" by the error linking X and x and Y and y. In particular, Costner pointed out the possibility of a *differential constant error,*
systematically built into the relationship between variable and indicator and
persisting through repeated measurement; for example, to use arrest rate
as an index of crime would exaggerate the abstract relationship between
social class and crime, because of the greater tendency of the police to
arrest persons from lower socioeconomic groups, regardless of the commis-
sion of a crime. To put the matter slightly differently, an indicator is the
product of a *causal process,* and this process may differ significantly and
systematically from the assumption that the indicator simply "reflects" the
variable.[27]

Now I should like to elaborate Costner's simplified model in two ways
that are important for the understanding of the comparative analysis of
dissimilar units. The first, not surprisingly, is the introduction of the assumption that the phenomena being studied occur in sufficiently dissimilar
social units (A and B in figure 6-2) that it cannot be assumed that the
indicators of the abstract variables are produced by the same process in
each. Or, as represented in figure 6-2, there may not be a correspondence

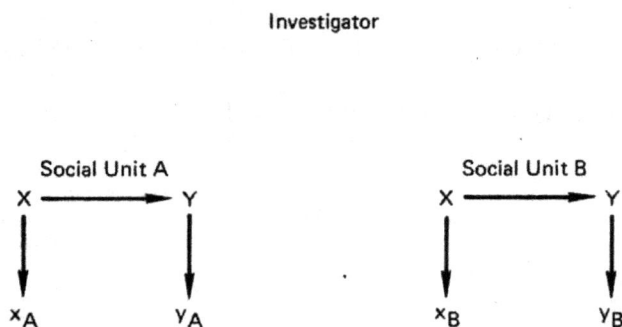

Investigator

Social Unit A

$X \longrightarrow Y$

$x_A \qquad y_A$

Social Unit B

$X \longrightarrow Y$

$x_B \qquad y_B$

FIG. 6–2   A Research Situation Involving Dissimilar Social Units

[26] Costner, "Theory, Deduction, and Rules of Correspondence," p. 247.

[27] That the choice of an indicator reveals certain assumptions, even a "theory,"
of the process by which it was produced was noted in my remarks on Weber's use of
religious documents as an indicator of a religious "spirit." See p. 122.

between $X \longrightarrow x_A$ and $X \longrightarrow x_B$ or between $Y \longrightarrow y_A$ and $Y \longrightarrow y_B$. For the moment it is not necessary to specify the precise character of the dissimilarity among units—for example, dissimilarity in cultural values, dissimilarity in level of economic development, or dissimilarity in type of political system—but only to acknowledge that there exists sufficient dissimilarity to complicate the variable-indicator relation. Needless to say, to introduce this assumption permits the possibility of more numerous and more complicated sources of unspecified error and differential constant error than the simple model presented by Costner.

The second elaboration is to introduce the investigator himself as part of the causal process that produces not only the indicators but also the other ingredients of the research model shown in figure 6-2.[28] The investigator must be regarded as an agent in identifying and selecting the appropriate social units; in identifying and selecting the general variables to be studied; and in identifying, selecting, and sometimes creating the indicators for those variables. As such he becomes a potential "operative variable" in various stages of the research process, and his causal role must be taken systematically into account in any methodological discussions.[29]

It is now possible to lay out the agenda for the remainder of this chapter. We may do so, moreover, with specific reference both to the representation of the comparative research setting in figure 6-2 and to Radcliffe-Brown's citation of the advantages of the comparative method.[30] He began with a specific example—the existence of exogamous moieties named after the eagle-hawk and the crow in a certain region in Australia. Instead of concentrating on the specific historical factors which might account for the evolution of the division of this particular region, Radcliffe-Brown adopted the comparative strategy. He turned to other societies, both in Australia and elsewhere, and discovered that the division into opposed groupings based on anomal identities was very widespread. By using this comparative strategy, Radcliffe-Brown substituted "certain general problems" demanding general explanations for "a particular problem of the kind that calls for a historical explanation." At the same time he moved in the direction of incorporating dissimilar social units into his analysis. The general problems he raised were the problem of totemism—or the association of a social group with a natural species—and the "problem of how opposition

[28] The role of the investigator in influencing the results of research is not limited to the comparative analysis of dissimilar social units, as the discussions of "experimenter bias" and "experimenter effect" in the psychological literature indicate.

[29] This formulation constitutes an explicit statement of preference for Weber's version of the role of the observer over that of Durkheim's.

[30] A. R. Radcliffe-Brown, *Method in Social Anthropology*, ed. M. N. Srinivas (Chicago: University of Chicago Press, 1958), pp. 126–27.

can be used as a mode of social integration." By using this strategy, more-over, Radcliffe-Brown was invoking certain abstract variables that could be brought back to explain the particular division between the eagle-hawk and crow moieties in Australia.

In following such a method, the investigator encounters a series of related problems, all of which fall under the general heading of "the prob-lem of comparability," which I discussed in a preliminary manner in chapter four. 1. Are the *social units* comparable with one another? In moving to societies outside the initial region in Australia, did Radcliffe-Brown select cases that were in the same general category, so that the instances of opposed groupings could be assumed to occur in a similar social context?[31] Or, more generally, is it legitimate to group highly com-plex nation-states like the United States and a hunting-and-gathering tribe in Australia together as "societies" when they appear to differ from one another in almost every respect? These questions raise the methodological issues associated with comparative *classification* and selection of appro-priate social units for comparison; these issues constitute the first item on the agenda remaining for this chapter. 2. Are the abstract *variables* ap-plicable to the dissimilar social units that have been selected for study? To follow Radcliffe-Brown's example, is it legitimate to interpret social divi-sions such as moieties as instances of the general variable of "opposition . . . used as a mode of social integration?" More generally, suppose we wish to compare the "political" aspects of two societies with different cul-tural traditions and social structures. In what sense is it appropriate to apply the word "political" to both the role of an African chieftain and that of an American legislator? The issue of choice of variables will be dis-cussed after the section on classification; under it we shall also cover many topics commonly discussed under the heading of "cross-cultural bias." 3. Are the *indicators* of the independent and dependent variables comparable from one sociocultural context to another? How can we compare groupings such as moieties with one another when their social meaning—that is to say, the causal processes by which they are produced —differ so much from society to society? Or, more generally, how can crime rates of a century ago be compared with crime rates now, given changes in recording procedures and in the social definition of crime? I shall conclude the chapter with a section on these issues, and, in so doing, shall cover the topics usually discussed under the heading of "the problem of equivalence." Throughout I shall also focus on the role of the investi-

---

[31] Recall Durkheim's admonition that meaningful comparisons can only be made among societies of the same species. See pp. 65–67.

gator, who—as an agent in selecting and classifying units, identifying variables, choosing and generating indices and imposing measures on them —constitutes an important source of variation that influences the ultimate correlations and causal relations that systematic comparative analysis strives to establish.

Then, in chapter seven, I shall turn to the problems more directly associated with establishing correlations between indicators (x_a and y_a, x_b and y_b in figure 6-2) and inferring causal relations ($X \longrightarrow Y$) from these correlations in comparative context. In that chapter I shall also raise the topic of different kinds of causal relations posited between X and Y and other variables—that is to say, different theories and paradigms— and trace the implications of these for the enterprise of comparative analysis.

Classification and the Units
to be Compared

In a methodological essay written several years ago, Kalleberg criticized Almond's classification of political systems that contained the following types: (1) Anglo-American, including some Commonwealth States; (2) Continental European (excluding Scandinavia and low countries); (3) pre-industrial or partially industrial; (4) totalitarian. Kalleberg argued that comparison among these types was impossible because "[Almond's] types do not have . . . common dimensions." Thus, to compare the systems by degree of consensus is impossible, because Almond did not "specify the criteria, *which can be found in* [*all*] *countries*, by means of which consensus is to be defined."[32] Totalitarian consensus is a different kind of consensus from that in democratic societies.

Having ventured this critique, Kalleberg went on to a general observation:

> The first requirement that must be kept in mind by students of comparative politics is the necessity for carefully distinguishing between classification and comparison. . . . The second requirement is the need for properly-defined comparative concepts. Truly comparative concepts . . . can only be developed after classification has been completed. Classification is a matter of "either-or"; comparison is a matter of "more or less." Two objects

[32] Arthur L. Kalleberg, "The Logic of Comparison: A Methodological Note on the Comparative Study of Political Systems," *World Politics* 19(1966):77–78.

being compared must already have been shown to be of the same class.
. . .[33]

While agreeing generally with Kalleberg's reasoning, I should like to examine the operation of classifying units for comparison in more detail.

Traditionally the units of analysis within which comparisons have been
made are cultures (mainly by anthropologists), societies (mainly by
sociologists), and nations (mainly by political scientists), though there is
great overlapping both among these types of units and in the choice of
basic social units by investigators from different disciplines. In defining
such a social unit, the investigator makes a claim, often implicit, that *the
units so defined do not, for purposes of subsequent analysis, vary with
respect to the characteristic defining the class.* Viewed in this way, classification emerges as a way of reducing and thereby controlling sources of
variation in the social context of the phenomena to be subsequently investigated. Classification renders phenomena comparable by asserting that
they inhere in a common context. Thus classification is a species of the
operation of converting possibly operative variables into parametric constants.

Consider, for example, Naroll's observation on the appropriate social
units for study in cultural anthropology. Noting that anthropologists use a
diversity of criteria to define societies—distribution of particular traits, territorial contiguity, political organization, language, ecological adjustment,
and local community structure—he proposed what he called a "cultunit,"
defined as "people who are domestic speakers of a common distinct language and who belong either to the same state or the same contact group."[34]
This definition incorporated three of the several criteria he listed. Such a
definition, moreover, set up criteria for inclusion and exclusion of possible
units, with the included units having common characteristics—that is,
considered as having no significant variation with respect to those characteristics.[35] Most analyses rest on definitions of units of analysis that are

[33] Ibid., p. 81. This also repeats Durkheim's statement that comparisons should
be made among societies of the same species. Kalleberg listed a "third requirement"
which is the "specification of operational definitions of the criteria or dimensions
utilized in the framework." Ibid. Note that Kalleberg's list of requirements—classification, comparative concepts, and operational definitions—parallels my headings of
social units, variables, and indicators.

[34] Raoul Naroll, "Some Thoughts on Comparative Method in Cultural Anthropology," in Blalock and Blalock, eds., *Methodology in Social Research*, p. 248.

[35] It is possible to refine a type concept of this sort by introducing subtypes—for
example, those cultunits in the same state as distinguished from those in the same
contact group—but the larger identifying category remains the same.

not nearly so explicit; the concept of "society," for example, normally implies commonality with respect to a degree of economic self-sufficiency, territorial sovereignty, and common culture, but these characteristics are not often systematically applied, nor is their variation made a subject of detailed empirical investigation.[36] More modest classificatory schemes also strive to reduce potential sources of variation. As we saw in chapter five, Weber's notion of the ideal type constituted an effort to lump together diverse instances into a category that could, for purposes of analysis, be considered common.

What is true for classifying basic social units for comparative analysis is also true for dividing them into subtypes. Gross dichotomous classifications into categories like "traditional" and "modern" involve a series of empirical assertions that the various sectors—such as economic, political, or intellectual—of the two types of societies are structured in definite relation to one another in each type of society; one result of applying such a classification is to simplify the investigator's view of the world by reducing its possible patterns of variation.[37] Russett argued that by grouping relatively homogeneous societies by region, the comparative analyst could be more confident that phenomena compared within regional clusters are more nearly comparable; their meaning is similar because of the similarity in social and political context gained by subtyping.[38] And in studying the determinants of civil violence, Gurr and Ruttenberg made explicit the parameteric control that is gained by subclassifying:

> The research design here presented incorporates a method of controlling for systematic variation . . . : division of the total universe of polities into "clusters," the polities of each of which are relatively homogeneous with respect to some constellation of political or socioeconomic conditions. Once such clusters are distinguished, separate multiple correlation analyses

[36] Following the suggestions of Parsons and Johnson, Marsh defined a society as having the following four characteristics:
"1. A definite territory;
  2. Recruitment in large part by sexual reproduction;
  3. A comprehensive culture; that is, cultural patterns sufficiently diversified to enable the members of the society to fulfill all the requirements of social life;
  4. 'Political' independence; that is, a society is not a subsystem of any other system, except perhaps in a very partial sense."
Marsh himself devoted some discussion to the practical difficulties involved in applying such a definition. Robert M. Marsh, *Comparative Sociology*, pp. 12–15.

[37] An example of such a classification is found in C. E. Black, *The Dynamics of Modernization* (New York: Harper & Row, 1966), pp. 6–26.

[38] Bruce M. Russett, *International Regions and the International System—A Study in Political Ecology* (Chicago: Rand McNally, 1967), p. 9.

can be made for each one, a procedure that constitutes a partial control for those variables on the basis of which they are discriminated.[39]

The proposition that classification is an effort to control suspected sources of variation by converting them into parameters is demonstrated clearly by the line of criticisms levelled at the resulting classificatory schemes. Addressing Naroll's notion of "cultunit," Leach complained that "any system of cross-cultural comparison which can be so used as to make 'the Tikopia' and 'the Chinese' units of comparable type is self-evidently absurd, and I do not see that the absurdity is reduced by calling the units 'cultunits' instead of tribes."[40] In effect, Leach was arguing that the societies so grouped by the criteria for identifying "cultunit" varied too much to be legitimately grouped together. Many of the criticisms of simplified dichotomies such as "traditional" and "modern" have argued that societies classified in each category both are heterogeneous in character and resemble societies placed in the other category in significant respects—arguing, in effect, that it is illegitimate to freeze their variability by simplified typing.[41] Finally, a number of careful empirical studies have decomposed type-notions and shown considerable variability among component parts that had previously been grouped together. Udy, for example, extracted seven ingredients from Weber's ideal types of "bureaucracy" and "rationality," attempting to devise measures for them, and examined different patternings of these components in 150 preliterate societies.[42] Freeman and Winch, using Guttman's scaling model, found that a sample

[39] Ted Robert Gurr with Charles Ruttenberg, "The Conditions of Civil Violence: First Tests of a Causal Model," in John V. Gillespie and Betty A. Nesvold, eds., *Macro-Quantitative Analysis: Conflict, Development, and Democratization* (Beverly Hills: Sage Publications, 1971), p. 189.

[40] Quoted in John W. M. Whiting, "Methods and Problems in Cross-Cultural Research," in Gardner Lindzey and Elliot Aronson, *The Handbook of Social Psychology*, 2nd ed. (Reading, Mass.: Addison-Wesley, 1968), 2:697.

[41] See, for example, Joseph R. Gusfield, "Tradition and Modernity: Misplaced Polarities in the Study of Social Change," in Jon M. Shepard, ed., *Organizational Issues in Industrial Society* (Englewood Cliffs, N.J.: Prentice-Hall, 1972), pp. 35–49; Reinhard Bendix, "Tradition and Modernity Reconsidered," *Comparative Studies in Society and History* 9(1967):292–346.

[42] Stanley H. Udy, Jr., " 'Bureaucracy' and 'Rationality' in Weber's Organization Theory: An Empirical Study," *American Sociological Review* 25(1959):791–95. For another piece of research, one aim of which was to demonstrate that "the components of Weber's ideal type [of bureaucracy] do not form an inherently connected set of variables" but that "some of the components of the ideal type are relatively uncorrelated with others, while some are highly correlated," see Arthur L. Stinchcombe, "Bureaucratic and Craft Administration of Production: A Comparative Study," *Administrative Science Quarterly* 4(1959–60):168–87.

of societies appeared to scale consistently on items traditionally grouped under the *Gemeinschaft-Gesellschaft* dichotomy (items such as type of punishment against crimes, complexity of government administration, and formality of education), thus arguing that "societal complexity" is in fact an appropriate basis for classifying societies, since it appears to be a dimension on which societies can be consistently located in relation to one another. Two other items—mode of mate selection and exogamy—did not scale, however, and Freeman and Winch suggested accordingly they be dropped from the dimension of societal complexity.[43]

Classification and sub-classification may also be considered from the standpoint of the role of the investigator. One of the standard criticisms raised against type concepts, such as Weber's ideal types, is that they are "subjective"—that they are the product of the perceptions and intuitions of the individual investigator, and that there is no guarantee that another investigator—or the same investigator on another occasion—would produce the same classification. Such a criticism asserts that the investigator is a source of uncontrolled variation, and, as such, can constitute a "contaminating" influence, both on the adequacy of the classification of units to be compared, and on any subsequent empirical associations established in utilizing it. Many classificatory techniques and procedures recommended in the literature may be regarded as efforts to control this variation, to neutralize the effect of the investigator—to convert him into a parameter, as it were. Suggestions for the consistent and unambiguous identification of units of analysis—such as Naroll's specification of criteria for the "cultunit"—are, in part, efforts to standardize classificatory efforts on the part of investigators.

The subclassifications arising from the applications of standardized statistical techniques such as factor analysis also may be seen as an effort to generate types by formal, technical, investigator-free methods. Driver and Schuessler, for example, attempted to factor out patterns of correlations within 16 northwest California Indian cultures, in order "to arrive at an *objective* classification or typology from square tables (matrices) of correlation coefficients."[44] Sawyer collected 236 items relating to social, economic, political, and other characteristics for 82 independent nations (in 1955) of more than 800,000 population. After correlating, factoring, and rotating the factors orthogonally, Sawyer found that 40 percent of the variance among the nations could be accounted for by reference to the

[43] Linton C. Freeman and Robert F. Winch, "Societal Complexity—An Empirical Test of a Typology of Societies," *American Journal of Sociology* 62(1956–57):461–66.

[44] Harold E. Driver and Karl F. Schuessler, "Factor Analysis of Ethnographic Data," *American Anthropologist* 59(1959):655–63. Emphasis added.

dimensions of size, wealth, and political orientation (Communist, neutral, or Western).[45] Emerging from this list was a three-dimensional classification within which the 82 nations were arranged. Similar types of analysis have appeared in the recent literature on comparative politics.[46]

The main features recommending such factor-analytic techniques are that they constitute a way of controlling investigator bias by a standardized technique, and that they seek to base classifications on empirically-established, rather than posited, dimensions. As they have been applied, however, they have yielded a corresponding number of weaknesses. Even this system of subtyping rests on a prior, and usually unexamined, grouping of units on the basis of their being "nations," a grouping which may itself conceal a great deal of significant variation.[47] In addition, the selection of items—which affects the ultimate character of the factors—has tended to be somewhat "mindless" in the sense that selection is based on an unsystematic mixture of criteria, such as what dimensions social scientists have in the past considered to be important, what is available in official reports, and the like; and that, correspondingly, the selection of items to be factored has no, or little, or unknown theoretical basis.[48]

From a methodological point of view, then, what criteria should determine the choice of units of analysis to be compared? Five criteria have emerged from the preceding discussion:

First, the unit of analysis must be appropriate to the kind of theoretical problem posed by the investigator. Blau, for example, has pointed out that if an investigator wishes to study the impact of different environments on

[45] Jack Sawyer, "Dimensions of Nations—Size, Wealth, and Politics," *American Journal of Sociology* 73(1967–68):145–72.

[46] Russett utilized factor analysis to group his sample of nations into regional clusters. *International Regions and the International System*, ch. 2. See also Phillip M. Gregg and Arthur S. Banks, "Dimensions of Political Systems: Factor Analysis of a Cross-Polity Survey," *American Political Science Review* 59(1965):602–14; Arthur S. Banks and Phillip M. Gregg, "Grouping Political Systems: Q-Factor Analysis of *A Cross-Polity Survey*," *The American Behavioral Scientist* 9, no. 3(November 1965):3–6.

[47] A review of this line of criticism is found in Charles L. Taylor, "Further Problems: A Consideration of Other Views," in Charles L. Taylor, ed., *Aggregate Data Analysis: Political and Social Indicators* (Paris-The Hague: Mouton—International Social Science Council, 1968), pp. 115–21.

[48] See Kingsley Davis, "Problems and Solutions in International Comparison for Social Science Purposes," reprint no. 273 of Population Reprint Series (Berkeley: International Population and Urban Research, Institute of International Studies, and Department of Demography, University of California, Berkeley; originally published in 1965); Erik Allardt, " 'Basic' Dimensions in the Comparative Study of Social Structures," *Transactions of the Sixth World Congress of Sociology* (International Sociological Association, 1966), 1:178–86.

formal organizations, the units of analysis to be compared are organizations themselves—not their component roles and internal relations—since the problematic *theoretical* preoccupation is at the former level.[49]

Second, the unit of analysis should be *causally* relevant to the phenomena being studied. On a number of different occasions Kuznets has argued that nation-states are the appropriate unit for the analysis of economic growth; his argument, furthermore, is mainly that the state constitutes an important set of influences on the fortunes of economic life. Nation-states set the "institutional conditions within which economic activities are pursued, the boundaries within which markets operate and within which human resources are relatively free to handle material capital assets and claims to them." Further, the sovereign government is "the overriding authority that resolves conflicts generated by growth and screens institutional innovations, sanctioning those believed essential and barring others."[50] In the light of these considerations, he continued, a complex and widespread process such as economic growth

> can best be studied if its manifestations are grouped around units that affect its course, rather than around units that bear little perceptible relation to the process. Thus, it would obviously make little sense to study economic growth for groups of families classified by the initial letter of their family names, for this particular classification has no obvious bearing upon the process of economic growth.[51]

The same argument—only the other way around—was made by Eberhard, who argued that the unit of "social system" (with its implication of functionally interrelated parts) is in many respects inapplicable to classical Asian societies, largely because the notion of system as a whole is less important in understanding social processes than the complex and more autonomous "layers" of those multiple societies.[52]

Third, the units of analysis themselves should in fact be empirically invariant with respect to their classificatory criterion—their "society-ness"

[49] Peter M. Blau, "The Comparative Study of Organizations," *Industrial and Labor Relations Review* 18(1964–65):323–38.

[50] Simon Kuznets, *Quantitative Economic Research: Trends and Problems* (New York: Columbia University Press, 1972), pp. 1–2. See also Simon Kuznets, "The State as a Unit in Study of Economic Growth," *Journal of Economic History* 2(1951):25–41.

[51] Simon Kuznets, *Modern Economic Growth: Rate, Structure, and Spread* (New Haven: Yale University Press, 1969), p. 17. Essentially the same argument for the national unit is presented by Kingsley Davis in "Problems and Solutions in International Comparison for Social Science Purposes," p. 1.

[52] Wolfram Eberhard, *Conquerors and Rulers: Social Forces in Medieval China*, 2nd, rev. ed. (Leiden, Holland: E. J. Brill, 1965), pp. 2–11.

or their "culture-ness"—so as not to conceal significant sources of variation.

Fourth, the choice of the unit of analysis should reflect the degree of availability of data referring to this unit. For the study of aggregative aspects of economic history, for example, the analyst is virtually forced to choose the nation as the unit of analysis, because "statistics and many other types of evidence can usually be obtained only in national terms."[53] But as Kuznets has pointed out, this criterion is not an independent one, but rather a "reflection of the more basic arguments . . . as to the importance of nation-states in making secular decisions directly bearing upon the course of economic growth."[54] Most data refer to national units because of the fact that national units are important parts of the causal process that produce them.

Fifth, insofar as possible, decisions to select and classify units of analysis should be based on standardized and repeatable procedures, provided that these procedures do not themselves introduce important sources of uncontrolled error.

The most important methodological conclusion of this brief essay on classification is that the processes of classification and subclassification are not operations distinct from scientific explanation, but are in many respects identical to it. The point of identity is that both classification (deciding what all cases have in common) and explanation (accounting for variance by reference to independent variables) rest on the procedures of converting sources of variation into parameters. In classifying, the investigator asserts that certain contextual features of a phenomenon should be treated as parametric constants for purposes of analysis. Classificatory schemes, moreover, are more or less powerful insofar as this claim is valid and the criteria for classification do not contribute sources of variation to the subsequent investigation of causal relations among the phenomena occurring within the social units.

Variables in Comparative Study

The general aim of comparative analysis—as of scientific analysis in general—is to generate logically rigorous causal explanations of regularities and variations in empirical phenomena. We have just seen that the selection of units of analysis—*classification*—involves *assigning* regularity in

[53] Rondo Cameron et al., *Banking in the Early Stages of Industrialization: A Study in Comparative Economic History* (New York: Oxford University Press, 1967), p. 5.

[54] Kuznets, *Modern Economic Growth*, p. 17.

the manifestation of attributes to a class of objects, subsequent variations among which are then to be explained.

To round out this chapter, I turn to the problems involved in *describing* and *measuring* variables in social units, whether these variables be regarded as dependent or independent. (Discussion of the issues involved in inferring causal relations among variables will be reserved until the next chapter.) I shall proceed by two phases. I shall first focus on the abstract variables, or comparative dimensions themselves; or, referring to figure 6-2, I shall be concerned with the kinds of concepts X and Y that are selected by the investigator for comparative analysis, and on the capacity to characterize empirical phenomena in dissimilar social units A and B. The second phase will focus on the selection of empirical indicators for such variables; referring to figure 6-2 again, it will concern the relations $X \longrightarrow x_a$, $Y \longrightarrow y_a$, $X \longrightarrow X_b$, and $Y \longrightarrow Y_b$, and will also include consideration of the role of the investigator in selecting such indicators. It will prove difficult, however, to keep the two phases separate from one another, since one criterion for assessing variables is to ask how they are manifested (what are their indicators), and one criterion for assessing indicators is to ask what they reflect (what are their corresponding concepts or variables). Accordingly, the discussion in each phase will continuously turn toward the other, and the entire discussion in the remainder of the chapter should be regarded as an examination of the concept-indicator relationship from two different angles.

It has long been recognized by investigators that comparative analysis "requires a generalized system of concepts which will enable the scientific observer to compare and contrast large bodies of concretely different social phenomena in consistent terms";[55] that the identification of such concepts is not a simple matter of discovering the empirical uniformities that dictate them, but is in large part conceptual, depending on "the level of generality of the language that is applied to express observations";[56] and

[55] See D. F. Aberle, A. K. Cohen, A. K. Davis, M. J. Levy, Jr., and F. X. Sutton, "The Functional Prerequisites of a Society," in Roy C. Macridis and Bernard E. Brown, eds., *Comparative Politics: Notes and Readings*, 4th ed. (Homewood, Ill.: The Dorsey Press, 1972), p. 61; Clyde Kluckhohn, "Universal Categories of Culture," in Frank W. Moore, ed., *Readings in Cross-Cultural Methodology*, pp. 507–23; Gideon Sjoberg, "The Comparative Method in the Social Sciences," *Philosophy of Science* 22(1955):106–11. Elias H. Tuma, *Economic History and the Social Sciences: Problems of Methodology* (Berkeley and Los Angeles: University of California Press, 1974), pp. 74–75.

[56] Adam Przeworski and Henry Teune, *The Logic of Comparative Social Inquiry* (New York: Wiley, 1970), p. 10; see also Michael Armer, "Methodological Problems and Possibilities in Comparative Research," in Michael Armer and Allen D. Grimshaw, eds., *Comparative Social Research: Methodological Problems and Strate-*

dealing with the problem of the "uniqueness" and "idiosyncrasy" of individual historical cases rests not only on empirical judgments but also on the invention of a language capable of assessing apparently unique features in more general terms.[57]

To make concepts more widely comparative, then, is simultaneously to make them more abstract and inclusive:

> The rules for climbing and descending along a ladder of abstraction are . . . very simple rules—in principle. We make a concept more abstract and more general by lessening its properties or attributes. Conversely, a concept is specified by the addition (or unfolding) of qualifications, i.e., by augmenting its attributes or properties.[58]

To facilitate comparisons, then, the investigator should avoid concepts that are so peculiar to a single culture or group of cultures that no instance of the concept can be found in other cultures. The concept "civil service," for example, is so closely linked to a bureaucratic administrative form that it cannot be instantiated in societies without a formal governmental apparatus. The concept "administration" is superior, since it is not bound so closely to particular forms of bureaucracy, but even this term is quite culture-bound. Weber's concept of "staff"[59] is even more helpful, since it can encompass political arrangements based on kinship and other forms of particularistic loyalties. "Staff" is more nearly satisfactory than "administration," then, and "administration" more satisfactory than "civil service," because the former allow for more nearly universal instantiation.

The recent social-scientific literature gives evidence of the search for categories that are more widely inclusive and comparative than traditional ones. In an influential work in comparative politics, Almond and Coleman expressed discontent with the comparative potential of traditional concepts in political science—concepts limited to the complex constitutional and parliamentary systems of Western society in the 19th and 20th centuries; they did not find these concepts useful "for the comparison of political systems differing radically in scale, structure, and culture."[60] In their search for more comprehensive categories, they turned to anthropology and

gies (New York: John Wiley & Sons, 1973), pp. 54–57; Giovani Sartori, "Concept Misinformation in Comparative Politics," *American Political Science Review* 64(1970): 1038.

[57] Przeworski and Teune, *The Logic of Comparative Social Inquiry*, p. 13.

[58] Sartori, "Concept Misinformation in Comparative Politics," p. 1041.

[59] See pp. 120–21.

[60] Gabriel A. Almond and James S. Coleman, eds., *The Politics of Developing Areas* (Princeton: Princeton University Press, 1960), pp. 3–4.

sociology and selected concepts such as political system, interest aggregation and interest articulation, and political socialization, which, they argued, could be extended to cover emerging polities as well as traditional Western ones.[61] Berreman, finding stratification, cultural pluralism, and social interaction too restricted as bases for defining caste, attempted to generate a definition that incorporated elements of all three and was thereby improved as a conceptual tool for cross-cultural comparisons.[62] Often the adoption of a more abstract set of comparative categories leaves a previously employed, more specific category as a special case of the more abstract concept.

[In conventional comparative government analyses] . . . we find a major distinction being made between parliamentary and presidential systems. . . . Difficulties arise . . . when [the distinction] is used where it is not appropriate. For example, if there is no legislature, and if voting is not practiced, then the distinction is clearly irrelevant. . . .

The solution to our problem is not to reject these established categories, but to provide a broader structural framework within which they can be shown to be special cases. If, for example, we distinguish between polities having legislatures and those that do not, then the parliamentary-presidential system dichotomy clearly applies only to polities with legislatures.[63]

The search for appropriate comparative categories reflects a kind of double-tension: on the one hand, as just indicated, if the comparative analysis of dissimilar systems is desired, the investigator is under pressure to generate more abstract and inclusive concepts; on the other hand, the movement toward more abstract concepts creates a counterpressure for respecification of rules for identifying empirical indicators as they might manifest themselves in the dissimilar systems that have been encompassed by the more general categories. For example, Zelditch, interested in the extent to which kinship systems of the world showed a sexual differentia-

---

[61] In a related complaint, Oliver and Miller found anthropological writings lacking in "definitions that would make possible a point-by-point comparison of analogous features of . . . political systems," and the concepts of political science similarly lacking because they were limited in their reference to complex political systems and "have barely nodded in the direction of nonliterate societies." Douglas Oliver and Walter B. Miller, "Suggestions for a More Systematic Method of Comparing Political Units," *American Anthropologist* 57(1955):118.

[62] Gerald D. Berreman, "Stratification, Pluralism and Interaction: A Comparative Analysis of Caste," in Anthony de Reuck and Julie Knight, *Caste and Race: Comparative Approaches* (London: J. & A. Churchill, 1967), pp. 45–73.

[63] Fred W. Riggs, "The Comparison of Whole Political Systems," in Robert T. Holt and John E. Turner, eds., *The Methodology of Comparative Research* (New York: The Free Press, 1970), pp. 90–91.

tion of roles along task-adaptive and socio-emotional lines, utilized the quite general concepts "instrumental" and "expressive" as variables to be investigated in the comparative context of role-behavior. But these abstract concepts are not immediately recognizable by a simple indicator in highly diversified cross-cultural contexts. Accordingly, Zelditch constructed a series of "designation rules for the rating of the cases," with instructions to the rater to classify a role as "instrumental" if the role-incumbent is described in the ethnographic report as "boss-manager of the farm; leader of the hunt, etc.; . . . the final court of appeals, final judge and executor of punishment, discipline, and control over the children of the family."[64] (It might be objected that this range of indicators is not satisfactory, since they mix a dimension of authority in with task-adaptive responsibility. For the moment, however, that objection is neither here nor there, since the main point is that the use of abstract comparative terms calls for a set of specifying procedures.)

The comparative investigator can thus be regarded as fighting a continuous struggle between the "culture-boundedness" of system-specific categories and the "contentlessness" of system-inclusive categories. Moreover, many of the issues, problems, and controversies of comparative analysis may be understood as emanating from different efforts to resolve this double-tension.

One line of resolution of the tension is to employ system-specific or "culture-bound" conceptualization and export it as a measure into inappropriate contexts.[65] Perhaps the clearest example is found in the conceptualization of economic activity as market activity with money transactions. Clearly the term *economic* is a concept that is universally identifiable in principle. All societies face the problem of scarcity of resources, and all societies must come to terms in some institutionalized way with this problem. All societies thus have an "economic problem" and manifest "economic behavior." To say this, however, is only to begin to identify economic behavior comparatively. It is also necessary to ask how economic behavior is manifested empirically.

[64] Morris Zelditch, Jr., "Role Differentiation in the Nuclear Family: A Comparative Study," in Talcott Parsons et al., *Family, Socialization and Interaction Process* (Glencoe, Ill.: The Free Press, 1955), p. 318.

[65] For a sample of discussions of cross-cultural bias in comparative studies, see Gunnar Myrdal, "The Beam in Our Eyes," and Charles Savage, Alexander H. Leighton, and Dorothea C. Leighton, "The Problem of Cross-Cultural Identification of Psychiatric Disorders," in Warwick and Osherson, eds., *Comparative Research Methods*, pp. 89–115; Erwin K. Scheuch, "Society as Context in Cross-Cultural Comparisons," *Social Science Information*, 6(1967):7–23. Sartori discusses the phenomenon of "conceptual stretching" in "Concept Misinformation in Comparative Politics," pp. 1034–36.

One convenient and widely used method of identifying "the economic" is to limit the empirical referents of the term to those aspects of persons' attitudes and activities that are subject to measurement in terms of money.[66] From the standpoint of empirical precision, the monetary index has advantages. From the standpoint of encompassing economic behavior on a uniform basis, however, the market-price model of economic activity has severe limitations. Even in our own society, many economic activities —housewives' labor, lending a hand to a friend, and so forth—are seldom transferred in the market and expressed in monetary terms. In the case of economies based on subsistence farming and domestically consumed household manufacture, the limitations of the market model are even more significant, since many kinds of economic behavior—such as the production, distribution, and consumption of foodstuffs—never involve markets. In addition, use of a market model is limited when comparing a growing economic system with its past, since one of the characteristics of economic growth is the entry of an increasingly larger share of economic activities into the market; therefore, if the market definition of *economic* is used, the rate of growth is inflated by the transformation of nonmarket economic activity into market economic activity.

Another definition of economic activity has been suggested by Polanyi, Arensberg, and Pearson.[67] Reacting against the tradition of formal economics, they argued that economic activity should be defined as that instituted process that results in a "continuous supply of want-satisfying *material* means." This materialistic definition introduces a bias precisely opposite to that of the market definition of economic activity—a bias in favor of the primitive and peasant societies. In such societies, it appears that most economic activity is devoted to a sort of material subsistence based on food, clothing, and shelter. In advanced market societies, however, in which expressive behavior, ideas, personalities, and other "nonmaterial" items have economic value, the formula of the "economic" as the "supply of want-satisfying material means" is not an adequate comparative measure. It is as illegitimate to try to force a physical or material bias on all economic activity as it is to impose a fully developed market analysis on all economic activity.

Any encompassing definition and measurement of economic activity, it seems clear, must involve more than the limited conception of market activity as physical production, or some other concrete activity. It must

[66] See Alfred Marshall, *Principles of Economics*, 8th ed. (New York: Macmillan, 1920), bk. 1, ch. 2.

[67] K. Polanyi, C. M. Arensberg, and H. W. Pearson, eds., *Trade and Market in the Early Empires* (Glencoe, Ill.: The Free Press and The Falcon's Wing Press, 1957).

involve a definition of the production, distribution, and consumption of scarce goods and services *in relation to individual and social goals.* As quantitative a comparative analyst as Kuznets has noted that "no economic measure is neutral, that is, unaffected by economic theories of production, value, and welfare, and the broader social philosophy encompassing them."[68] Economic activity, he went on to argue, "like other individual or social human activities, is purposive; its results can be meaningfully measured only in relation to some clearly defined goals and in terms of costs and returns."[69] Economic measures and economic analysis "reflect a broad consensus, sharply defined in theory and vaguely perceived in practice, on the basic purposes of economic activity and on the acceptable rules and feasible ways by which such purposes are met."[70] It follows that comparative economic measures of items like capital, consumption, and the like are limited to societies that share such purposes and rules. To make the comparative scope of economics wider would have to take the goals and rules —or we might say, the value and normative contexts—as themselves subject to variation. This would call for different conceptualization and operationalization of economic activity according to different contexts. It would make for a more abstract definition of economic activity combined with a series of respecifications of indicators in heterogeneous societies. Kuznets recognized the necessity for such generalization in principle, but refused to yield to it in practice:

> One might argue that limiting the choice of assumptions to those reflecting the consensus of society, and the choice of theories to those based on observable, if simplified, reality, is indispensable if any empirical counterparts are to be found and economic measurement is to be possible. It is extremely difficult to find empirical counterparts to a set of basic purposes and rules *radically* different from those prevailing—which, incidentally, may explain the weakness of empirical bases and formulations in the writings of critics who stand outside the basic framework of the economic system.[71]

Rather than making the move toward the more abstract characterization and its necessarily more complicated set of respecifications, however, Kuznets argued that economists' assumptions *do* reflect accepted goals and rules in many societies, *do* provide reliable measures, and *can* be modified appropriately as the parametric—value and normative—conditions of societies change.[72] If the investigator makes such a claim—how realistic

[68] Kuznets, *Quantitative Economic Research,* p. 18.
[69] Ibid., p. 19.
[70] Ibid.
[71] Ibid., p. 20.
[72] Ibid., pp. 20–22.

it is is always open to question—the problems of comparability become relatively simple insofar as they involve procedures of representing economic indicators consistently within the parametric framework rather than varying that framework and incorporating it into diverse empirical indicators. The problems of selecting appropriate indicators thus are made more narrowly technical.

Kuznets' solution to the tension between abstraction and specification may be regarded as a sort of "middle-of-the-road" solution insofar as he recognized the relativity of concrete measures to their sociocultural context—and thus departs from the "hard-line" positivist who would insist that it is possible to compare by using concrete, context-free indicators—but at the same time refused to make the conception so abstract as to encompass all contexts. Two alternative solutions to Kuznets' have been developed, but each generates its own difficulties. The first might be termed the "relativistic" alternative. It takes the variability of the context of any phenomenon into account, thus remaining faithful to the meaning of the phenomenon and not distorting it by superimposing any culture-bound conceptions. To stay with the economic example for the moment, investigators like Mauss wished to respect and give adequate representation to the ways in which individual cultures themselves define the "economic." He characterized his own comparative methodology as follows:

> *Since we are concerned with words and their meanings,* we choose only areas where we have access to the *minds of the societies* through documentation and philological research. This further limits our field of comparison. Each particular study has a bearing on the systems we set out to describe and is presented in its logical place. In this way we avoid that *method of haphazard comparison in which institutions lose their local colour and documents their value.*[73]

Numerous expressions of this position have appeared, especially in the anthropological literature; perhaps the most recent is Clarke's objection to conceptualizing *any* sort of general "basic needs, problems, drives, etc." as cross-cultural constants. Even these are to be treated as "functions of the related cultural superstructure."[74] The problem generated by such a position, however, is that the investigator tends to treat every phenomenon in the same way that any society chooses to define it, and, as a consequence, tends to lose a grasp on any general comparative concepts altogether.

[73] Marcel Mauss, *The Gift: Forms and Functions of Exchange in Archaic Societies,* trans. Ian Cunnison (Glencoe, Ill.: The Free Press, 1954), pp. 2–3. Emphasis added.

[74] J. J. Clarke, "On the Unity and Diversity of Cultures," *American Anthropologist* 72(1970):545–54.

The issue posed here is a very general one, and reflects—in different form—the same sort of methodological tension as that between Durkheim's sociological positivism and Weber's configurational analysis. It is the tension between positivistic objectivism on the one hand—a position that would define concepts and indicators without reference to cultural context and individual meaning—and phenomenological subjectivism on the other—a position that would make phenomena identical to the meanings that groups and individual actors impart to them. My own position is that there can be no general solution to this tension. General variables or dimensions *must* be chosen if comparative analysis is to be possible; but these should be varied in their degree of abstraction according to the scope of comparison required. A comparison of the economies of advanced capitalist societies can realistically be based on simplified parametric assumptions and equivalent indicators, whereas the incorporation of economies embedded in different value and normative contexts must vary the definition of the economic—and its measurement—systematically in accord with the variations in this context.

The second alternative solution is the one Kuznets envisioned but refused to embrace—that is, the attempt to make the definition of general concepts more abstract and thereby to take account of a wider range of variations of contexts. This solution—as well as its accompanying problems—appears in that part of the social science literature that is vaguely designated as "functionalist." Certain invariant points of reference—for example, the "functional requisites" of society—are posited, and these form the basis for identifying "structures," which are variable manifestations of the invariant categories:

> Functional prerequisites refer broadly to the things that must get done in any society if it is to continue as a going concern, i.e., the generalized conditions necessary for the maintenance of the system concerned. The specific structural arrangements for meeting the functional prerequisites differ, of course, from one society to another and, in the course of time, change in any given society.[75]

Examples of functional prerequisites are "role differentiation and role assignment," "shared cognitive orientations," "socialization," and so on.[76] In a recent formulation, Parsons has argued that the notion of function, as an invariant point of reference, constitutes the basis of comparability of structures and processes:

[75] Aberle, Cohen, Davis, Levy, and Sutton, "The Functional Prerequisites of a Society," p. 61.
[76] Ibid., pp. 65–72.

Function is the master concept for analysis of the organization of living systems. As such it is superordinate to both "structure" and "process." That structures and processes should be differentiated along functional lines within the same system implies their *comparability.* If they were in principle incomparable the system could not be rationally understood, and, second, it would not be possible to account for its integration as a system.[77]

Comparisons are made according to the degree of differentiation of structures in systems in relation to a common, less differentiated point of origin.[78]

The functionalist formulation of society has been subjected to many critical assessments, but for the moment I shall concentrate on the difficulties of respecifying such inclusive categories as "invariant functions." Consider an empirical example. One of the most consistent differences between Western and non-Western political systems, according to Pye, is that in the latter "the political sphere is not sharply differentiated from the spheres of social and personal relations."[79] In functional terms, this says that different structures contribute to the same function in different polities. Evidently such a characterization calls for a different series of indicators and a different set of rules for specification in each set of societies. In the more differentiated form, processes of political influence would be more likely to be recorded in the form of *formal* exchanges among politically-relevant units—votes, lobbying, party bartering—whereas in the less differentiated, the investigator would have to look into the subtle patterns of kinship and tribal interaction to draw out the corresponding patterns of political influence. The same would hold for economic activities. Market and other transactions between differentiated units provide the empirical indicators—level of production, investment, inventories, etc.—that would have to be measured on a different basis—for example, the detailed account of how people allocate their time with respect to economic tasks—since the former kind of data are neither available nor relevant to the less complex setting.

Scholars working within the functionalist tradition have not yet developed sufficiently precise rules for respecification of the various indicators for the performance of different functions in different settings. The task is not made easier by the recognition that "no structure is unifunctional, i.e., performs only one function; . . . the same structure can be multifunctional, i.e., can perform across different countries widely different func-

[77] Talcott Parsons, "Comparative Studies and Evolutionary Change," in Vallier, ed., *Comparative Methods in Sociology*, pp. 100–101.

[78] Ibid., p. 102.

[79] Lucian W. Pye, "The Non-Western Political Process," in Eckstein and Apter, eds., *Comparative Politics*, p. 657.

tions; . . . and therefore, the same function has structural alternatives, i.e., can be performed by very different structures."[80] Or, as Levy has phrased the issue:

> Such is the flexibility of concrete structures with regard to the functions that they can perform that it is difficult to make any statement with regard to a minimal list of concrete structures necessary in any society. This flexibility makes it difficult to establish the requisite basis of concrete structures on this general level. Even when concrete structures are universally found in empirical cases of societies (e.g., the family), it is impossible at present to state that this ubiquity is not as the result of a certain lack of imagination in the creation of alternative social arrangements.[81]

An investigator like Kuznets opted to "freeze" certain of the contextual variability of a given "function"—such as the economic—by assuming that it takes place *within* a setting of common goals and rules; this restricted the scope of comparison, to be sure, but permitted the assumption that certain standard indicators generated in that setting were equivalent. Those who posit completely universal and invariant versions of that function relax all such restricting assumptions, and have to build all the variability back into the process of specifying indicators. Such a task poses enormous difficulties. These difficulties probably account for the fact that the empirical literature produced by functional analysts tends to be taxonomic—that is, citing and describing different structural arrangements in different functional spheres—and for the fact that propositions relating limited numbers of variables according to simplified assumptions have been relatively sparse in that literature. They probably also account for the fact that many of the major advances in comparative knowledge have been in areas like kinship, in which empirical structures, while theoretically highly variable, are in fact limited in number in different societies.[82] And finally, they probably account as well for the fact that some, impatient with the generality of functional categories, have called for "concepts applicable to some (rather than all) societies."[83] Such a call is, in effect, an appeal to resolve the dilemma between abstraction and specification in the direction of the latter. As we have seen, however, such a solution cannot be defended on entirely

[80] Sartori, "Concept Misinformation in Comparative Politics," p. 1048.

[81] Marion J. Levy, Jr., "Comparative Analysis of Societies in Terms of 'Structural-Functional Requisites,' " *Civilizations* 4(1954):195. See Also M. J. Levy, Jr., and L. A. Fallers, "The Family: Some Comparative Considerations," *American Anthropologist* 61(1959):647–51.

[82] Whiting, "Methods and Problems in Cross-Cultural Research," pp. 709–10.

[83] Reinhard Bendix, "Concepts in Comparative Historical Analysis," in Stein Rokkan, ed., *Comparative Research Across Cultures and Nations* (Paris-The Hague: Mouton, 1968), p. 78.

general grounds, for movement either in the direction of abstraction or specification always entails both some gains and some corresponding costs. The dilemma must be resolved in relation to the specific theoretical purposes at hand and the level of comparative scope desired.

The Comparability of
Empirical Indicators

Let me refer again to the empirical indicators x_A, y_A, x_B, and y_B in figure 6-2. As we have seen, the degree to which these phenomena (x_A and x_B, y_A and y_B, respectively) are comparable depends in part on the mode of *classification* of the social unit in which they are regarded as occurring and in part on the character of the *dimension* or *variable* that they are regarded as representing. Both the selection of social units and the selection of dimensions, moreover, can be regarded as efforts to control, by conceptual means, sources of variation in the context of the phenomena. As such, they represent operations similar to explanation itself—part of which is an effort to manipulate and isolate sources of variation in the relationship between two indicators, one defined as independent and one defined as dependent. In this final section of the chapter, I shall look at the problem of comparability once again, this time concentrating directly on the indicators themselves. The distinction between the focus of the preceding section and that of the present one parallels the distinction between "conceptual equivalence" and "measurement equivalence" often made in the literature on comparative studies.[84] The distinction cannot be hard and fast, however, because variables are assessed in large part in terms of the indicators called for, and the indicators are assessed in relation to the kinds of variables they are presumed to indicate. For this reason, many of the arguments made in this section will resemble those made in earlier sections—points dealing fundamentally with the control of sources of variation—though the arguments will arise from a different perspective.

The issue of comparability of indicators can be represented in the form of two closely related questions dealing with correspondences: (a) Does the process by which an indicator is generated correspond to the theory of that process that is explicit or implicit in the mind of the investigator? (From the measurement standpoint this raises the problem of validity, or the degree to which an indicator measures what it purports to measure.) (b) Does the process by which an indicator is generated in social unit A correspond to the process by which it is generated in social unit B?

---

[84] Donald P. Warwick and Samuel Osherson, "Comparative Analysis in the Social Sciences," in Warwick and Osherson, eds., *The Methodology of Comparative Research*, pp. 11–28.

(This is the problem of equivalence proper, and from the standpoint of measurement it concerns the problem of the reliability of a measure in different contexts.) We shall consider these two questions in the order presented.

Two problems of incompleteness frequently plague comparative research. The first is an outright paucity of data, in which case a dimension or variable cannot have an indicator at all, no matter how clearly it is defined; in such cases substitute indicators of varying degrees of adequacy are often chosen.[85] The second is the incompleteness or vagueness of conceptualization of a variable, so that the "what" that an indicator purports to represent remains unknown. In introducing his volume on the comparative study of political opposition, Dahl tentatively defined "opposition" as follows:

> Suppose that A determines the conduct of some aspect of the government of a particular political system during some interval. We need not specify the interval exactly; it may be a period in the past, the coming year, etc. Suppose that during this interval B cannot determine the conduct of the government; and that B is opposed to the conduct of government by A. Then B is what we mean by "an opposition."[86]

But at the same time he noted that the term "conduct of the government" was left "deliberately broad and vague," even "undefined." Similarly, he left the term "oppose" undefined, giving only a few general illustrations of the forms it might take.[87] While the definition established some practical guidelines, its incompleteness nevertheless left the investigator without adequate criteria to determine whether one empirical instance or another constitutes an indicator of "opposition." Other concepts in common currency in comparative studies—concepts such as "development" and "modernization"—also suffer from vagueness and multiplicity of connotation.[88]

---

[85] Kurt Finsterbusch, "The Sociology of Nation-States: Dimensions, Indicators, and Theory," in Armer and Grimshaw, eds., *Comparative Social Research*, pp. 427–31.

[86] Robert A. Dahl, "Preface" to Robert A. Dahl, ed., *Political Oppositions in Western Democracies* (New Haven: Yale University Press, 1966), p. xvi.

[87] Ibid., pp. xvi–xvii.

[88] See Retzlaff's comment on Cutright's measure of "political development," as employed in Phillips Cutright, "National Political Development: Measurement and Analysis," *American Sociological Review* 28(1963)253–64: "Apart from suggesting measurement criteria, Cutright does not explicitly define the concept of political development as he uses it. Does he mean to imply that the existence of stable, democratic government is the sole measure of political development, or even *a* measure of it?" Ralph Retzlaff, "The Use of Aggregate Data in Comparative Political Analysis," *Journal of Politics* 27(1965):811.

Another order of problem arises when a comparative dimension is defined more or less clearly, but the investigator chooses an indicator for it which apparently represents a different variable or set of variables from that which it is purported to represent. Consider the following examples: (a) In his synthetic work on comparative sociology, Marsh took societal differentiation as his central variable and defined this as "the number of structurally distinct and functionally specialized units in a society."[89] Such a definition evidently calls for some measure of roles and collectivities performing in functionally distinct spheres of social action. The indicators Marsh chose for differentiation, however, were "population of political unit" and "degree of social stratification" for societies from Murdock's *World Ethnographic Sample,* "percentage of males who are in nonagricultural occupations," and "gross energy consumption in megawatt-hours per capita for one year" for contemporary national societies.[90] While a case might be made that these are useful indirect indicators for societal differentiation—insofar as they are correlated with it—nevertheless far more "slippage" between variable and indicator is introduced than if a direct measure of differentiation or complexity were used.[91] (b) In attempting to devise a measure for domestic political aggression, Feierabend, Feierabend, and Nesvold made use of the following scaling device:

> Dismissals or resignations of officeholders are assigned to scale position 1; peaceful demonstrations and strikes are ascribed scale position 2; riots and assassinations are at position 3; and large-scale arrests and imprisonments, at position 4. Revolts are included in scale position 5, while guerrilla and civil war and revolution are located at scale position 6. This last scale position represents the most serious aggressive events.[92]

Aside from evident problems such as coding and the comparability of such events across national lines, the scale contains a questionable "theory" concerning the amount of aggression manifested in different events (are an assassination and a "riot" equally aggressive, for example?) and the seriousness of threat to a polity (a strike in a vital industry is often a more serious threat to a government than a peasant revolt). (c) A more subtle example is found in *The Civic Culture,* by Almond and Verba. Their central variable was "political culture"; culture was defined as a "psychological orientation toward social objects"—with the political culture as a

[89] Marsh, *Comparative Sociology,* p. 31.
[90] Ibid., p. 35.
[91] Such measures are available. See the reference to the Freeman and Winch study of societal complexity, pp. 170–71.
[92] Ivo K. Feierabend with Rosalind L. Feierabend and Betty A. Nesvold, "The Comparative Study of Revolution and Violence," *Comparative Politics* 5(1973):396.

subvariant[93]—and political culture was measured by interviewing a sample of individual citizens in five societies and examining the results of those interviews. What is problematical is that the concept of "culture" is usually conceived of as a "global" property of a social unit, a property which is not based on aggregated information about individual members of the social unit but rather on the unit considered as a whole.[94] Admittedly, direct indices of global properties—indices such as constitutions or sacred documents of various sorts—are themselves difficult to come by and are frequently questionable indicators; but the measure of a "culture" on the basis of percentaging individual responses to a questionnaire rests on a questionable theoretical version of that concept.

It is well known that the choice of different indicators for general variables yields different empirical results. For example, in a re-analysis of data on cross-national rates of manual-nonmanual mobility by Fox and Miller, Cutright pointed out that by excluding "nonclassified respondents" from the denominator and by treating farmers as manual workers, the figures yield rates of five percent greater upward mobility and five percent less downward mobility in Italy, as well as three percent more upward and six percent more downward mobility in the United States. Furthermore, Cutright noted that in their analysis Fox and Miller did not remove structural changes—for example, the steady expansion of nonmanual sectors in developing societies—and found that a corrected measure of manual-nonmanual mobility yielded a rank-order correlation of only 0.54 with uncorrected rates.[95] Evidently, too, empirical associations between various independent variables and economic inequality differ, depending on whether measures of intersectoral or measures of individual inequality are chosen.[96] The choice among indicators—and their respective validity—rests not only on intrinsic features of the indicator or on criteria of how much measurement error is present in each. The choice also depends on the theoretical purposes for which the measure is to be employed, and on its correspondence with the meaning of the variable expressed—a meaning endowed by that theoretical purpose. Uncorrected manual-nonmanual indicators may

[93] Gabriel Almond and Sidney Verba, *The Civic Culture: Political Attitudes and Democracy in Five Nations* (Boston: Little, Brown, 1963), pp. 13–14.

[94] Paul F. Lazarsfeld and Herbert Menzel, "On the Relation between Individual and Collective Properties," in Amitai Etzioni, ed., *Complex Organizations: A Sociological Reader* (New York: Holt, Rinehart and Winston, 1961), pp. 28–29.

[95] Phillips Cutright, "Studying Cross-National Mobility Rates," *Acta Sociologica* 11(1968):170–76.

[96] See the discussion in C. T. Husbands and Roy W. Money, "The Cross-National Study of Inequality: A Research Note," and Phillips Cutright, "Getting Ready to Get Ready: Reply to Husbands and Money," *American Sociological Review* 35 (1970):319–27.

be appropriate if gross occupational turnover is of theoretical significance; corrected manual-nonmanual indicators are appropriate if some measure of residual mobility—for example, mobility dependent on differential socialization and motivation—apart from structural realignments in the economy is desired; neither may be appropriate if the theoretical interest is in finer movements *within* the nonmanual sphere. The validity of an indicator, in short, depends upon an implicit understanding of the *relation* between the process by which the indicator is produced and the theoretical purposes of the investigator.[97]

The problem of equivalence—or the comparability of measures drawn from different social units—has received exhaustive discussion in the literature on comparative analysis. Basically the problem is whether a phenomenon measured in a similar way in different settings can be regarded as an indicator of the same variable. Converse and Dupeux highlighted the problem in a series of observations on the French and American polities a number of years ago:

> Broad differences in institutions and political practices in the two societies can serve to channel public interest in different directions. The French political poster, often a full-blown campaign document, is addressed to other goals than the American political billboard, and hence the reading of such posters in the two societies is in no sense comparable activity. Similarly, the national control of the domestic airwaves in France means that two media of communication are given a totally different cast than in the United States. This fact, coupled with reduced access to radio or television sets in France, renders the attention paid by the two publics to such political broadcasts fundamentally incomparable.[98]

This familiar problem appears in all types of research involving dissimilar units, no matter what the character of the data or what the research instrument employed. The particular form of the problem varies from case to case, however, because in using different research methods the investigator intervenes in the production of his data in different ways. Consider first the analysis of various social aggregates that are produced and recorded in the course of societal transactions in ways that are not significantly affected by the activities of the investigator himself—market transactions, voting statistics, census data, and the like. Comparative investigators of such data are plagued by problems such as the following: different degrees of monetization of economies means that differential

[97] Cf. International Urban Research, *The World's Metropolitan Areas* (Berkeley and Los Angeles: University of California Press, 1959), pp. 15–17.

[98] Philip E. Converse and Georges Dupeux, "Politicization of the Electorate in France and the United States," *Public Opinion Quarterly* 26(1962):3–15.

proportions of the total amount of economic activity are recorded; fluctuating exchange rates make it difficult for the economic measures of one country to be compared consistently with those of another;[99] recording conventions differ significantly among different nations on items such as unemployment figures, crime statistics, literacy, with the result that comparisons are plagued by problems of unavailability, inaccuracy, under-enumeration, unrepresentativeness, and the like;[100] compilations of aggregates such as conflicts or "riots" by newspaper scanning also yield highly variable results.[101]

In research where the investigator becomes actively involved in generating data—for example, in survey research—he is, in principle, able to control certain sources of error by drawing a representative sample, standardizing the stimulus situation for respondents, and so on. But the introduction of the investigator into the research situation is likely to introduce new sources of error. Standard questions administered in different cultural settings run into the following types of problems: different meanings are assigned to questions by virtue of linguistic differences;[102] comparable "samples" are difficult to draw; citizens of developing countries may not have been exposed to the "culture" of answering questions, are likely to be inclined to give "acquiescent" responses, or to regard the interview situation either as inquisitorial or as a situation possibly to be exploited.[103] At-

[99] For a discussion of representative problems, see Goran Ohlin, "Aggregate Comparisons: Problems and Prospects of Quantitative Analysis Based on National Accounts," and Phyllis Deane, "Aggregate Comparisons: The Validity and Reliability of Economic Data," in Stein Rokkan, ed., *Comparative Research across Cultures and Nations* (Paris-The Hague: Mouton, 1968), pp. 163–75.

[100] For a review of such problems, see Erwin K. Scheuch, "Cross-National Comparisons Using Aggregate Data: Some Substantive and Methodological Problems," in Richard L. Merritt and Stein Rokkan, eds., *Comparing Nations: The Use of Quantitative Data in Cross-National Research* (New Haven: Yale University Press, 1966), pp. 131–67.

[101] Michael C. Hudson, "Data Problems in Quantitative Comparative Analysis," *Comparative Politics* 5(1973):617–19.

[102] Susan Ervin and Robert T. Bower, "Translation Problems in International Surveys," *Public Opinion Quarterly* 16(1952):595–604.

[103] The literature on the issue of bias in cross-cultural surveys is voluminous. The reader is referred to Elmo C. Wilson, "Problems of Survey Research in Modernizing Areas," *Public Opinion Quarterly* 22(1958–59):230–34; Lloyd Rudolph and Susanne H. Rudolph, "Surveys in India: Field Experience in Madras State," *Public Opinion Quarterly* 22(1958–59):235–44; Erwin K. Scheuch, "The Cross-Cultural Use of Sample Surveys: Problems of Comparability," and Robert E. Mitchell, "Survey Materials Collected in the Developing Countries: Obstacles to Comparison," in Stein Rokkan, ed., *Comparative Research across Cultures and Nations*, pp. 176–238; Frederic W. Frey, "Cross-Cultural Survey Research in Political Science," in Holt and Turner, eds., *The Methodology of Comparative Research*, pp. 173–294.

tempts to replicate experimental laboratory findings in cross-cultural settings have indicated that the "experiment-effect" for different cultures may
be a more important source of variation than any of the variables manipulated within the experiment.[104] Finally, the process of gaining access to
research sites in different social settings not only poses serious ethical,
political, and practical issues for the investigator, but it may also introduce
wide ranges of "error" into the data that he ultimately collects.[105]

Even this cursory scan of problems of equivalence yields a general conclusion: all such problems, no matter what their particular guise, concern
the variation in the context of indicators within different social units—
variation that somehow contaminates a desired relationship between a
variable and its presumed indicator.[106] We reach the same conclusion in
examining various efforts to *overcome* problems of equivalence in comparative research. Again, to choose only a scattering of possible illustrations:
(a) Economists have developed a variety of devices for incorporating "non-monetary" economic indicators into national income accounts
in order to gain more adequate measures of "real" income in different
societies; in effect they have attempted to eliminate the "error" introduced
into income accounts by not counting these indicators.[107] For example,
in his effort to take account of "unpaid family labor" in the
shares of major industrial sectors in national product and labor force,
Kuznets calculated industrial distributions of measures both including and
excluding estimates of such labor, thereby making an effort to approximate

[104] See, for example, Richard S. Lazarus, Edward Opton, Jr., Masatoshi Tomita,
and Masahisa Kodama, "A Cross-Cultural Study of Stress Reaction Patterns in Ja-
pan," *Journal of Personality and Social Psychology* 4(1966):622–33; also Jay Haley,
"Cross-Cultural Experimentation: An Initial Attempt," *Human Organization* 26
(1967):110–17.

[105] For a sample of three very different discussions of these issues, see William
H. Form, "Field Problems in Comparative Research: The Politics of Distrust,"
Joseph W. Elder, "Problems of Cross-Cultural Methodology: Instrumentation and
Interviewing in India," and Alejandro Portes, "Perception of the U. S. Sociologist and
Its Impact on Cross-National Research," in Armer and Grimshaw, eds., *Comparative
Social Research*, pp. 83–169.

[106] Przeworski and Teune suggested that only by "controlling intervening vari-
ables" can "the cross-national equivalence of relationships be established." Adam
Przeworski and Henry Teune, "Equivalence in Cross-National Research," *Public
Opinion Quarterly* 30(1966):557.

[107] See M. K. Bennett, "International Disparities in Consumption Levels," *American Economic Review* 46(1966):452–61; Wilfred Beckerman, *International Comparisons of Real Incomes* (Paris: Organization for European Economic Cooperation,
1966); Wilfred Beckerman and Robert Bacon, "International Comparisons of Income Levels: A Suggested New Measure," *Economic Journal* 76(1966):519–36.

the amount of variation contributed by the more elusive unpaid laborers.[108] (b) Political scientists and others have developed measures designed to build likely sources of error—errors resulting from under-reporting and under-enumeration, for example—into aggregate indices in order to increase their comparability.[109] (c) In cross-cultural psychological research, to use "language-free" instruments and "projective tests" constitutes an effort to enhance cross-cultural comparability by eliminating—and thereby controlling—linguistic and related forms of variation that affect responses to verbal stimuli.[110] Still other efforts to overcome the same problem are the "back-translation" of survey or test items to insure comparability of test-stimuli, and interviewing by bilinguals.[111] (d) Others have argued that *different* indicators should be used to measure the same variable in different contexts; Przeworski and Teune, for example, attempted to design different measures for political activeness in different societies (including those as different as Poland, Yugoslavia, and the United States); such an approach attacks the problem of unwanted contextual variance by *incorporating* it into the measure.[112] Verba has suggested a variety of strategies at different stages of survey research—in wording of questionnaire items, in sampling procedures, in providing multiple measures, etc.—all designed to incorporate context into the comparative study design.[113] (e) Rommetveit and Israel made some preliminary attempts to control for cross-cultural differences in meaning in the replication of experiments.[114] (f) Naroll has

[108] Simon Kuznets, "Quantitative Aspects of the Economic Growth of Nations. 2. Industrial Distribution of National Product and Labor Force," *Economic Development and Cultural Change* 5(October 1956):19ff.

[109] See Ted Robert Gurr, *New Error-Compensated Measures for Comparing Nations* (Princeton: Center of International Studies, 1966); see also Ted Robert Gurr, *Polimetrics: An Introduction to Quantitative Macropolitics* (Englewood Cliffs, N. J.: Prentice-Hall, 1972), pp. 49–59.

[110] Charles E. Osgood, "On the Strategy of Cross-National Research into Subjective Culture," *The Social Sciences: Problems and Orientations* (Paris-The Hague: Mouton/UNESCO, 1968), pp. 487–88; for an assessment of the limited success of projective tests in cross-cultural settings, see Gardner Lindzey, *Projective Techniques in Cross-Cultural Research* (New York: Appleton-Century-Crofts, 1961).

[111] Bruce W. Anderson, "On the Comparability of Meaningful Stimuli in Cross-Cultural Research," *Sociometry* 30(1967):124–36.

[112] "Equivalence in Cross-National Research," pp. 558–59; "International Studies of Values in Politics," *Values and the Active Community: A Cross-National Study of the Influence of Local Leadership* (New York: The Free Press, 1971), pp. 49–50.

[113] Sidney Verba, "The Uses of Survey Research in the Study of Comparative Politics: Issues and Strategies," in Rokkan, Verba, Viet, and Almasy, *Comparative Survey Analysis*, pp. 80–99; Verba, "Cross-National Survey Research: The Problem of Credibility," in Vallier, ed., *Comparative Methods*, pp. 309–56.

[114] Ragnar Rommetveit and Joachim Israel, "Notes on the Standardization of Experimental Manipulations and Measurement in Cross-National Research," *Journal of Social Issues* 10(1954):61–68.

devised a scheme for estimating and correcting for—and thereby reducing variability in—ethnographic reports in the various stages of their design, execution, and interpretation.[115]

Though diverse in method and differing in effectiveness from case to case, all these efforts have in common the attempt to make parametric some source of variation—whether this emanates from the investigator or others who produce the data, or in the interaction between them—that may affect the validity and the reliability of data, and thereby affect the quality of causal inferences based on associations among those data.

Concluding Remarks

Though I have organized this chapter as a sequence of separate discussions of classification, abstract variables (or comparative dimensions), and indicators, it has proved difficult to keep these three operations separate for two reasons. First, while the operations—selecting units, selecting variables, selecting indicators—differ with respect to the aspect of the research process each concerns, all have in common the investigator's attempt to minimize the influence of variation in context—including himself as context—on empirical phenomena by converting this context into some sort of parametric constant. Second, in assessing the adequacy of one of the three operations it invariably becomes necessary to invoke the other two as criteria. In assessing the adequacy of comparative dimensions, for example, it is necessary to know what social units are being compared, and what kinds of indicators the dimensions are meant to call forth.

Because of the interdependence of these various research operations, some of the polemics involving the appropriate and most strategic "entering wedge" for comparative analyses seem on the fruitless side. I have in mind, for example, the two conjoined discussions of Riggs and LaPalombara, in which the former recommended the identification of "whole political systems" or patterns of government, as a basis for comparative study,[116] while the latter, rejecting the "whole systems" approach as "scholastic," called for research on segments of the political process such as "decision-making" in a variety of political units.[117] The reason why such controversies are fruitless is that Riggs, while opting to deal initially with the most general lines of contextual variation of phenomena, could not proceed

[115] Raoul Naroll, *Data Quality Control—A New Research Technique* (New York: The Free Press of Glencoe, 1962), pp. 80–105.

[116] Fred W. Riggs, "The Comparison of Whole Political Systems," in Holt and Turner, *The Methodology of Comparative Research*, pp. 73–121.

[117] Joseph LaPalombara, "Parsimony and Empiricism in Comparative Politics: An Anti-Scholastic View," in ibid., pp. 151–72.

to his desired goal of generating "rigorous statements of testable and interesting hypotheses about the causes and consequences of diverse forms of government"[118] without selecting certain comparative dimensions and indicators less general than "whole systems"; and LaPalombara not only would invariably be driven to find indicators for dimensions such as decision-making, but also would be forced to consider variability in the contexts of decision-making. The latter would push him in the direction of coming to terms—by some scheme of classification—with larger social units to assure comparability of the dimension of decision-making in different systems. No matter where the wedge enters in the comparative analysis of dissimilar societies, the investigator sooner or later confronts an identical series of issues which he must resolve either directly and self-consciously or by default. I have attempted to lay out these issues in this chapter.

In focusing on classification, description, and measurement as forms of establishing parametric control over suspected sources of variation ("error"), I have also demonstrated the essential parallel between these operations and the operation known as explanation. (We shall see further evidence of this parallel when we focus directly on explanation in the next chapter.) At the beginning I identified the essence of scientific explanation as the establishment of logical and empirical controls over sources of variation, and identified a variety of methods—differing in their adequacy—of gaining such control. But it is also the case, as this chapter has shown, that classification, selecting variables, and selecting indicators—often seen as preceding and differing from explanation—are various forms of explanation as I have defined the term. Indeed, it is possible to regard an empirical indicator as a special type of dependent variable, and to regard the different operations that an investigator goes through in representing it as so many independent variables affecting it. For example, the array of responses to a survey instrument administered cross-nationally (the outcome, or dependent variable) is a function of the investigator's selection of nations, his choice of conceptual dimensions, his writing of items, his mode of administration, and his efforts to control for contextual and other contaminating influences. The research operation, in short, is an empirical phenomenon, and it is amenable to assessment by means of the same sorts of methods that are applicable to the analysis of the associations among any group of empirical phenomena.

Appreciating this fundamental parallel, we may also note how undeveloped is the "science" of assessing the impact of different forms of classification, different variables, and different indicators on the results of research. We have seen in this chapter only modest use of the statistical methods to

118 Riggs, "The Comparison of Whole Political Systems," p. 121.

arrive at subclassifications and to improve the validity and reliability of indices by systematically taking into account sources of error. And while a reading of the vast literature on the methodology of comparative analysis reveals a general awareness on the part of investigators that their own strategies can contribute substantial and sometimes overwhelming error, only sparse efforts systematically to assess and control those strategies are evident.[119] With the exception of a few empirical studies which indicate that some gross classification systems are overly simple, little has been done systematically to assess the impact of choice of different kinds of units on the research process by varying the units and tracing the consequences. The choice of one set of units over another—for example, Kuznets' and others' emphasis on the nation-state—rests on a series of empirical assertions that the nation is more important than regions within the nation or groupings of nations. While often plausible, methodologically these assertions stand as imaginary experiments, with the investigator imagining, on the basis of his general knowledge, that the choice of other units would be less appropriate because of their lesser impact on economic variables. Virtually no systematic variation of the selection of dimensions has been attempted; most of the critical discourse about comparative variables is negative in the sense that critics point out that one or another variable is culture-bound or otherwise inappropriate. In other cases methodological discussions of the research process consist of a report on the part of the investigator as to how careful he was to secure appropriate entry to the research site, to train interviewers, and so on; again, the methodological status of such descriptions is that of the imaginary experiment, with the investigator asserting in general ways how it would have been otherwise if he had not taken such precautions. Evidently, if the research operations can be regarded legitimately as causal processes that produce indicators, and if these operations contribute as much error in the comparative analysis of dissimilar units as they appear to do, then comparative investigators should assign priority to bringing the best available scientific methods to bear on the systematic assessment of the research process itself, much as they have done in the analysis of causal relations considered as operating external to the research operation.

[119] This remark parallels Wiggins' observation that "[whereas] an experimental design can control most of the extraneous variables which are present prior to the experiment . . . , there are many extraneous variables occurring *during* an experiment which until recently have been unperceived or uncontrolled." "Hypothesis Validity and Experimental Laboratory Methods," p. 393.

7

Association, Cause, Explanation, and Theory

We may recapitulate the arguments of chapter six by again referring to figure 6-2, reproduced here. That figure represents the research situation of the investigator studying two or more social units with evident parametric differences. The parametric differences between the units (A, B) constitute contexts which have causal significance for the empirical phenomena under study (x_A, y_A, x_B, y_B) and which are likely to make them incomparable with one another. By "incomparable" I mean that the phenomena (x_A, x_B, and y_A, y_B, respectively) cannot be regarded as identical indicators for the general variables (X and Y, respectively). If incomparable, the associations among the phenomena ($x_a \longrightarrow y_A$, and $x_B \longrightarrow y_B$, respectively), cannot be regarded as manifestations of causal relations among the general variables ($X \longrightarrow Y$).

Looked at another way, the parametric differences among different social units constitute sources of error in estimating the relations between independent (X) and dependent (Y) variables. My task in chapter six was to treat the procedures of classification, description, and measurement as attempts to render parametric differences similar, thereby rendering the empirical phenomena comparable. Thus:

1. Classification involves the assertion that social units (cultures, societies, communities, formal organizations, and the like) are identical—or resemble one another sufficiently for purposes of analysis—with respect to certain definitional criteria. In venturing such an assertion the investigator, in effect, attempts to hold constant or makes parameters of the classificatory criteria, and rules out those criteria as sources of variation (or error) in the phenomena studied. Insofar as the units actually vary empirically with respect to the criteria of classification, the investigator has correspondingly failed to control this variation.

2. The selection of descriptive variables (X and Y) involves the assertion that there are, in principle, instances of these variables in units A and B. Insofar as the investigator chooses variables that are in some degree unit-specific—that is, cannot be instantiated in all the units under study—an additional source of error is introduced into the effort to establish relations among these variables.

3. The selection of measurable indicators (x_A, y_A, x_B, y_B) involves the assertion that the causal processes generating these indicators in different systems are sufficiently similar that they may be regarded as representing the same respective variables in units A and B. Insofar as this assertion is unfounded, error is introduced into the relations $X \longrightarrow x_A$, $Y \longrightarrow y_A$, etc., and the relations between X and Y as expressed by the relations between their indicators.

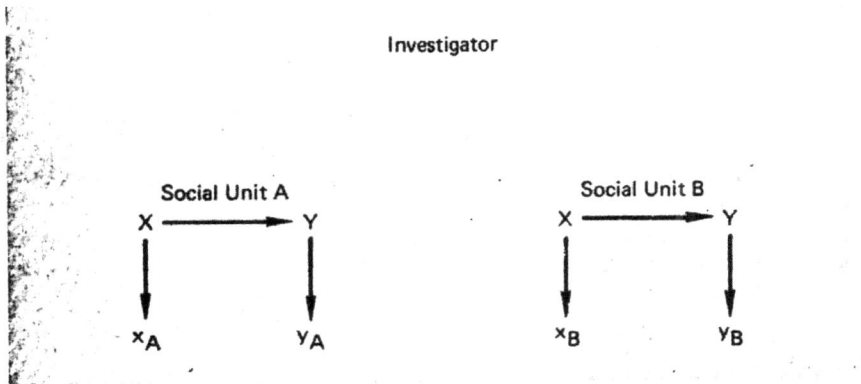

Investigator

Social Unit A

X ⟶ Y

x_A y_A

Social Unit B

X ⟶ Y

x_B y_B

FIG. 6–2 A Research Situation Involving Dissimilar Social Units

Furthermore, though the various operations of classifying, describing, and measuring involve procedures at different stages and levels of analysis, they share the objective of bringing the correlations between variables and observed indicators to "[unity] or else very high and subject only to minor random errors."[1]

In this chapter I leave these issues aside and concentrate directly on establishing associations and causal relations between X and Y, as observed through the associations between x and y in a number of different social units. I shall consider first the difficulties of establishing association and cause in the study of a single case, and the ways that the addition of other cases helps overcome these difficulties. After digressing briefly on the recurrent issue of the idiographic versus the nomothetic mode of investigation, I shall discuss the phenomenon of empirical correlation, as well as the difficulties in making the inferential transition from correlation to cause. Most of the chapter will be devoted to identifying the available ways of increasing the level of confidence in causal inferences. Toward the end I shall show how associations and causal inferences are invariably embedded in a network of "other knowledge"—assumptions and assertions not directly based on the empirical phenomena at hand but often having other empirical reference and varying in validity. And though the focus now shifts from issues related to classification and measurement to issues related to causality and theory, the distinction between parameters and operative variables[2] will prove as helpful in this chapter as it did in the last.

The Limitations of Case Study

Numerous observers have pointed out that a single, cross-sectional constellation of empirical phenomena does not afford the possibility of establishing causal relations among those phenomena. To use Zelditch's example, "it could not be said from a study of the family in the United States that industrialization is a cause of the isolated nuclear family." Why not? Basically, because the isolated nuclear family is associated with possibly causal phenomena other than industrialization as well; "urbanization, the frontier, or a puritan heritage might equally well have caused it."[3] With no variation in either the presumed effect or the possible causes, there is no immediate empirical basis for either eliminating or establishing a preference for any one of the possible causes. Or, as Campbell and Stanley put it, the

---

[1] See p. 164.

[2] See pp. 154–55.

[3] Morris Zelditch, Jr., "Intelligible Comparisons," in Ivan Vallier, ed., *Comparative Methods in Sociology. Essays on Trends and Applications* (Berkeley and Los Angeles: University of California Press, 1971) pp. 288–89.

one-shot case study has "such a total absence of control as to be of almost no scientific value."[4]

Campbell and Stanley appeared to overstate the argument against case studies, for in the social sciences they have proved to be of great value in generating hypotheses, refining relations among variables, and the like.[5] But they were correct with respect to the limits on drawing causal inferences from them. Such inferences, when emanating from a case study, generally rest on the implicit comparison "with other events casually observed and remembered."[6] More generally, these inferences rest on the appeal to "other knowledge" and the imaginary experiment. Given the available data, these are the only methods for estimating causal relations; and since these methods do not permit rigorous empirical control, they are among the most fragile of the comparative methods.

The crucial factor determining the limitation of the case study lies not in the actual number of cases studied but in the lack of variation in possible causes and effects. Thus, though Durkheim included many tribes in his study of primitive religion, he treated them as invariant with respect to the relevant social-structural and religious phenomena to be treated as causes and effects; so, in effect, he analyzed a single case. And as we saw, his main arguments for establishing causal relations among these phenomena rested on "other knowledge," mainly psychological generalizations that provide plausible links among the phenomena. To make the point the other way around, consider Nadel's effort to rescue the case study from Radcliffe-Brown's indictment that while "the study of a single society may . . . afford occasion for hypotheses, which then need to be tested by reference to other societies, it cannot give demonstrated results." That need not be the case, Nadel argued, if "we include time perspective and cultural change in our enquiry" and if we consider "internal variations" in the case in question.[7] In so arguing, however, Nadel was in effect expanding the number of cases—whether by comparing the society with its own

[4] Donald T. Campbell and Julian C. Stanley, *Experimental and Quasi-Experimental Designs for Research* (Chicago: Rand-McNally, 1966), p. 6.

[5] Arend Lijphart, "Comparative Politics and the Comparative Method," *American Political Science Review* 65(1971):691–93.

[6] Campbell and Stanley, *Experimental and Quasi-Experimental Designs for Research*, p. 6. Hyman has designated this procedure as "pseudo-comparative sociology." Herbert H. Hyman, "Research Design," in Robert E. Ward, ed., *Studying Politics Abroad: Field Research in the Developing Areas* (Boston: Little, Brown, 1964), pp. 153–88.

[7] S. F. Nadel, *The Foundations of Social Anthropology*, (London: Cohen and West, 1949), p. 240.

past or by subdividing it—thereby introducing the possibility of investigating empirical co-variation.

Expanding the Number of Cases

The addition of cases permits the beginning of empirically-informed assessments that can supplement and improve on the reliance on other knowledge and the imaginary experiment. Its basic continuity with these weaker forms of comparison, however, is illustrated by Rhoads:

> Why did not the Shaker communities in America become denominationalized after a generation? The hypothesis of the denominational transformation [transition from sect to denomination] would make such a prediction. The logic of the imaginary experiment would perhaps direct one to imagine the introduction of an intra-worldly ethic of asceticism as a substitute for the actual extra-worldly (Shaker withdrawal into self-contained communities) asceticism, making probably an identification with the work ethic, material success, and accommodation to the economic order. Such an imagination in the light of Weber's thesis of the *Protestant Ethic* "makes sense," the latter thesis functioning as a rough guide for such an imaginative reconstruction. Yet the role of asceticism as an answer to the question of the Shaker sect becomes more probable when that sect is compared with the course of development of American Methodism. Both sects shared features in common as to time and place of origin, matters of doctrine, etc., yet Methodism began with an ascetic ethic applied *within* the secular order, whereas the Shakers physically separated from society into more or less self-contained communities. In this example the comparison of the two religious groups serves as a check on the application of the imaginary experiment. It can readily be observed that the application of the comparison of cases is a logical extension of the imaginary experiment, the two procedures being closely related.[8]

In the cross-sectional observation of the single case, there is, strictly speaking, no variation in either dependent or independent variables, since what is observed is a fixed pattern of relationships. Expanding the observations over time provides additional cases—that is, different patterns of the variables—that increase the variation of all variables. Greater variation in outcome is achieved; for example, Moran contrasted Argentine and Australian political development, the former leading to political disinte-

---

[8] John K. Rhoads, "The Type as a Logical Form," *Sociology and Social Research* 51(1967):353–54.

gration, the latter to political integration—outcomes not observable in the study of either case alone.[9] Greater variation in possible causes is also achieved; for instance, Gerhard attempted to assess the historical validity of Turner's "frontier thesis" by examining frontier societies other than America—for example, Russia, Canada, and Australia—and pointing to variations in the frontiers' apparent impact.[10]

Equally important, the addition of cases provides an initial lever for gaining control over the extended variation, so that certain causes may be ruled out—with varying degrees of effectiveness—and a presumption may be established in favor of others. Thus, in his comparative study of political development, Moran pointed to certain broad similarities between Argentina and Australia:

> Both are primarily agricultural countries whose economies rely on commercial export of wheat, beef, and wool. Both had a "big man's frontier" and early developed a small landholding class which dominated the economy. Each boasts of its large industrial base, yet complains of being a "dependent" or "periphery" economy. . . . Australia and Argentina are situated in the temperate latitudes of the Southern Hemisphere. While each has seemingly abundant agricultural land, more than a third of their populations are concentrated in the largest cities. Both are nationalistic and show a pride matched with highly ambivalent feelings about the older and more crowded Northern Hemisphere.[11]

By such observations he suggested that the search for conditions affecting political stability in the two societies is best directed to *other* conditions, in which the societies differ. Similarly, in his comparative essay on American and Canadian political parties, Epstein pointed out evident similarities between the two societies—similarities in literacy rates; universal suffrage; social and economic class structure; a single-member, simple-plurality election system—thus ruling out or at least playing down these conditions as factors explaining the differences between the party systems of the two societies.[12] In both illustrations the investigators' arguments constitute an effort to establish parametric control over potential operative variables,

[9] Theodore H. Moran, "The 'Development' of Argentina and Australia: The Radical Party of Argentina and the Labor Party of Australia in the Process of Economic and Political Development," *Comparative Politics* 3(1970–71):71–92.

[10] Dietrich Gerhard, "The Frontier in Comparative View," *Comparative Studies in Society and History* 1(1958–59):205–29.

[11] Moran, "The 'Development' of Argentina and Australia," p. 71.

[12] Leon D. Epstein, "A Comparative Study of Canadian Parties," *American Political Science Review* 68(1964):46–48.

and, as such, approximate the logic of Mill's method of difference—ruling out points of agreement as operative causes of different outcomes.

I shall carry this line of argument further when discussing the method of controlled comparison later in the chapter. For the moment, I should note that the advantages of adding one or a few cases to extend variation and increase the probability of control should not be exaggerated. In any event the number of potentially operative variables still far exceeds the number of cases studied. Furthermore, if only a few cases are added, only certain nonparametric statistical techniques become available to establish the strength or significance of suspected associations among causes and effects. And finally, the asserted similarities between cases may obscure important differences along the very dimensions on which the cases are claimed to be similar. For example, to assert that both Argentines and Australians "are nationalistic and show pride matched with highly ambivalent feelings about the older and more crowded Northern Hemisphere" may conceal salient differences: Australian ambivalence is mainly toward Britain, Argentine ambivalence mainly toward Spain. Furthermore, this and other cultural differences in nationalistic expression may be related causally to the dependent variable, that is, type of political integration. Care must be taken that potential sources of variation are not "assumed away" by a claim that cases resemble one another, without undertaking the requisite empirical investigation.

A Digression on the
Idiographic-Nomothetic Dilemma

Earlier I noted a tension between Durkheim's and Weber's programs for sociology with respect to the conceptualization of human society and the status of "laws" governing it. In chapter four we saw that Durkheim regarded social facts as social reality—facts represented in empirical, hopefully measurable, indices; and facts to be related causally and lawfully to one another by the study of concomitant variation in the indices representing them. Weber, on the other hand, as noted in chapter five, regarded social reality as the *"real,* i.e., concrete, individually-structured configuration of our cultural life." And while laws might be helpful as heuristic devices to generate explanations of concrete configurations, the configurations themselves cannot be derived or deduced from the laws. And while both scholars relaxed these positions somewhat in the course of their further methodological reflections and their comparative research, Durkheim adopted an initial position that has been referred to as "nomothetic," whereas Weber's position is closer to that which has been called the "idiographic."[13]

The contrast between—and the debate over the advantages and liabilities of—these two approaches have appeared in different guises in many academic disciplines. For example:

—In psychology, in the debate concerning the statistical and clinical modes of prediction.[14]

—In the contrast between history and the social sciences, in which it is commonly supposed that "[historians] deal with the unique while social scientists look for generalizations. The historian tries to describe and explain specific events such as the Puritan or French revolutions, while the social scientist is interested in the causes of revolution in general."[15]

—In the contrast between anthropology and sociology. Leach maintained that "[the] sociologist with his statistical orientation presupposes that the field of observation consists of 'units of population,' 'individuals'; in contrast, the social anthropologist, with his non-statistical prejudices, thinks of his data as being made up of 'systems of relationship.' "[16]

—In political science, in which Verba has distinguished between the "configurational" and "aggregate" approaches to macropolitical phenomena.[17]

—In the comparative study of societies generally, in which the "area study" or "uniquist" approach has been contrasted with the more general "comparativist" approach.[18]

[13] Following Windeband, Allport referred to "nomothetic" disciplines as those which "seek only general laws and employ only those procedures admitted by the exact sciences. . . . The idiographic sciences, such as history, biography, and literature, on the other hand, endeavor to understand some *particular* event in nature or in society." Gordon W. Allport, *Personality: A Psychological Interpretation* (New York: Henry Holt, 1937), p. 22.

[14] The classical discussion of this issue in psychology is Paul E. Meehl, *Clinical vs. Statistical Predictions: A Theoretical Analysis and a Review of the Evidence* (Minneapolis: University of Minnesota Press, 1954).

[15] Guenther Lewy, "Historical Data in Comparative Political Analysis," *Comparative Politics* 1(1968):103. See also Austin T. Turk, "The Sociological Relevance of History: A Footnote to Research on Legal Control in South Africa," in Michael Armer and Allen D. Grimshaw, eds., *Comparative Social Research: Methodological Problems and Strategies* (New York: Wiley, 1973), pp. 286–90.

[16] E. R. Leach, "An Anthropologist's Reflections on a Social Survey," *The Ceylon Journal of Historical and Social Studies* 1(1958):11.

[17] Sidney Verba, "The Uses of Survey Research in the Study of Comparative Politics: Issues and Strategies," in Stein Rokkan, Sidney Verba, Jean Viet, and Elina Almasy, *Comparative Survey Analysis* (Paris-The Hague: Mouton, 1969), p. 57–60.

[18] Allen D. Grimshaw, "Comparative Sociology: In What Ways Different from Other Sociologies," in Armer and Grimshaw, eds., *Comparative Social Research*, pp. 18–20.

Little would be served by a lengthy review of the debates on the relative merits of these two approaches. But since I have just discussed the transition from the one-shot case study to the study of aggregated cases, I might note a number of characteristics that mark this transition, thus pinpointing the relations between the idiographic and nomothetic approaches, and perhaps making the opposition between them not quite so diametric as is often supposed.

First, and by definition, the two approaches differ in the number of cases brought under study.

Second, the mode of comprehension often differs. In considering the individual case, the investigator frequently attempts to attain an "understanding" of the pattern of the unit, a grasp of the relations among its constituent parts. In this operation the investigator may not invoke any causal model; he may identify neither an event nor class of events to be explained nor any causal factors. The operation may be more akin to an "appreciative" or "aesthetic" act, an effort to understand the principles by which the parts consistently fit together. On the other hand, in the study of aggregated cases, the investigator is typically oriented from the outset toward "variables" which affect one another causally.

Third, when explanations *are* attempted, the investigator of the individual case is typically interested in the explanation of a single event, the investigator of aggregates in a distribution of events. As a result, the status of the attempted explanation differs. In the former there is an effort to account either for why an event occurred or why it did not; in the latter, the interest is typically in statistical or probabalistic relations between causes and effects.

Fourth, and as a result of the third, the idiographic mode of explanation typically *incorporates* different orders of causal variables; many factors are brought to bear to increase the plausibility of the explanation of a given event; "accidental" factors are given play.[19] The aggregative mode of explanation aims to *exclude* extraneous causes to establish the precise strength of the supposed causal relation between two or more phenomena.

Fifth, as we have seen, in the one-shot study of a case the only means of establishing control over variables is by appeal to other knowledge or by imaginary experiment. Expanding the number of cases—and thereby expanding the range of variation of both dependent and independent variables—opens the way to the use of comparative illustration and statistical or situational manipulation to gain parametric control.

---

[19] Lafferty has referred to the idiographic mode as a "conjuncture" of different causal factors. William M. Lafferty, "Contexts, Levels, and the Language of Comparison," *Social Science Information* 11(1972):67.

Sixth, the two approaches typically involve different research techniques. The idiographic analyst relies more on the observation of a wide span of events and relationships to discern a complex pattern and its implications. The investigator with a nomothetic bent tends to use quantifiable indices—through survey, census, sampling, etc.—of the variables chosen for study.[20]

Finally, however, the two approaches—insofar as both attempt to explain—do *not* necessarily differ substantively with respect to the nature of causal forces invoked. The same psychological generalization—for example, relative deprivation—may be called upon to explain why an individual shopper decided at a given moment to purchase an automobile and to explain why an entire class of downwardly-mobile individuals tend to be more intolerant of minorities than others. That is to say, the idiographic and nomothetic approaches do not call for different theoretical grounding-points. The differences between them lie more in the mode of explanation, the mode or organizing variables, and the techniques of research employed.

Some Remarks on Correlation

With the further addition of cases, a point is reached where classical parametric statistical techniques can be employed to establish the strength of association between variables (Mill's method of concomitant variation). Such techniques may also be employed to rule out extraneous independent variables by holding constant or otherwise controlling sources of variation, thus creating a presumption in favor of other independent variables (Mill's method of difference). I shall summarize a single correlational study— any of several hundred others could have been selected—to illustrate these advantages:

Otterbein was interested in locating certain variables that account for different rates of internal war in societies.[21] He defined "internal war" as "warfare between political communities within the same cultural unit"; "community" was defined operationally, as was "cultural unit"; and the frequency of war was coded on a three-point scale as "continual," "frequent," and "infrequent or never." On the side of the independent variables, he selected and operationalized several types:

1. Social-structural variables: the existence of fraternal interest groups (it was predicted that internal war would correlate positively with this variable).

[20] Leach, "An Anthropologists's Reflections on a Social Survey," pp. 11–12.
[21] Keith F. Otterbein, "Internal War: A Cross-Cultural Study," *American Anthropologist* 70(1968):277–88.

2. Political variables: type of party who can initiate war—"official" or "any-one" (it was predicted that "internal" war would be associated with the latter); degree of centralization of political system (it was predicted that the less centralized, the more internal war).
3. Intersocietal variable: external war (it was predicted that this would be negatively correlated with internal war).

These relations were tested on a sample of 50 societies drawn from the *Ethnographic Atlas* compiled by Murdock. Using the X^2 and Fisher's exact test as measures of significance, Otterbein found that neither fraternal interest groups, presence of unauthorized raiding parties, nor centralization of political system was consistently and significantly associated with the prevalence of internal war. When, however, level of centralization was held constant, he found that both fraternal interest groups and unauthorized raiding parties influence the frequency of internal war in decentralized political systems, but not in centralized ones. Finally, the incidence of external war was not significantly correlated with internal war, even when a variety of other conditions was held constant.

If the possibility of sampling and measurement error, as well as the possibility of the presence of other variables, are set aside for the moment, the associations uncovered by Otterbein suggest that the hypotheses linking social-structural variables with internal war—particularly when a crucial dimension of political structure is controlled for—are more plausible than the social-psychological hypothesis that involvement in conflict with external enemies leads to a closing of the ranks and diminished conflict within a society. Furthermore, because the number of societies studied was sufficiently large, certain statistical techniques could be utilized to estimate more precisely whether the results could have been expected by chance alone.[22]

It should be noted that factors *other* than the simple discoverable strength of empirical association often affect the magnitude of correlation coefficients in comparative studies. For one thing, if two variables, independent and dependent, constitute facets of some more global variable, the investigator will likely be measuring two aspects of the same phenomenon and will, as a result, obtain strong apparent correlations between these aspects. For example, in a study of Dutch and Belgian high school and university students (as well as a small group of French students), Pinner undertook to establish a positive relation between a measure of parental overprotection of subjects and subjects' expressions of political distrust.

---

[22] For a brief characterization of some of the problems involved in applying statistical techniques to a sample drawn from a universe with unknown characteristics, see the comment by Sjoberg later in the chapter.

In administering the study he asked the students to respond to questions dealing with attitudes toward government institutions and processes, as well as family relations.[23] It is less than remarkable that he found a strong positive association between memories of being socially confined by parents and attitudes of political distrust, largely because the two are probably facets of a more general attitude set toward authority figures.

Higher associations also are obtained when variables are defined at global levels, particularly if indices for them contain a number of decomposable variables. I have in mind, for example, certain comparative studies that use "national culture"—or some similar measure—as an independent variable. An illustration is the study by Devereaux, Bronfenbrenner, and Suci, which uncovered consistent national differences in estimates by American and German children concerning the relative importance of the father and the mother in family affairs, the amount of parental intervention in their lives, and so on.[24] Evidently, however, the variables "American" and "German" are composed of a multitude of organized variables that overdetermine the results, as it were; furthermore, reliance on such general variables tends to obscure the precise features of family structure and processes that might account for the differences. Considerations such as these prompted Przeworski and Teune to suggest that the goal of comparative research is "to substitute names of variables for the names of social systems, such as Ghana, the United States, Africa, or Asia."[25] Arguing by analogy, they pointed out that it would be inappropriate to attribute the fact that water boils at different temperatures in Denver and New York to "Denver-ness" and "New York-ness." Rather, it is necessary to select a crucial feature of the differences between the two—atmospheric pressure —that accounts for the difference, and disregard the other differences between the two cities.[26] Similarly, they called for decomposing proper names of different social systems into more specific dimensions, such as level of literacy, rural-urban ratios, and the like.

Some of the associations between quantitative indices of variables such as economic development, literacy, development of communications, have

[23] Frank A. Pinner, "Parental Overprotection and Political Distrust," *Annals of the American Academy of Political and Social Science* 361(September 1965):58–70.

[24] Edward C. Devereux, Jr., Urie Bronfenbrenner, and George J. Suci, "Patterns of Parent Behavior in the United States of America and the Federal Republic of Germany: A Cross-National Comparison," *International Social Science Journal* 14 (1962):488–506.

[25] Adam Przeworski and Henry Teune, *The Logic of Comparative Social Inquiry* (New York: Wiley, 1970), p. 8.

[26] Ibid., p. 9. See also Henry Teune and Krzysztof Ostrowski, "Political Systems as Residual Variables: Explaining Differences Within Systems," *Comparative Political Studies* 6(1973):3–21.

emerged as impressively high. Cutright, for example, found a Pearson zero order association of 0.81 in a sample of 77 nations between his index of communications development and an index of political development that incorporated measures of political complexity and political stability; he found a correlation of 0.95 between the communications-development index and economic development. Such high correlations, Cutright noted, reflect "the highly interdependent nature of national social organization . . . the score a nation receives on communications development is itself highly dependent on the national level of educational development, urbanization, labor force movement out of agricultural employment, and economic development."[27] Such findings are not without general interest. Because they are pitched at such a high level of generality, however, the inferences that can be drawn from them must be correspondingly general; and little can be inferred with respect to the specific mechanisms that link, say, political stability and level of economic development.

The conclusions to be drawn from these illustrations are two: first, that "hypotheses relating variables of wide conceptual generality are more readily verified";[28] and second, inferences drawn from such hypotheses must remain at the level of conceptual generality at which the hypotheses are pitched. Surely, moreover, one of the most appropriate research strategies at the present time is to press further toward the decomposition of multivariable composites into more specific forms.[29]

The most commonly cited difficulty of working with correlations among variables in a number of social units—no matter what the level of conceptual generality of variables and no matter what kinds of social units studied—is the difficulty of moving from the establishment of correlation to the assignment of causal relation among variables. Even so strong an advocate of correlational methods as Durkheim acknowledged that on the basis of concomitant variation alone it cannot be known which variable is cause and which effect or whether both are effects of a third cause. Indeed, the case against inferring cause from correlation may be extended further: even if variables are *not* correlated across different social units, they may be causally related to one another. Consider the recent research of the project on the International Studies of Values in Politics. In an ambitious

[27] Phillips Cutright, "National Political Development: Measurement and Analysis," *American Sociological Review* 28(1963):260.

[28] Jonathan M. Higson, "Different Emphases in the Social Scientist's Conception of Comparative Method," *International Journal of Comparative Sociology* 9(1958): 143–44.

[29] See Ivan Vallier's review of such efforts in "Empirical Comparisons of Social Structure: Leads and Lags," in Vallier, ed., *Comparative Methods*, pp. 230ff.

comparative effort, the investigators were interested in establishing the conditions which account for differences in the level of leaders' activity in community politics in the United States, India, Poland, and Yugoslavia. After an extended analysis, no single set of determinants appeared to account for level of activeness in the several countries studied; that is to say, there was not significant comparative co-variation. Instead, a distinctive pattern of determinants for activeness appeared in each society. Activeness in Poland, for example, depended heavily on the vicissitudes of national policy and little on the characteristics of local leadership; furthermore, in Poland, unlike the other three countries, a high level of conflict in a community appeared to diminish the activeness of leaders. In the United States a different constellation of factors appeared to account for leaders' activeness:

> Wealthy cities, with a middle-class population, are active; poor cities, often with a working-class population, are not active. The leaders in active cities value economic development and the avoidance of conflict. In the poorer cities there are active party organizations in which the leaders perceive themselves as influential. In the less active cities there are divisions between labor and management. The most salient finding about the American cities is that almost all of the relationships between characteristics of the socio-political structure and individual leaders and activeness disappear when the economic level of the city is removed from consideration.[30]

Quite different "structures of explanation" were also found for India and Yugoslavia. Methodologically, this means that although various factors (level of urbanization, level of economic development, ideological values, and so on) are apparently causally related to leaders' activeness, correlations between these variables and activeness did not appear when the different countries were compared. The parametric differences among the countries are apparently so strong that different variables gain salience, recede, or become irrelevant in each country.[31]

We reach the same conclusion when we take into account the phenomenon of functional equivalence. If we assume (as did Durkheim) that a single cause is responsible for a single effect, then a correlation between

---

[30] International Studies of Values in Politics, *Values and the Active Community: A Cross-National Study of the Influence of Local Leadership* (New York: The Free Press, 1971), pp. 304–5.

[31] For a general discussion of the impact of multicausality and pluricausality on correlations, see André J. F. Köbben, "The Logic of Cross-Cultural Analysis: Why Exceptions?" in Stein Rokkan, ed., *Comparative Research across Cultures and Nations* (Paris-The Hague: Mouton, 1968), pp. 35–39.

the two presumably reflects the strength of the causal relation between them. If, however, we assume that a variety of different effects may emerge from a common complex of conditions, the relationship between correlation and cause is changed. As Köbben illustrated it:

> We may ask ourselves when [prophetic movements] will occur. Some factors may be named: oppression; internal tensions; sudden changes; catastrophes; diseases; poverty. It is true that, where all or some of these factors occur, prophetic movements will frequently arise. Sometimes, however, a secular revolutionary (nationalistic) movement may arise instead, or else an organized attempt at economic betterment, for instance through the founding of cooperatives. . . . These are functional equivalents which weaken the rule: "where such and such conditions are fulfilled, a prophetic movement will arise."[32]

Under these circumstances, low-level correlations between causes and effects may be expected, but this does not diminish their status as causes. In an earlier work I noted that low correlations are to be expected between various kinds of explanatory conditions (strain, structural conduciveness, for example) and different kinds of collective behavior (hostile outbursts, norm-oriented movements, value-oriented movements). The strategy I adopted to gain association between causes and effects was to attempt to assess the causal force of *combinations* of causes through the logic of "value-added."[33]

On the basis of the foregoing, I must agree with Zelditch's conclusion that "just as the existence of a correlation is no proof of causation, nor even of genuine correlation, so absence of a correlation is no proof *against* causation or the existence of genuine correlation. It is possible for u to be present and v not, or for v to be present and u not, and still for u to be a cause of v."[34] The reason for this, moreover, is that in different social units parametric differences may obscure, overwhelm, reverse, or otherwise change the pattern of correlation and causation in the different units. It follows that any effort to overcome this indeterminacy in the relations between correlation and causation must consist in gaining control over the context that is responsible for the indeterminacy. This effort, moreover, consists of a variety of techniques for converting operative variables into parametric constants. Let us now review some of those techniques.

[32] Köbben, "The Logic of Cross-Cultural Analysis: Why Exceptions?" p. 39.

[33] Neil J. Smelser, *Theory of Collective Behavior* (New York: The Free Press of Glencoe, 1962), ch. 3.

[34] Zelditch, "Intelligible Comparisons," in Vallier, ed., *Comparative Methods,* p. 300.

Increasing Confidence in
Causal Inference

Sampling

One of the aims of sampling is to randomize or otherwise control un-wanted sources of variation. In drawing a random sample, for instance, the objective is to assure that each item in the universe has an equal chance of being drawn, thus attempting to assure that sources of variation affecting the sample are the same as those affecting the universe as a whole. How-ever, random sampling has not in fact led to the objectification of data or the elimination of bias, as would be expected.

Three distinct problems of sampling have plagued cross-cultural and cross-national research: (1) the unknown nature of the universe; (2) the degree of independence of individual cases from one another; and (3) the difficulty of obtaining comparable samples *within* social units that display evident parametric differences.

1. Sjoberg has identified some of the difficulties involved in attempting to draw a sample of societies from the universe of all known societies. The immediate target of his remarks was Murdock's comparative study of kin-ship in preliterate societies:[35]

> His comparative analysis of kinship systems is one of the studies which has drawn upon the data amassed by the Human Relations Area Files . . . on numerous literate and nonliterate societies. . . . [Certain] difficulties arise when probability statistics are applied on a cross-cultural basis. Murdock's sampling design with respect to world societies invites some serious criti-cisms. Just what is the universe from which his sample has been selected? The fact that he has included within his sample some historically "extinct" societies means that his universe embraces all societies which have ever existed. But we lack sufficient knowledge about this universe. It consists of societies for which we have adequate data, others upon which our knowl-edge is limited, and finally those about which we really know nothing. There is no way of determining how societies for which we lack informa-tion are related to those upon which we have information. Under these circumstances it is most difficult to consider his sample as "random"; some major "biases" may in fact be present. And if a random sample is not em-ployed, extreme caution must be exercised in interpreting (if not actually applying) inductive statistical techniques—e.g., the chi-square test which Murdock utilizes to generalize from his "sample" to the universe. Too often

[35] George Peter Murdock, *Social Structure* (New York: Macmillan, 1949).

social scientists employ statistical procedures without examining the assumptions upon which their analyses necessarily rest.[36]

Nor does the attempt to include the entire universe—for example, all independent nation states now existing as indicated by some criterion such as United Nations membership—solve the problem of selection bias.[37]

2. Closely related is the problem of what constitutes the appropriate units to be sampled from the universe—tribes, societies, cultures, nations, "cultunits," or whatever. Murdock's original *World Ethnographic Sample* was criticized because it contained "units which vary in level from the major regions such as Asia and Africa, and nations such as Korea and Uganda, to tribes and subtribes. Even 'the world' is listed as a case."[38] His *Ethnographic Atlas,* compiled subsequently, attempted to represent units more consistently at the societal level. Even so, ambiguities still remained. When should a unit be treated as a subunit of another? For example, should Egypt be considered a unit in itself, or not counted because it is a part of the United Arab Republic? No final resolution to such ambiguities is available; as always, the definition of units depends in large part on the purposes of study, and should be expected to vary as the research occasion demands.

The sampling problem that has plagued anthropologists most is "Galton's problem," so-named because it was he who, in 1899, challenged Tylor's study of correlations (adhesions) between cultural traits. Could it not be, he argued, that the correlations between items were the product of borrowing and diffusion of traits, and thus did not reveal any causal or functional relation among them? To put the implications of Galton's question in the framework I have been using, he asked if the process of diffusion did not constitute a set of operative variables that accounted for the association between the correlated variables. If diffusion is as important as Galton's question implied, serious doubts are cast on efforts to correlate items cross-culturally, because the correlations are inflated on account of the interdependence of cases.

Many of the strategies adopted by anthropologists sensitive to Galton's problem have aimed at minimizing—that is, gaining parametric control

[36] Gideon Sjoberg, "The Comparative Method in the Social Sciences," *Philosophy of Science* 22(1955):112.

[37] Charles L. Taylor, "Further Problems: A Consideration of Other Views," in Taylor, ed., *Aggregate Data Analysis: Political and Social Indicators in Cross-National Research* (Paris-Mouton: International Social Science Council, 1968), pp. 117–21.

[38] John W. M. Whiting, "Methods and Problems in Cross-Cultural Research," in Gardner Lindzey and Elliot Aronson, eds., *The Handbook of Social Psychology,* 2nd ed. (Reading, Mass.: Addison-Wesley, 1968), 2:702.

over—the variable of diffusion by attempting to assure independence. In constructing his *Ethnographic Atlas,* for example, Murdock, aware that common historical origin and geographical proximity are common bases for diffusion, adopted two rules of thumb:

1. The universe from which a world sample should be drawn consists, not of the totality of the world's culture-bearing units, but of clusters of such characterized by close genetic relationships. . . .
2. No world sample should include any two societies located geographically so close to one another that diffusion is likely to have jeopardized the essential independence of their cultures.[39]

Naroll has devised five separate standardized methods to control for geographical propinquity in the selection of cases,[40] and McNett and Kirk have suggested a grid method to approximate randomness in drawing samples of cultures.[41]

Most cross-cultural investigators acknowledge that because of the unknown extent of historical diffusion, sampling problems in cross-cultural analysis cannot be entirely overcome; accordingly, they typically settle for a number of practical steps designed to minimize unwanted sources of association that might result from a process of diffusion. Swanson, for instance, in his study of the correlates of various features of primitive religions, took Murdock's sample of 556 societies, which contains no more than a few societies from similar and neighboring peoples, and is grouped into 50 regions of the world. Swanson eliminated certain cases not likely to contain information relevant to the subject of his research (he based the elimination on interviews with specialists who knew the societies in question); and he omitted societies that had been converted to one of the great world religions (such as Christianity or Mohammedanism), once again to reduce associations that might be traceable to diffusion. By taking these precautions Swanson hoped to assure

that [the list of peoples] represent a wide range of the world's simpler peoples, that some of the lack of independence produced among the sample's members by their borrowing from neighbor societies has been removed, that they are not concentrated in one or a few geographic regions, and that

[39] George Peter Murdock, "Ethnographic Atlas: A Summary," *Ethnography* 6 (1967):110–11.
[40] Raoul Naroll, "Galton's Problem: The Logic of Cross-Cultural Analysis," *Social Research* 32(1966):428–51.
[41] Charles W. McNett, Jr., and Roger E. Kirk, "Drawing Random Samples in Cross-Cultural Studies: A Suggested Method," *American Anthropologist* 7(1968): 50–55.

the method by which they were chosen was not knowingly biased in favor of the hypotheses we shall test in later chapters.[42]

3. In some cross-cultural and cross-national research an effort is made to draw a sample of cases *within* two or more units, and compare the samples with one another with respect to associations of their attributes. This technique raises all the issues of comparability and equivalence reviewed in the previous chapter. In some instances the samples themselves have not been drawn in the same manner from social unit to social unit. The study of attitudes toward occupational prestige conducted by Inkeles and Rossi included a national sample of American adults 14 years and over; a sample of Japanese males 20 to 68 years of age in six large cities; a sample of written questionnaires distributed through adult-education centers and other organizations in England; and a sample of persons displaced from the Soviet Union—clearly non-comparable samples, though the precise extent of bias cannot be ascertained.[43] In other instances, however, the attempt to attain comparability by using some standardized means of sampling creates new problems. For example, to draw a sample stratified by number of years of education for the United States and Argentina would not yield comparable data because of the different structure of the educational systems and the different significance of education in the two societies. Some investigators have drawn samples by using *different* procedures for different societies, thereby hoping to incorporate certain parametric differences and to make the samples functionally but not formally equivalent. Manaster and Havighurst, for example, constructed six-level scales of educational attainment for the United States, Brazil, and England, making different formal (for example, number of years of school completed) cut-off points in the different societies, and basing their decisions on the cut-off points on their "knowledge of the social structure of the [countries]."[44] The success of such efforts, of course, corresponds to the validity of that knowledge. In any event, such efforts constitute efforts to control for variation in the sociocultural contexts of units that might render the samples incomparable.

[42] Guy E. Swanson, *The Birth of the Gods: The Origin of Primitive Beliefs* (Ann Arbor: University of Michigan Press, 1960), p. 37.

[43] Alex Inkeles and Peter H. Rossi, "National Comparisons of Occupational Prestige," *American Journal of Sociology* 61(1955–56):330–32.

[44] Guy J. Manaster and Robert J. Havighurst, *Cross-National Research: Social-Psychological Methods and Problems* (Boston: Houghton-Mifflin, 1972), pp. 164–65. For an account of how Almond and Verba developed a stratified, multistage, probability sample for the cross-national study of political culture, see Gabriel A. Almond and Sidney Verba, *The Civic Culture* (Princeton: Princeton University Press, 1963), appendix A.

Controlled comparison and the use of "near cases"

The systems of sampling just reviewed attempt to control variation either by attempting to randomize its effects or eliminate it by guaranteeing independence of cases, or both. The aim of such cross-unit research, moreover, is to obtain a sufficiently large number of representative instances to be able to establish confidence in the observed associations. A number of years ago, however, Eggan registered reservations about this strategy of generating knowledge by means of a "systematic comparison of a world-wide variety of instances." Instead, he proposed a more modest "method of controlled comparison":

> My own preference is for the utilization of the comparative method on a smaller scale and with as much control over the frame of comparison as it is possible to secure. It has seemed natural to utilize regions of relatively homogeneous culture or to work within social or cultural types, and to further control the ecology and the historical factors so far as it is possible to do so. . . . After comparing the Australian moiety structures [with one another] and finding their common denominators, I would prefer to make a comparison with the results of a similar study of moiety structures and associated practices of the Indians of Southern California, who approximate rather closely the Australian sociocultural situation. The results of this comparison could then be matched against comparable studies of Northwest Coast and other similar moiety systems, and the similarities and differences systematically examined by the method of concomitant variations. . . . I suggest the method of controlled comparison as a convenient instrument for [the exploration of middle-range theory], using covariation and correlation, and avoiding too great a degree of abstraction.[45]

The logic behind this and related suggestions[46] is that potential sources of variation are converted into parameters by selecting cases that resemble one another in significant respects. The resemblances can then be regarded as "ruled out" as explanatory factors, and explanations based on other variables can be generated within the framework provided by the resemblances. The issue of how the resemblances arose—whether by historical accident, common geographical setting, diffusion, or whatever—is not

---

[45] Fred Eggan, "Social Anthropology and the Method of Controlled Comparison," in Frank W. Moore, ed., *Readings in Cross-Cultural Methodology* (New Haven: HRAF Press, 1966).

[46] See John Walton, "Standardized Case Comparison: Observations on Method in Comparative Sociology," in Armer and Grimshaw, eds., *Comparative Social Research*, pp. 173–91.

relevant, because the resemblances are treated as given and controlled, not operative variables.

Numerous applications of this method of controlled comparison are found in the social-science literature. In analyzing differences in social organization on British and American merchant ships, Richardson regarded it as an advantage that both types of ships resembled one another in so many ways—common purposes, similar formal hierarchies of authority, low labor turnover, isolation of men from families, and the like. Arguing implicitly that because the ships were similar in these respects, variations potentially stemming from them were thereby controlled. In this way the research setting was particularly appropriate for demonstrating the importance of distinctive national training, the style of exercising authority, and informal systems of stratification.[47] Vallier, in a study of the different paths of development of two Latter-day Saint bodies (the Mormons and the Reorganites), noted that those bodies "share a basic religious value tradition and major goals but are located in widely different situations or social environments." By selecting his cases in this way he attempted to "gain, from the beginning, maximum control over cultural factors that are known to be a major source of variation," and to locate the operative sources of variation in development in the "external situation" of the groups, especially in their use of missionaries and voluntary labor.[48] West undertook to study the differential impact of British, French, and American colonial practices by selecting the small island groups of Fiji, Tahiti, and French Polynesia, and Eastern Samoa, respectively. Among the advantages of this procedure, he felt, were that these island communities shared the characteristics of being small, isolated, and under colonial rule for a relatively short period. As such, they presented the investigator with a series of "clear, isolated problems in which other colonial areas are obscure and much more complex."[49] Such a strategy seems preferable— from the standpoint of isolating the impact of specific variables—to the comparison of, say, elites in Indonesia and Ghana, which represent different continents, different cultural traditions, and different colonial traditions.[50]

[47] Stephen A. Richardson, "Organizational Contrasts on British and American Ships," *Administrative Science Quarterly* 1(1956):189–207.

[48] Ivan Vallier, "Church, Society, and Labor Resources—an Interdenominational Comparison," *American Journal of Sociology* 68(1962–63):21–33.

[49] F. J. West, *Political Advancement in the South Pacific: A Comparative Study of Colonial Practice in Fiji, Tahiti, and American Samoa* (Melbourne: Oxford University Press, 1961), p. vii.

[50] Thom Kerstiens, *The New Elite in Asia and Africa: A Comparative Study of Indonesia and Ghana* (New York: Praeger, 1966), pp. 22ff.

Another way of gaining the same sort of control is to narrow the focus of inquiry from between-unit variation to within-unit variation. What must be treated as variable between systems—because of their sociocultural differences—can be treated as parametric if only one system, subdivided into sectors or units, is considered. In intranational comparisons, "the system characteristics can be held relatively constant."[51] Thus, in analyzing the considerable political differences between northern and southern California, Wolfinger and Greenstein were able to "control" system-characteristics such as legal and constitutional structure—control of which would be lost if differences in political attitudes between two nations were compared.[52] Studying relations within homogeneous areas increases the investigator's confidence that "the functional relationship between the variables studied [is] more or less the same,"[53] unlike the study of different societies, in which a unique structural configuration of variables may account for the same phenomenon in each.

Another advantage of including within-system analyses is that the chronic problem of the limited number of cases can be overcome to a degree, and that suspected associations can be investigated at different levels. We observed this in Durkheim's analysis of altruistic suicide, in which he attempted to replicate military-civilian differences in suicide rates by investigating a number of differences among different categories of military personnel. To choose another example, let us suppose that we are interested in explaining the causes of differential student unrest in Latin American countries. After comparative investigation, we are able to rank-order a dozen countries in terms of general level of unrest among students. Suppose further that a plausible hypothesis to account for the rank-ordering is that the less uncertainty there is in the transition from student role to occupational role, the less the likelihood of unrest. Those Latin American countries with educational systems "out of line" with occupational structures in terms of this transition appear consistently to manifest higher levels of student unrest. But with an N of 12, and so many plausible hypotheses available, we cannot have much confidence in the "transition" theory. To further test this theory, we turn to replication, both at more general and less general analytic levels. We might observe, for

[51] Juan Linz and Amando de Miguel, "Within-Nation Differences and Comparisons: The Eight Spains," in Richard L. Merritt and Stein Rokkan, eds., *Comparing Nations: The Use of Quantitative Data in Cross-National Research* (New Haven: Yale University Press, 1966), p. 269.

[52] Raymond E. Wolfinger and Fred I. Greenstein, "Comparing Political Regions: The Case of California," *American Political Science Review* 63(1964):74–85.

[53] Bruce M. Russett, *International Regions and the International System—A Study in Political Ecology* (Chicago: Rand McNally, 1967), p. 9.

example, that in general Latin American countries have a greater incidence of student unrest than North American countries. In the latter, moreover, education tends to be more technical, vocational, and geared to specific occupational lines than in Latin America. This finding would be consistent with the comparisons *among* Latin American countries themselves. At a less general level, we might attempt to locate unrest according to the same association *within* each Latin American country. Thus, within each country, engineering and architectural students appear to be low in unrest because as a rule they move easily into occupational positions; law students are very high because, in Latin tradition, they are trained in general education and not prepared for any particular occupational role; economics students intermediate with respect to future occupational changes should be intermediate with respect to level of unrest. *Within* the United States, students in engineering, medicine, and law—with relatively smooth transitions into adult occupational roles—should be politically quiescent, whereas students in the liberal arts should be more prone to unrest, even though the overall level of unrest is lower in the United States than in Latin American countries. Should these hypothetical replications turn out as anticipated, they would generate greater confidence in the "transition" theory, which could not be strengthened, no matter how refined the analytic techniques, if we remained at the level of comparing Latin American countries among themselves.

Advantageous as is replication at different analytic levels in increasing confidence in comparative findings, the investigator should proceed judiciously in its use. Systems at different analytic levels—nations, regions, communities—are characterized by different parametric conditions, so that the causal significance of associations may be expected to vary.[54] As in all comparisons, the investigator must attempt to establish that the parametric conditions governing the interunit comparisons be made as nearly alike as possible to the parametric conditions governing the intraunit comparisons. Otherwise the investigation of the large relation in the small, or vice versa, would involve a comparison of incomparables.

An additional point of vulnerability of the method of controlled comparison—whether it takes the form of comparing "near cases" or the form of comparing phenomena within units—lies in the questionability of the assumption that parametric control is actually gained over a variable by pointing out that two systems resemble one another with respect to that

---

[54] As Blalock noted, "in shifting units of analysis we are likely also to affect the degree to which other uncontrolled factors may vary." Hubert M. Blalock, Jr., *Causal Inferences in Nonexperimental Research* (Chapel Hill: The University of North Carolina Press, 1964), p. 113.

variable. To point out that America, Canada, and Australia are large countries is one thing; to assume that size has the same *causal* significance in explaining, say, political arrangements in the three countries is another. Geographical size, like other variables, interacts with a plurality of other sociocultural variables in exercising its influence as a condition, and the three countries vary considerably with respect to these other variables. The significance of size varies over time, too. At a period of early expansion size may constitute an opportunity factor for a society; as it reaches a high level of development the same size becomes a limiting condition on population and economic growth. Furthermore, to assert that two systems resemble one another in some respect—as Vallier claimed for the cultural values and goals of the two Latter-day Saint groups he studied—involves an *empirical* assertion of resemblance between the two groups that should be established systematically rather than by simple assumption or impression. Concerning comparative community studies, Reiss observed: "In each case where a community context is selected as a means of controlling variation we will need to demonstrate just what particular variation is controlled in studying the problem in this community."[55] The point might well be generalized: To posit resemblances between systems and claim that control is thereby gained involves both an assertion of similarity that must be established empirically and an assertion of causal significance that must be assessed by means of the same battery of research methods that are applied to any other causal statement.

Thus far I have noted two types of strategy in attempting to control sources of variation in comparing diverse social units: one is to randomize or eliminate variation by systematic methods of sampling, the other to hold certain variables constant by arranging for the systems to resemble one another in significant respects. In another context Przeworski and Teune have called these the "most different systems" design and the "most similar systems" design.[56] The former studies causal relations among associated phenomena in different systems without regard to system-specific differences; thus if "rates of suicide are the same among the Zuni, the Swedes, and the Russians, those factors that distinguish these three societies are irrelevant for the explanation of suicide."[57] The strategy of control in these studies is to reduce "irrelevant systemic factors," mainly by techniques of sampling. The "most similar systems" design takes cognizance of differences among systems, but attempts to reduce the significance of these

[55] Albert J. Reiss, Jr., "Some Logical and Methodological Problems in Community Research," *Social Forces* 33(1954–55):53.
[56] Przeworski and Teune, *The Logic of Comparative Social Inquiry*, pp. 32–39.
[57] Ibid., p. 35.

differences by grouping systems together on the basis of certain resemblances—thereby controlling for those features of resemblance—and attempting to establish causal relations by studying associations among those features in which the systems differ. Both methods are efforts to approximate—by different strategies—a combination of Mill's methods of difference and concomitant variation; both attempt to make systems similar in as many respects as possible, thereby creating a presumption in favor of the causal significance of those respects in which they co-vary. And as we have observed, each strategy carries its distinctive strengths and vulnerabilities.

Multivariate analysis

One feature of the method of controlled comparison is an effort to hold certain variables constant in order to isolate and observe the operation of others. When extended, it leads to more complicated techniques of standardization and multivariate analysis. The main methodological objective of these techniques, like controlled comparison, is to determine, by holding different variables constant, which of several competing explanatory factors might be ruled out. In our account of Durkheim's and Weber's comparative explanatory strategies, we noted that both attempted to rule out "minority status" as explanations for different propensities for suicide and rational economic activity, respectively. Both did so by pointing to groups that occupied minority status but did not commonly display the kind of behavior in question. This type of argument survives in much contemporary analysis. For example, in an effort to explain differences in the research productivity of medical scientists in 19th-century France, Germany, Britain, and the United States, Ben-David systematically pointed to the ways in which the scientific environment in these countries did *not* differ—in access to scientific ideas, in growth of population, and national income—thereby attempting to rule out these factors, and buttressing his case that distinctive national differences are attributable to the different patterns of organization of the scientific enterprise.[58]

Formal techniques of standardization and multivariate analysis rest on the same logic, but they are generally applied to larger samples and use mathematical and statistical techniques. An example of standardization is found in Duncan's effort to refine regional comparisons by correcting for urbanization. Noting that in many efforts to compare regions much of the

---

[58] Joseph Bed-David, "Scientific Productivity and Academic Organization in Nineteenth-Century Medicine," *American Sociological Review* 25(1960):832–33.

difference among them is contributed by rural-urban differences, he developed two methods, one direct and the other indirect, for measuring regional differences in ratios of physicians to 10,000 population. Both methods took into account differences in urbanization. The differences between the standardized ratios and the crude ratios were considerable. The Pacific region of the United States, for instance, ranked first in ratio of physicians to 10,000 persons on a crude measure, but when standardized for degree of urbanization, dropped to fourth and third, respectively, on the direct and indirect methods.[59] Methodologically, standardization renders the units being compared similar with respect to a potential source of variation. As such it is a sophisticated form of the method of controlled comparison.

Multivariate analysis typically involves assessing the simultaneous relations among a number of significant independent variables (including direct and indirect effects, second and higher-order interactions, and so on) as causes of the dependent variable. Though multivariate analysis assumes a variety of forms, I present only two examples of its use in comparative research here. In a cross-sectional analysis of data for 114 polities, Gurr found several measures of civil strife correlated consistently and strongly with (a) several indices relating to short-term deprivation; (b) several indices relating to persisting deprivation; (c) a measure of level of legitimacy afforded a regime; (d) several measures of the coerciveness of a regime; (e) measures of institutionalization of channels of protest other than strife; and some other measures. Taken together, the measures of his independent variables accounted for about two-thirds of the variance among nations in magnitude of civil strife.[60] Continuing his analysis, he calculated a number of partial correlations, in which several of the independent variables were treated as "intervening" between another independent variable and the measures of civil strife. When other variables were controlled, short-term deprivation and institutionalization of alternatives declined in their ability to account for strife. Only "persisting deprivation" remained consistently unaffected by the introduction of control variables. On the basis of these and other partial correlations, Gurr developed a revised causal model, giving different salience to each variable

[59] Otis Dudley Duncan, "Regional Comparisons Standardized for Urbanization," in Jack P. Gibbs, ed., *Urban Research Methods* (Princeton: D. van Nostrand, 1961), pp. 534–39.

[60] Ted Robert Gurr, "A Causal Model of Civic Strife: A Comparative Analysis Using New Indices," in John V. Gillespie and Betty A. Nesvold, eds., *Macro-Quantitative Analysis: Conflict, Development, and Democratization* (Beverly Hills: Sage Publications, 1971), pp. 217–26.

according to its predictive strength *in relation to* the remaining independent variables.[61]

Among the tasks undertaken in Inkeles' study of the modernization of individuals in six countries—Argentina, Chile, East Pakistan, India, Nigeria, and Israel—was his effort to account for differences within a sample of individuals in each country according to their disposition to participate as citizens in the affairs of their country. Though Inkeles devoted much effort to devising an appropriate index for "participant citizenship," my concern is with his causal analysis—that is, his treatment of "social factors fostering active citizenship." Factors such as education, exposure to mass media, and work experience correlated individually with participant citizenship with varying degrees of strength.[62] But Inkeles was interested in disentangling these influences, many of which were evidently related to one another. In particular, he was interested in the impact of experience in the factory on participant citizenship, when other potential explanatory variables were held constant. Using a complicated matching technique by which as many as eight variables could be controlled, Inkeles attempted to calculate the residual effect of each with all others held constant. Thus, education continued to be highly correlated with the index of participant citizenship in all six countries (coefficients from 0.35 to 0.57, all significant at the 0.01 level), even when region of origin, occupation, years of factory experience, years of urban experience, exposure to mass media, and other variables were controlled. Experience in the factory and exposure to mass media also continued to exert an effect. By using this and other matching techniques, Inkeles was also able to demonstrate that urban experience was apparently insignificant as a determinant of participant citizenship. This kind of analysis is extremely powerful in establishing the relative importance of different variables, and has found extensive use in cross-national analyses of quantitative data. Even when such elaborate controls are used, the causal significance of the associated variables may remain uncertain. Speaking of the persistent association between exposure to mass media and participant citizenship—even when the other variables are controlled—Inkeles remarked that this "does not, of course, resolve the ambiguity as to whether exposure to the mass media inculcates citizenship values, or whether those with an interest in politics look into the press and radio."[63] Like all methods of control, multivariate

---

[61] Ibid., p. 241.

[62] Alex Inkeles, "Participant Citizenship in Six Developing Countries," *American Political Science Review* 63(1969):1131–34.

[63] Ibid., pp. 1138–39.

analysis does not succeed in establishing causal relations; it only increases confidence in the plausibility of such relations by ruling out the effect of other possible causes.[64]

The introduction of time

Most of the efforts to establish presumption of causality reviewed thus far rely on manipulations of cross-sectional comparisons. Despite the sophistication of some techniques, such comparisons continue to be plagued with problems of incompleteness of control, inability to assign causal priority to one or another of a pair of associated variables, and an inability to assign temporal priority to one or another of several correlated variables.[65] A number of supplementary strategies have been devised in the social sciences, however, to establish a presumption in favor of causal relations by examining temporal relationships. The most common is to study the relations among a number of different time-series, often with an assumption of time-lag.

One line of analysis is to examine the level of association among variables over an extended period of time. A sociological example of the attempt to establish causal priority by assuming a lag is found in the effort of Henry and Short to discover relations between the fluctuations in the suicide rate and fluctuations in business activity. Beginning with Durkheim's assertion that extraordinary windfalls in periods of speculation are disorienting and give rise to anomic suicide, Henry and Short predicted that if this were the case, suicide would be positively correlated, especially among males, with rapid increases in the business index. Examining their own data, Henry and Short found that in general, the trough or low point of male suicide was reached just *before* the peak of business expansion. The slight general increase of suicide just before the peak, moreover, was

[64] A number of additional formal means of testing causal relationships in models have been reviewed in Blalock, *Causal Inferences in Nonexperimental Research*, ch. 3. Because the models in question involve quite strict assumptions about the causal relations among variables and the freedom of the models from the confounding influence of outside variables (ibid., p. 62), such techniques have found limited use in the analysis of phenomena in social units with evident parametric differences, for example, societies.

[65] See p. 162. For a discussion of the "cross-section fallacy"—that is, imputing temporal relationships on the basis of correlations, see Matilda White Riley and Edward E. Nelson, "Research on Stability and Change in Social Systems," in Bernard Barber and Alex Inkeles, eds., *Stability and Social Change* (Boston: Little, Brown, 1971), pp. 418–19.

contributed primarily by the female, not the male rate.[66] This led Henry and Short to reject Durkheim's hypothesis relating business prosperity and anomic suicide. Furthermore, the grounds on which they rejected it rested on the logic of the time lag: if prosperity were genuinely causal, suicide rates should have accompanied business activity upward, perhaps with a slight lag; but since the opposite relation held, the causal inference could not be drawn.

To turn to another example, Flanigan and Fogelman analyzed longitudinal comparative data on 44 countries from 1800 to 1960 in an effort to "identify the patterns of social and economic conditions associated with successful and unsuccessful attempts to introduce and maintain democratic systems through time."[67] For each decade of that period, they found urbanization consistently and positively related to their measure of democratization and proportion of labor force in agricultural employment consistently and negatively related to democratization. In addition, they discovered that urbanization and proportion in agricultural employment were similarly related to indices of successful attempts to introduce or establish democratic regimes. Furthermore, an examination of rates of change in these independent variables during the two decades before the attempt to establish democratic regimes revealed that success was negatively related to the rates of change in the indices of urbanization and proportion in agricultural employment.[68] When, however, they attempted to supplement the cross-sectional correlations with serial correlations—that is, correlating the variables by decade, country by country—they found the correlations differing in strength, decade by decade, yielding different patterns of association over time.[69] In a subsequent analysis Pride also found cross-sectional and longitudinal correlations among similar variables in considerable disagreement.[70] Attempting to unravel the confused results produced by these two methods, Pride applied a technique of "pattern analysis," which built in lead-lag relationships between estimates of urbanization and

[66] Andrew F. Henry and James F. Short, Jr., *Suicide and Homicide: Some Economic, Sociological and Psychological Aspects of Aggression* (Glencoe, Ill.: The Free Press, 1954), pp. 42–44.

[67] William Flanigan and Edwin Fogelman, "Patterns of Democratic Development: An Historical Comparative Analysis," in Gillespie and Nesvold, eds., *Macro-Quantitative Analysis*, p. 475.

[68] Ibid., pp. 485–87.

[69] Ibid., pp. 489–91. See above, pp. 208–9 for evidence of different "structures of explanation" for different societies.

[70] Richard A. Pride, "Pattern Analysis: An Alternative Approach to Quantitative Historical Data," *Comparative Political Studies* 4(1971):363–64.

democratization. On the basis of this array, Pride was able to discover a number of typical sequential patterns relating indices of socioeconomic variables and democratization in a comparative study of 26 countries:

> Virtually all the countries which accomplished democratization before significant social change are classified as stable democratic systems in the twentieth century; or to put it another way, fully eight of the nine countries which are classified as stable democratic regimes in the twentieth century were those that became democratic early in their mobilization phase before significant social and economic change began. A democratic system was developed while these countries had low levels of urbanization and high levels of agricultural work force . . . rather than accompanying or following significant mobilization. The second striking finding is that wherever substantial mobilization occurred first . . . the countries never sustained democratic government over several decades.[71]

This line of analysis, while based on quite crude measures, permits more solid inferences about the causal relations between democratization and various mobilization measures because it, unlike cross-sectional or longitudinal correlations, built time in as a factor.

There are substantive reasons for believing that the analysis of lead-lag relations in different institutional sectors can produce much knowledge concerning the dynamics of fundamental processes of economic and social development.[72] Furthermore, there are sound methodological reasons for believing that the discovery of repeated cross-sectional associations over time, of longitudinal correlations within social units, and of consistent patterns of lead-lag relations among time series are powerful bases for increasing confidence in causal relations. Nevertheless, one caution should be introduced. Uncontrolled sources of variation and intervening variables render relations among time-series as vulnerable to error as cross-sectional analyses, and efforts to standardize and control are as essential in temporal analysis as in all other types.[73]

---

[71] Ibid., p. 368.

[72] Moshe Lissak, "Some Theoretical Implications of the Multidimensional Concept of Modernization," *International Journal of Comparative Sociology* 11(1970): 195–207.

[73] See White and Nelson, "Research on Stability and Change in Social Systems," in Barber and Inkeles, eds., *Stability and Social Change*, pp. 422–23; also Wolfgang Zapf and Peter Flora, "Some Problems of Time Series Analysis in Research on Modernization," *Social Science Information* 10(1971):53–102.

Cross-level fallacies in establishing association and cause

I have noted a number of strategies that are available for establishing association and cause in relating social variables. It now remains to stress that variables and their indicators in the social sciences are represented at a number of different analytic levels, and that a common source of error in comparative—and other types of—research is to infer association or cause at one level from observed association at another.

In social analysis variables—and data representing them—are commonly framed at the following levels of analysis:

1. Variables concerning the attributes of individual persons—their age, sex, attitudes, patterns of behavior, and so on.

2. Variables referring to the aggregated attributes of the population of a social unit. Here I refer to what Lazarsfeld and Menzel termed "properties of collectivities which are obtained by performing some mathematical operation upon some property of each single member."[74] The mathematical operation may be adding, percentaging, averaging. As examples of aggregated attributes of a population I might mention proportions of persons of different ages, persons voting Democratic, persons unable to read, and so on.

3. Variables concerning patterned social interaction (also referred to as roles or social structure). This conception of structure is similar to what Lazarsfeld and Menzel referred to as "structural properties" of social units—those properties "which are obtained by performing some operation on data about the relation of each member to some or all of the others."[75] In one sense the notion of social structure is close to aggregated attributes, since we often identify social structure by referring to regularities in a population's attributes and behavioral patterns. In using the term "family structure," for example, we refer to the empirical fact that the same people—adult male categorized as husband and father, adult female categorized as wife and mother, and several young classified as son, daughter, brother, and sister—regularly sleep under the same roof, share economic goods, and so on. The difference between regularities in a population's attributes and behavior on the one hand, and its social-structural arrangements on the other, lies in the ways the notions are conceptualized. Social structure is characterized on the basis of the *relational* aspects among members of a social unit, not on some aggregated version of attributes of behavior of the

---

[74] Paul F. Lazarsfeld and Herbert Menzel, "On the Relation between Individual and Collective Properties," in Amitai Etzioni, ed., *Complex Organizations: A Sociological Reader* (New York: Holt, Rinehart and Winston, 1961), p. 427.

[75] Ibid., p. 428.

individual members. Furthermore, the conception of social structure implies that the relations among members are not merely fortuitous or statistical but are regulated by the operation of certain social forces. These forces are sanctions, including both rewards and deprivations, and norms, or standards of conduct that indicate the occasions on which various kinds of sanctions are to be applied.

4. Variables concerning cultural patterns—values, world views, knowledge, symbols, and so on—which supply systems of meaning and legitimacy for patterned social interaction. Examples of concrete cultural patterns are the Judeo-Christian religious heritage, the values of democratic constitutional government, the Baroque musical style, and so on. Cultural patterns are examples of what Lazarsfeld and Menzel called "global" properties of collectives;[76] they are not based either on aggregated information about individual members of a social unit or on specific relations among the members but on properties of the collective considered as a whole.

The most widely-discussed fallacy of inference regarding associations at different levels is the "ecological" or "group" fallacy, which involves the inference of correlations at the level of individual persons on the basis of correlations among aggregated attributes. In Robinson's classic example, the correlation coefficient between percentage of colored population and illiteracy (based on census data) was 0.946 when census area subdivisions for the entire country were used as a basis for calculating the correlation; when calculated on the basis of individual data, however, Robinson arrived at a correlation of only 0.20.[77] Others have pointed to the obverse fallacy —the individualistic fallacy—which involves inferring relations at higher levels of generality on the basis of observations recorded at lower levels.[78]

Keeping the four levels of analysis in mind, but without attempting to exhaust all possible types of fallacies, I might mention the following:

To generalize from individual regularities to societal characteristics may be illegitimate:

> . . . it is generally the case that an individual who receives an increase in his income saves proportionately more of his income following the increase than he saved before; but it is apparently not the case that as the national

[76] Ibid., pp. 428–29.

[77] W. S. Robinson, "Ecological Correlations and the Behavior of Individuals," *American Sociological Review* 15(1950):351–57. See also the observations on the ecological fallacy in Durkheim's *Suicide*, mentioned in ch. 4 of this book.

[78] A good discussion of both the group and individualistic fallacies can be found in Erwin K. Scheuch, "Cross-National Comparisons Using Aggregate Data: Some Substantive and Methodological Problems," in Merritt and Rokkan, eds., *Comparing Nations*, pp. 131–67; see also Howard R. Alker, "A Typology of Ecological Fallacies," ibid., pp. 69–86.

income of a society increases over time, proportionately more of it is saved. The difference here may be owing to the different time-scales at the two levels, to price-level changes in the second case but not the first, perhaps to different methods of measurement, and so forth.[79]

The same might be said of the generalization from aggregated individual responses to global or social-structural characteristics. I noted earlier the problems involved in imputing differences in "political culture"—a global characteristic of a society—on the basis of percentage differences among *individual* responses to questions on an attitude survey, as employed by Almond and Verba. In the same cross-cultural study, Almond and Verba asked some individual respondents to say what they considered the most successful forms of protest against bureaucratic procedures. But as Scheuch pointed out, "these aggregated opinions are most certainly not the most direct measure of citizens' ability to influence authorities [a social-structural characteristic]."[80] Similarly, the stability of institutions or the integration of society as a whole (social-structural characteristics) cannot be inferred from, for example, measures of high value-consensus on the part of the citizenry, though the level of consensus may be one of the factors affecting stability and integration.

Reading the other way around, it is often fallacious to make inferences regarding individuals on the basis of evidence at the cultural and social-structural levels. An example of the "cultural fallacy" would be to characterize the personalities of individual members of a society on the basis of themes that emerge in received myths and folklore. Whiting and Child, for example, in their comparative study of patterns of child-rearing, "filled in" various psychological correlations and processes occurring in childhood—for which they had no direct measures—on the basis of associations among cultural traits.[81] Thus Inkeles and Levinson were correct in insisting that generalizations about "national character" or "modal personality" be based in the first instances on data about individual personality attrib-

[79] Terrence K. Hopkins and Immanuel Wallerstein, "The Comparative Study of National Societies," in David E. Apter and Charles F. Andrain, eds., *Contemporary Analytical Theory* (Englewood Cliffs, N. J.: Prentice-Hall, 1972), p. 434.

[80] Erwin K. Scheuch, "Social Context and Individual Behavior," in Mattei Dogan and Stein Rokkan, eds., *Quantitative Ecological Analysis in the Social Sciences* (Cambridge: The MIT Press, 1969), p. 141.

[81] John W. M. Whiting and Irvin L. Child, *Child-Training and Personality: A Cross-Cultural Study* (New Haven: Yale University Press, 1953), ch. 2. Subsequently Whiting proposed that the cross-cultural method of study "rests on the assumption that the customs of a society are truly comparable to the habits of an individual." "The Cross-Cultural Method" in Moore, ed., *Readings in Cross-Cultural Methodology*, p. 291.

utes (since the concepts are framed in terms referring to individuals), though they regarded cultural productions as useful ancillary sources of data.[82]

I shall return to the problem of articulating different levels of analysis later in the chapter. At the moment, I should like to indicate why it is often unwarranted to make inferences to levels of analysis different from the level at which data are observed. Different levels of analysis refer, in fact, to different principles of *systemic organization* (personality, social system, culture), and, in consequence, the different levels are governed by different parametric constraints. In chapter four I noted that to argue by analogy from biological to social systems is to argue, in effect, that because the two types of system resemble one another in systemic organization, the same processes and causal relations prevail in both; but when the principles of systemic organization differ, argument by analogy is likely to be fallacious. The same error is committed when association and cause are inferred from any system-level different from that which the association is observed. The resulting types of errors constitute what we have called the cross-level fallacies. The corresponding methodological moral, moreover, is that assertions of association and cause should be established, when possible, on the basis of data from the same analytic level at which the assertion is made.

Referring Associations to
Theoretical Context

Explanation as an appeal to other knowledge

Early in the chapter I noted that one of the shortcomings of the one-shot case study was that, given the inability to control variation in the possibly causal factors, imputation of cause necessarily rests on the relatively weak comparative methods of imaginary experiment and appeal to other knowledge. I should now like to stress that these kinds of methods are also in evidence in interpretations of association in aggregated cases, despite the fact that the possibility of establishing valid associations and ruling out alternative causal factors is much greater than when dealing with only one case. I shall do this by giving two illustrations of correlational analysis:

1. Apple was interested in two explanations of the relations of "friendly

[82] Alex Inkeles and Daniel J. Levinson, "National Character: the Study of Modal Personality and Sociocultural Systems," in Lindzey and Aronson, eds., *Handbook of Social Psychology*, pp. 423–28.

equality" between grandparents and grandchildren that have been noted by numerous anthropological investigators:

—Radcliffe-Brown's thesis that " 'friendly equality' between grandparents and grandchildren exists as a relieving reaction to the tension caused between parents and children by parental authority and by the obligations each has toward the other."
—Nadel's thesis that "informality between grandfather and grandson is associated with lack of family authority by the grandfather."[83]

Apple argued that Radcliffe-Brown's thesis implied that "grandparents would be universally disposed to friendly equality with grandchildren." (It would be more nearly correct, I think, to have said that friendly equality between them would vary with the amount of tension generated between parents and children.) She argued further that Nadel's hypotheses predicted that friendly equality would be negatively associated with grandparental authority; and that in societies where grandchildren have less friendly equality with one set of grandparents (for example, on mother's side) than with the other, the former will be more involved in exercising authority in the household. On the basis of information obtained from ethnological reports on 75 societies, she tested for the associations emerging from Nadel's hypothesis by using χ^2 and Fischer's exact test, and found them significant in every case.[84] (It might be added that if "tension" as referred to by Radcliffe-Brown is positively correlated with "authority" as used by Nadel, her findings could be regarded as consistent with Radcliffe-Brown's interpretation as well.)

Apple referred to Radcliffe-Brown's thesis as "psychological" and Nadel's as "structural," but she acknowledged that the latter "does not rule out psychological analysis." In fact, when she stated one of the postulates informing her study, several implicit psychological generalizations surfaced: "The postulate . . . that the more closely associated a person in the status possessing the most jural authority in a hierarchy, the less likely he is to have an informal and equal relationship with subordinates in the hierarchy."[85] This postulate rests on general psychological propositions that authority breeds distrust and distance, that individuals are uncomfortable in the presence of authority, and that they resolve their discomfort by assuming correct and unrelaxed relations with people in authority. Such assumptions "make sense" of the apparent negative cross-cultural associa-

---

[83] Dorian Apple, "The Social Structure of Grandparenthood," *American Anthropologist* 58(1956):656.

[84] Ibid., pp. 658–62.

[85] Ibid., p. 657.

tions between relations of friendly equality and authority.[86] Indeed they *say why* authority is to be treated as independent and friendly equality as dependent variable; in a word, they provide the basis for assigning cause to the association.[87]

2. In his cross-national investigations of the sources of democracy and political stability, Lipset presented various types of data apparently showing that level of national income was negatively associated with radicalness of worker protest. Though Lipset did not systematically control for other factors that might affect radicalness, let us assume for the moment that the relationship is not a spurious one. How did Lipset interpret the association?

> Economic development, producing increased income, greater economic security, and widespread higher education, largely determines the form of the "class struggle," by permitting those in the lower strata to develop longer time perspectives and more complex and gradualist views of politics. A belief in reformist gradualism can be the ideology of only a relatively well-to-do lower class.[88]

Again, a host of psychological generalizations concerning the impact of wealth and education on political attitudes inform this interpretation— generalizations which are not inconsistent with the association but which are in no sense tested by it. Furthermore, if a different psychological "theory" were assumed—for example, that workers experienced rising

[86] Homans was correct in pointing out that his and Schneider's controversy with Levi-Strauss over the determinants of unilateral cross-cousin marriage was not only a disagreement about facts but also involved a disagreement between them on the psychological postulates used to interpret the facts: ". . . our explanation of our correlations is psychological in that it relies, among other things, on a proposition that men, as men, have some tendency to fear, avoid, and feel some constraint in the presence of, persons placed in authority over them. In the same way, Levi-Strauss's explanation of the fact that the matrilateral form of marriage occurs in a larger number of societies than does the patrilateral one relies . . . on the proposition that men as men have some tendency to recognize a particular institution as in some way good for their societies and adopted it for that reason." George C. Homans, "Marriage, Authority, and Final Causes: A Study of Unilateral Cross-Cousin Marriage" (with David M. Schneider) in George C. Homans, *Sentiments and Activities* (London: Routledge and Kegan Paul, 1962), pp. 252–53. That is to say, much of their debate over explanations was a debate over "other knowledge."

[87] One of the difficulties in Apple's study is that the term "authority" appears on the side of the independent variable and "equality" on the side of the dependent variable, thereby suggesting that the apparently separate measures for each might be measuring the same phenomenon, since "authority" implies "inequality."

[88] Seymour Martin Lipset, *Political Man* (Garden City, N.Y.: Doubleday, 1960), p. 60.

expectations and corresponding dissatisfactions as their income increases[89] —this would change the causal context and lead one to expect an association opposite to that observed by Lipset.

Causal knowledge hinges, then, not only on establishing relations and ruling out alternatives, but also on a network of parametric assumptions resting on "other knowledge" that varies in adequacy. Blalock referred to this other knowledge as an "auxiliary theory containing a whole set of additional assumptions, many of which will be inherently untestable."[90] We saw how important such assumptions were in the thought of Weber and Durkheim, even though Durkheim protested that explanations can be established through the examination of concomitant variation of social facts. The same holds true for highly complex, mathematical models in any branch of the social sciences. Note Kuznets' comment on formal economic explanations:

> To distinguish a set of wholes [e.g., nation-states] and parts within each [e.g., firms, consumers] does not carry us far in explaining economic behavior, even if we know that the parts are related to each other in cooperation, imitation, competition, and bargaining. We need some general knowledge concerning the "drives," the principles of operation, of these parts and wholes and concerning the characteristic conditions under which the parts cooperate, compete, and bargain. Indeed, economics, even at its most abstract level, includes a number of quasi-empirical generalizations on these topics, although they are often presented as formal assumptions with no immediate claim to empirical validity. Yet the fact that these particular assumptions [e.g., maximization of profit by the firm] are made is in itself an indication of reference to observable reality.[91]

We may agree with Swanson, then, that causality can never be definitively established, no matter how widely an association is observed, and how thoroughly alternative explanations are rejected by the manipulation and control of causal factors. He also went on to note, however, that in addition to using these procedures to establish cause, "we are [also] more confident that a causal relation exists if we have some logically valid reasons for thinking that it should."[92] Those reasons—which vary in their

---

[89] For a discussion of the importance of such a postulate in the work of Tocqueville, see ch. 2 of this book.

[90] Hubert M. Blalock, Jr., "The Measurement Problem: A Gap between the Languages of Theory and Research," in Hubert M. Blalock, Jr. and Ann B. Blalock, eds., *Methodology in Social Research* (New York: McGraw-Hill, 1968), p. 25.

[91] Simon Kuznets, "Parts and Wholes in Economics," in Daniel Lerner, ed., *Parts and Wholes* (New York: The Free Press of Glencoe, 1963), pp. 50–51.

[92] Swanson, *The Birth of the Gods*, p. 3.

logic and validity—constitute the network of ancillary assumptions and assertions that inform all investigations in the social sciences that attempt to establish causal relations.[93] To put it another way, those reasons constitute the *theoretical framework* that informs empirical investigations and demonstrations.

Explicitness and structure in theoretical context

The theoretical context in which empirical correlations are embedded may vary with respect to explicitness and structure. At one extreme is the presentation of all possible associations among several hundred variables as produced by a computer. This a-theoretical extreme is represented by computer printout volumes like *A Cross-Polity Survey* and *A Cross-Cultural Summary*.[94] The forward to the latter characterizes its method:

> This volume contains statements in sentences of English, of some 20,000 statistically significant correlations that tell us what classes of culture co-occur or overlap with other classes. The classes are arranged dichotomously (e.g., slavery present, slavery absent), and utilize, selectively, all available sources of coded cross-cultural data (38 all told) for the 400-culture sample developed by George Peter Murdock in the *Ethnographic Atlas*. The computer has winnowed out all "uninteresting" (nonsignificant) associations and Textor has winnowed out all the tautological and redundant ones. The 20,000 remaining are arranged in order congenial to anthropologists, e.g., location, linguistic affiliation, natural environment, settlement pattern, diet, subsistence base, technology, etc.[95]

Another method of discovering associations "by technique alone" is found in some factor analyses. Adelman and Morris attempted to "obtain a statistical explanation of the economic and noneconomic forces which directly and indirectly determine a country's capacity for economic growth." Their approach was what they described as "overtly empiricist," chosen because "there are no firmly validated theories of the process of socio-economic and political change." Instead, they "let the data specify the model," building it on the basis of the strength of associations obtained

[93] See Blalock: ". . . no main body of deductive theory can ever be tested without the use of some . . . auxiliary theory, whether explicitly formulated or not." "The Measurement Problem," p. 25.

[94] Arthur S. Banks and Robert B. Textor. *A Cross-Polity Survey* (Cambridge: The MIT Press, 1963); Robert B. Textor, comp., *A Cross-Cultural Summary* (New Haven: HRAF Press, 1967).

[95] George P. Spindler, "Forward" to Textor, comp., *A Cross-Cultural Summary*, pp. vi–vii.

by the use of a step-wise regression method applied to 74 underdeveloped noncommunist nations between 1957 and 1962.[96]

It is perhaps too harsh to characterize such methods as "the study of society . . . without a . . . focus and very often without a . . . question."[97] It is true, however, that the kind of theory—if it may be dignified by that term—that informs such wholesale statistical operations is found in (a) the investigator's general "sense" of what variables are important and relevant to the study of society, economy, polity, or whatever; this is in turn informed by his "sense" of what important theorists have considered to be important dimensions; (b) the "reasons" in the minds of policy-makers and other generators of official data for deciding to record these data in certain ways; and (c) the formal characteristics of the type of associational method (for example, factor analysis) employed. As such, the "theory" is unknown for the most part. Knowledge generated by these means is correspondingly a-theoretical.

> It is apparent that in factor analysis the set of factors will vary when different observed variables are selected for analysis. When the observed variables are the same it is likely that the use of postulated unmeasured factors will mean that many plausible alternative models, both factor-analytical and others, will satisfy the observed data equally well. It is also clear than [sic] even when a factor analysis leads to a simple, clear and meaningfully interpretable structure its usefulness, if used for explanations, will vary very much depending on what is to be explained. All this means that no set of fundamental and basic factors can be established once and for all by factor analysis. In fact, there is an almost infinite number of sets of basic structural dimensions of a society if the sole method of systematic conceptualization is provided by a statistical multivariate technique.[98]

Other correlational studies provide a more explicit theoretical basis for expecting indicators to co-vary, though in many cases the reasoning is quite eclectic. An instance of semi-structured theoretical reasoning can be found in Weber's mode of explanation within the framework of ideal-typical analysis. A more contemporary instance can be found in an in-

[96] Irma Adelman and Cynthia Taft Morris, "An Economic Model of Socio-economic and Political Change in Underdeveloped Countries," *American Economic Review* 58(1968):1184.

[97] Roy C. Macridis, "Comparative Politics and the Study of Government," *Comparative Politics* 1(1968):103–10.

[98] Erik Allardt, "'Basic' Dimensions in the Comparative Study of Social Structures," *Transactions of the Sixth World Congress of Sociology* (International Sociological Association: 1966), 1:176.

fluential paper by Deutsch on political development.[99] He regarded social mobilization as the systematic change in variables such as exposure to mass media, change of residence, urbanization, change from agricultural occupations, literacy, and per capita income. He argued that in processes of economic development these and other indicators changed in much the same direction, though at different rates. By a series of inferences, moreover, he stressed that these changes have implications for *political* development. The growing numbers of politically relevant strata, for example, "produces mounting pressures for the transformation of political processes." More needs become politically relevant, and traditional political structures are thereby made archaic. As a result "[the] growing need for new and old government services implies persistent political pressures for an increased scope of government and a greater relative size of the government sector in the national economy." Similarly pressure grows for a broadened base for the political elite; political participation increases; and more voluntary associations form.[100] Clearly Deutsch did not produce a theory in any deductive sense, but he more or less systematically brought a great number of assumptions to bear to "make sense" of the pattern of changing indicators of economic development, social mobilization, and political change.

Other associational studies are much more narrowly theoretically focused. Otterbein's correlational study of the incidence of internal war, for example, was informed by fairly definite social-scientific hypotheses such as that relating out-group aggression to in-group aggression. Otterbein made an effort to relate his findings directly to such hypotheses. Much of the "culture-and-personality" literature in anthropology is similarly closely patterned after hypotheses in psychoanalytic theory. Rosenblatt, for example, in studying co-variation in 21 societies between early childhood frustration of oral and dependency needs on the one hand, and "importance of romantic love" on the other, was directly addressing Freudian hypotheses relating childhood traumas to adult fixations.[101]

Finally, some theories in the social sciences approach the ideals for formal deductive structures which are explicit in their conceptual structure, determinate in the posited relations among variables, and formally "closed" to additional variables. Such theories are rare in the social sciences. It has been pointed out, however, that Durkheim's theoretical structure in *Suicide*

[99] Karl W. Deutsch, "Social Mobilization and Political Development," *American Political Science Review* 55(1961):493–514.
[100] Ibid., pp. 498–500.
[101] Paul C. Rosenblatt, "A Cross-Cultural Study of Child Rearing and Romantic Love," *Journal of Personality and Social Psychology* 4(1966):336–38.

comes close to the model of logical deduction;[102] and many contemporary theories, especially in economics, are formally derived mathematically. It should be stressed, however, that in the social sciences all efforts to explain rest on some kind of "other knowledge" or "auxiliary theory"; they differ formally, however, with respect to the degree to which this is made explicit and structured.

The substance of theoretical context and the status of different classes of variables

In addition to differences in degree of formalization, the theoretical contexts of studies of empirical variation differ in *substance.* These substantive differences, moreover, emanate from several kinds of choices—not necessarily self-conscious—that are made with respect to the ingredients of theoretical context we have identified:

1. Contexts may vary in terms of *dependent variables,* or outcomes, or, more simply, according to what the theory is "about." Most topical areas —the study of political development, the study of bureaucracy, the study of socialization—are identified in this way; that is to say, they are identified with respect to the variation to be explained.

2. Contexts may vary in terms of *independent variables.* For example, in a classification of approaches to the study of political development in the past two decades, Packenham identified the legal-formal approach, which singles out formal constitutional features as decisive factors in developing political institutions; the economic approach, which stresses the importance of a high level of economic development in supporting advanced political institutions; the administrative approach, which stresses the causal role of governmental effectiveness; the social systems approach, emphasizing the importance of popular participation; and the political culture approach, which stresses the supporting attitudes of the citizenry as decisive in the maintenance of a developed polity.[103] Typically different "schools" of thought are identifiable by reference to the causal variable chosen for special emphasis.

3. Less evident but equally important as bases for noting differences among theories are the differences in their dependence on "other knowledge"

[102] Robert K. Merton, *Social Theory and Social Structure,* enl. ed. (New York: The Free Press, 1968), pp. 150–53.

[103] Robert A. Packenham, "Approaches to the Study of Political Development," *World Politics* 17(1964–65):108–20.

—the context of the causal relations between independent and dependent variables. Among these are:

—Special assumptions about factors that are potentially operative causes but which, for purposes of analysis, are assumed not to vary. For most social analyses biological, climatological, and other non-social factors are typically treated as "givens."
—Special assumptions about factors that "intervene" as processes or mechanisms, and "explain" why causes and effects are so related. I have repeatedly stressed the importance of psychological postulates in both the classical theories and the contemporary studies I have examined.
—Special assumptions about the mode of causality—whether causes are treated as simple and direct; as inherent in some kind of systematic whole, such as an equilibrium system; as constituting necessary conditions; as constituting facilitative conditions; as constituting inhibitions, and so on.
—Special assumptions about the nature of knowledge—for example, the differences displayed by Durkheim and Weber with respect to the role of the observer and the role of the actor in generating knowledge.[104]

The understanding of the substance of a theory—and the methodology that accompanies it—depends on a grasp of *all* these ingredients of the theoretical context; not only causes and effects but the network of assumptions that inform their relations; not only the "main" theory but also the "auxiliary" theory, to use Blalock's terminology. In examining the works of Tocqueville, Durkheim, and Weber I observed repeatedly how powerful the ancillary assumptions are as vehicles to bring coherence and meaning to their empirical investigations. It is especially important to identify what is "frozen" into parametric givens, not only because of the importance of these for the structure of explanation, but because these often constitute repositories of the kinds of weaknesses of theory that are often most difficult to discern—weaknesses involving unverified generalizations, questionable assumptions, and unmeasured variables.

One feature of the theory construction that is not always appreciated is that when an investigator chooses one or two sets of variables as the focus for study—for example, the relationship between customs of child-rearing and cultural explanations of the origin of disease[105]—he is not only com-

---

[104] For an effort to classify theories in sociology according to different special assumptions about society and knowledge, see James T. Duke, "Theoretical Alternatives and Social Research," *Social Forces* 45(1966–67):571–82.

[105] The illustration is from Whiting and Child, *Child-Training and Personality*, ch. 1.

miting himself to a proposition that these phenomena will co-vary, *he also simultaneously asserts that other phenomena will not vary;* that is to say, he makes certain assumptions about parameters. As Whiting observed, "the cross-cultural method, by studying cultural norms, holds individual variation constant. Psychological studies of individuals in a single society do just the opposite, in that cultural norms are held constant and individual variations are studied."[106] Furthermore, by making a decision on what independent and dependent variables to stress, he makes a simultaneous judgment on the methodological status of other variables. Apter and Andrain, for example, identified three foci of work in comparative politics —the normative, the structural, and the behavioral. Though they gave a special meaning to each one of these dimensions, they resemble what I earlier termed the cultural social-structural, and individual levels of analysis. Furthermore, they noted how the methodological status of these variables differed according to the theoretical perspective adopted:

> If the observer considers norms and values the independent with structure intervening and behavior dependent, then he would analyze the independent function of ideas in action, linked to action by stratification, organization, and so forth. Political philosophers often take this view. If an approach deals with structure as independent, with norms intervening and behavior dependent, then a bureaucracy may be viewed as imposing its normative imprint so as to change behavior. Marx held a theory in which participation in the material mode of existence (a structural situation) generalized man's condition into a shared sense of solidarity (normative bonds), developing a revolutionary motivation (a behavioral variable) which allowed groups of individuals to make choices not hitherto perceived possible in the system. The result was the transformation of the existing system (capitalism) into another structural type (socialism). If behavior is regarded as the independent variable, with normative concerns intervening and structure dependent, then we would expect to find theories about belief or attitude formation bringing about the internalization of values which then lead to changes in concrete structures. Thus the role of the Great Legislator or charismatic leader is to create a new set of values which will eventuate in structural changes, as in the stratification system. This pattern surely exists in "revolutionary" situations.[107]

More generally, studies attempting to trace the impact of culture on behavior usually make parametric assumptions about the institutional context

---

[106] "The Cross-Cultural Method," in Moore, ed., *Readings in Cross-Cultural Methodology*, p. 291.

[107] David E. Apter and Charles F. Andrain, "Introduction" to Apter and Andrain, eds., *Contemporary Analytical Theory*, p. 7.

in which this takes place;[108] studies attempting to trace the impact of social structure invariably make parametric assumptions about psychological processes by which this impact is mediated. But as we have seen repeatedly, these "invisible" assumptions about the workings of the social world are as essential for explanations as the operative variables themselves.

Given the restricted purposes of this book, I shall not attempt any comprehensive survey of substantive theories in the social sciences, nor shall I discuss canons by which theories can be evaluated from a logical point of view.[109] Instead, I should like to note a number of potential points of vulnerability of theory that have become evident in my effort to locate its role in the comparative study of diverse social units.

First, any theoretical framework must be assessed in terms of what it envisions as varying and what it envisions as constant. Not only does this yield a grasp of the substance of the theory in question, it also provides insight as to what a theory can and cannot be expected to do by way of explanation. If a theory freezes certain ranges of empirical variation into parameters, this is a legitimate and necessary procedure in order to generate a manageable framework. At the same time, the theory cannot be expected to cast much light on the variability of those phenomena (because they have been assumed to be constant); nor can it be expected to provide very detailed examination of the causal significance of those phenomena (for the same reason, namely that the phenomena are not permitted to vary.)[110] By examining a theory in this way, the limitations on its *scope* can be ascertained.

[108] Shils noted that the impact of intellectuals' ideas (a cultural variable) "is possible only through a complex set of institutional arrangements. The institutional system in which intellectual objects are reproduced or created has varied markedly in history. Its variations have at least in part been affected by the nature of the intellectual tasks, the volume of the intellectual heritage, the material resources necessary and available for intellectual work, the modes of reproduction of intellectual achievements, and the scope of its audience." Edward A. Shils, "The Intellectuals and the Powers: Some Perspectives for Comparative Analysis," *Comparative Studies in Society and History* 1(1958):11.

[109] For an assessment of theoretical structure from the standpoint of consistency, deduction of hypotheses, and other logical criteria, see Neil J. Smelser, *Sociological Theory: A Contemporary View* (New York: General Learning Press, 1971).

[110] See Eckstein's interesting contrast between the explanatory potential of structural-functional and Marxist frameworks, potential which depends in part on their differing parametric assumptions. Harry Eckstein, "A Perspective on Comparative Politics: Past and Present," in Harry Eckstein and David E. Apter, eds., *Comparative Politics: A Reader* (New York: The Free Press of Glencoe, 1964), pp. 27–28. See also the suggested list of phenomena that should be treated as operative variables in John C. Harsanyi, "Explanation and Comparative Dynamics in Social Science," *Behavioral Science* 5, no. 2(1960):136–45.

Second, whatever the mix of parameters and operative variables, any theoretical framework must be assessed in terms of what parts of it rest on empirical observation, what parts on various kinds of "other knowledge" that is not directly assessed. As we have seen, most theories that have been brought to bear on the comparative analysis of social units are shrouded in a maze of qualifying assumptions, most of which are advanced with little or no empirical demonstration—though they are often defended by logical argumentation and polemic. By examining a theory in this way it can be ascertained how much the theory rests on *speculation.* Blalock has complained that "[most] sociological theories, at present, seem to be so top-heavy with unmeasured variables and untestable assumptions that they yield only a very small number of imprecise predictions," and has suggested a number of strategies for incorporating these elements—which are, in effect, potential sources of error—formally into the theoretical framework as variables to be assessed directly.[111]

Third, any theoretical framework should be assessed in terms of what parts of the "other knowledge" on which it is based remain unspecified. As we have seen, the "theory" that informs most exercises in factor analysis is almost completely unspoken, and remains hidden in the operating assumptions of agencies that recorded the data series and the investigators that selected among all possible data series. And conceptual ambiguities are among the most common failings in various substantive theories; Sartori, for example, has complained that investigators working within the functionalist framework have had difficulty in ascertaining the interplay between "functions" and "structures" because the two overlap conceptually, the second often being defined implicitly by reference to the first.[112] Insofar as a theory fails to specify its major variables and parameters, or does so ambiguously, the corresponding theoretical weakness is that of *vagueness.*

Finally, and with special reference to the comparative studies of diverse units, any theoretical framework should be examined from the standpoint of whether its parameters—that which it regards as constant—are indeed generalizable empirically to all the units under study. Herskovitz, among others, has complained that classical economic assumptions of rationality are scarcely generalizable to traditional African societies;[113] Leys has subjected the underlying assumptions of Duverger's theory of political parties

[111] Hubert M. Blalock, Jr., "Theory Building and Causal Inferences," in Blalock and Blalock, eds., *Methodology in Social Research,* pp. 155–56.

[112] Giovani Sartori, "Concept Misinformation in Comparative Politics," *American Political Science Review* 64(1970):1046–48.

[113] Melville J. Herskovitz, "African Economic Development in Cross-Cultural Perspective," *American Economic Review* 46(1956):452–61.

and found them wanting in their general applicability;[114] and Theodorson has laid down the general accusation that "[correlations] in American society often are assumed to reflect natural laws and mechanistic causes."[115] The essence of these complaints is that differences among social units constitute intervening variables and, as such, change the significance of empirical correlations among other variables. Insofar as these complaints have merit, they point to a final source of weakness of theoretical frameworks, namely the *empirical variation in assumed constants*. A particularly pressing strategy for comparative studies, moreover, is to attempt to subject assumed constants to *direct* empirical tests, using comparative data, thereby establishing a more solid basis for treating these constants as parameters for purposes of further analysis.[116]

A Concluding Note

In two respects my mission in this volume has been a narrow one. First, I have focused more on methodological than on substantive issues, even though I have insisted throughout on the inseparability of the two. Second, within the methodological sphere, I have focused on research that has involved the comparative analysis of social units that are dissimilar from one another in important respects, even though I have insisted that my observations have general methodological significance. In another respect, however, my mission has been ambitious. I have begun with Tocqueville and ended with Blalock, as it were, and have attempted to encompass the work and vision of both—as well as all the others I have treated—within a

114 Colin Leys, "Models, Theories, and the Theory of Political Parties," in Eckstein and Apter, eds., *Comparative Politics,* pp. 306–9.

115 George A. Theodorson, "The Uses of Causation in Sociology," in Llewellyn Gross, ed., *Sociological Theory: Inquiries and Paradigms* (New York: Harper & Row, 1967), p. 148.

116 Note Seeman's effort to establish "alienation" as a variable that intervenes between various social-structural variables (especially type of organizational membership) and behavioral variables (especially acquiring information about the social environment. The psychological links he was interested in assessing were those implicit in mass-society theory and those in Rotter's theory of learning. American and Swedish survey data appeared to line up consistently with the psychological assumptions he invoked. Melvin Seeman, "Alienation, Membership, and Political Knowledge: A Comparative Study," *Public Opinion Quarterly* 30(1966):353–68. For a number of suggestions as to what psychological processes might be regarded as universal, see Robert R. Sears, "Transcultural Variables and Conceptual Equivalence," in Bert Kaplan, ed., *Studying Personality Cross-Culturally* (Evanston, Ill.: Row, Peterson and Co., 1961), pp. 445–56.

single methodological framework. To justify such an exercise in comprehensiveness, it seems appropriate, in concluding, to mention a number of threads of continuity that have informed my analysis.

1. The operation of classifying—or selecting units for analysis—involves the claim, sometimes implicit, that the social units in a given class (for example, societies) do not vary with respect to the classificatory criteria. As such, classification emerges as an effort to control certain sources of possible variation. We found this statement to apply to Tocqueville's division of societies into aristocratic and democratic types, to Durkheim's identification of different social species, to Weber's assignment of historical instances to an ideal type, and to modern efforts to deal with societies, nation-states, "cult-units," and the like, as units of analysis.

2. The choice of dimensions or variables for the analysis of evidently dissimilar systems involves the claim that indicators for these dimensions can be found in the social units under study. We found this statement to apply to variables such as liberty, despotism, and centralization as employed by Tocqueville; to concepts such as mechanical and organic solidarity as employed by Durkheim; to concepts such as charismatic and rational-legal authority as employed by Weber; and to modern efforts to generate comparative concepts, such as interest-articulation, political instability, and psychological modernity.

3. The selection of indicators in comparative analysis involves the assumption that the indicators have the same meaning, or are *comparable* across dissimilar social units. Examined further, this involves the assumption that the causal processes generating the indicators are sufficiently similar in different social units that the indicators may be regarded as representing the same general variables. We found this statement to apply to official statistics signifying the social suicide rates as analyzed by Durkheim; to religious documents signifying the development of rationality as analyzed by Weber, and to various indices of economic and social development—gross national product, literacy rates, rates of social mobility, and the like. Much of the research effort in comparative studies, moreover, involves the attempt to assure that indicators in dissimilar social units are indeed comparable.

4. The various methods of attempting to establish association among variables—and to impute causal significance to these associations—involves the effort to control potential sources of variation in causes, thereby ruling them out or rendering them constant, and thus strengthening the case for other selected causal factors. We found this statement to apply to Tocqueville's efforts to account for the differences in the French, American, and British nations; to Durkheim's battery of methods and arguments used to establish the causal link between type of society and type

of solidarity; to Weber's methods and arguments used to establish the causal link between a rational ethic and the rise of rational bourgeois capitalism; and to more modern research designs using more complicated methods such as multivariate analysis. It was also possible to establish that the various methods of research, generally conceived—experimentation, statistical manipulation, systematic comparative illustration, heuristic assumption, etc.—are in effect different ways of attempting to establish parametric control over possible sources of variation.

5. In moving from topic to topic that engages the attention of methodologists—classifying, selecting variables, selecting indicators, establishing associations, and so on—both in the examination of some classics and in the systematic examination of selected contemporary comparative studies, it has proved impossible to discuss these items *in vacuo*, in abstraction from the substantive ideas, or theoretical assumptions, that inform these procedures. As we have seen, the theoretical presuppositions of an investigator are important influences on what he chooses as variable, what as constant, what as causes, and what as effects. Those choices, moreover, determine where in the empirical world he looks for appropriate indicators, thus giving theoretical presuppositions an effect, once removed, on the data to be examined. As we also saw, causal assumptions also inform the decision to select the basic units for comparison; and the choice of indicators reveals at least an implicit causal theory of how such indicators are produced in the social unit. It must be underscored[117] in conclusion, therefore, that any methodological consideration, however technical, must always be referred to the conceptual or theoretical context within which investigation is proceeding.

[117] For two statements of the continuity between the conceptual and the methodological aspects of empirical research, see Arnold M. Rose, "The Relation of Theory and Method," in Gross, ed., *Sociological Theory*, pp. 207–19; and Paul F. Lazarsfeld, "Concept Formation and Measurements in the Behavioral Sciences: Some Historical Observations," in Gordon J. DiRenzo, ed., *Concepts, Theory and Explanation in the Behavioral Sciences* (New York: Random House, 1967), pp. 187–90.

Index

Actor, role of, in Durkheim's and Weber's methodology, 47–50, 49 fig.

Adelman, Irma, a-theoretical factor analysis by, 233–34

Allport, Gordon W., on definition of "nomothetic" and "idiographic," 203*n*

Almond, Gabriel
and classification of political systems, 167
concept formulation of, 176–77
and problem of cross-level fallacy, 228
use of empirical indicators by, 187–88

America. *See* United States

Analogy
in Durkheim's comparative methodology, 99–100
in Weber's comparative methodology, 148–49

Andrain, Charles F., and emphasis on select variables, 238

Anthropology
"Galton's problem" of sampling in, 212

idiographic approach to, 203
units of analysis in, 168

Appeal to other knowledge, 147–48
use of, in correlational analysis, 229–33

Apple, Dorian, and appeal to other knowledge, 229–31

Apter, David E., and emphasis on select variables, 238

Arensberg, C. M., concept of economic activity described by, 179

Associations
between indicators, 198
between variables, 198
cross-level fallacies in establishing, 226–29
related to theoretical context, 229–41

Banks, Arthur S., a-theoretical work by, 233

Ben-David, Joseph, multivariate analysis technique of, 220

Berreman, Gerald D., concept formulation of, 177

West, F. J., controlled comparison procedures of, 216
Whiting, Beatrice, and deviant case analysis, 159–60
Whiting, John W. M., 153
  and assumptions about nonvarying parameters, 238
  and problem of cross-level fallacy, 228

Winch, Robert F., on classification, 170–71

Zelditch, Jr., Morris
  concept formulation of, 177–78
  on limitation of case study, 198
  on problem of correlational causation, 210

¶P

Visit us at *www.quidprobooks.com.*

www.ingramcontent.com/pod-product-compliance
Lightning Source LLC
Chambersburg PA
CBHW070355270326
41926CB00014B/2556